Anti-Inflammatory Cookbook

170 Healthy & Delicious AIP Recipes for Beginners, 4-Week Diet Meal Plan with Shopping List to Boost Immunity and Reduce Inflammation + Bonus Vegetarian and Vegan Options

Lucy Malone

Copyright © 2024 by Lucy Malone. All rights reserved.

All rights reserved. No part of this publication may be reproduced, distributed, or transmitted in any form or by any means, including photocopying, recording, or other electronic or mechanical methods, without the prior written permission of the publisher, except in the case of brief quotations embodied in critical reviews and certain other noncommercial uses permitted by copyright law.

Disclaimer: The information contained in this book is for informational purposes only. It is not intended as a substitute for the advice provided by your healthcare professional. Always consult with your doctor or other qualified health provider regarding any medical condition. The author and publisher disclaim any liability for any damages or adverse effects arising from the use or application of the information contained in this book.

Table of Contents

INTRODUCTION 8
   Welcome and Purpose 8
   Reader's Problems and Solutions 8

PREPARING FOR THE ANTI-INFLAMMATORY DIET 10
   Basics of Inflammation and Effects on the Body 10
   Preparing for a Healthy Change 11
   How an Anti-Inflammatory Diet Helps 12
   Personal Stories and Testimonials 12
   Understanding Allergies, Intolerances, and Sensitivities 13
   Foods to Avoid 14
   From the Author 15

WEEKLY MEAL PLANS WITH RECIPES 16
   Meal Planning 16

SAMPLE WEEKLY MEAL PLANS 17
   Week 1: Introduction to Anti-Inflammatory Eating 17
   Shopping List for Week 1 18
   Week 2: Building on Basics 19
   Shopping List for Week 2 20
   Week 3: Expanding Your Repertoire 21
   Shopping List for Week 3 22
   Week 4: Maintaining and Enjoying Variety 23
   Shopping List for Week 4: 24

BREAKFAST & BRUNCH 25
      Turmeric Oatmeal with Berries 26
      Avocado Toast with Cherry Tomatoes 26
      Veggie Omelette 27
      Sweet Potato Hash 27
      Green Smoothie Bowl 28
      Quinoa Breakfast Bowl 28
      Berry Smoothie 29
      Coconut Yogurt with Fresh Fruit 29
      Almond Flour Pancakes 30
      Papaya Boat 30
      Turmeric Scrambled Eggs 31
      Buckwheat Porridge 31
      Zucchini Fritters 32
      Acai Bowl 32

Cauliflower Breakfast Skillet 33
Pumpkin Spice Smoothie 33
Stuffed Bell Peppers 34
Golden Berry Smoothie 34
Coconut Flour Muffins 35
Mushroom Spinach Frittata 35
Kale and Quinoa Salad 36
Beetroot Smoothie 36
Berry Chia Jam on Toast 37
Flaxseed Porridge 37
Blueberry Almond Smoothie 38
Cucumber Avocado Salad 38
Collard Green Wraps 39
Peach Quinoa Bowl 39
Eggplant Breakfast Skillet 40
Turmeric Coconut Porridge 40

LUNCH & DINNER RECIPES 41

Turmeric Chicken and Vegetable Stir-Fry 42
Quinoa and Black Bean Salad 43
Baked Salmon with Asparagus 43
Cauliflower Rice Stir-Fry 44
Lentil and Spinach Soup 45
Zucchini Noodles with Pesto 46
Miso Soup with Tofu and Seaweed 46
Greek Salad with Grilled Chicken 47
Spaghetti Squash with Marinara Sauce 48
Roasted Brussels Sprouts and Sweet Potatoes 49
Cabbage and Carrot Slaw with Tahini Dressing 49
Grilled Portobello Mushrooms 50
Moroccan Chickpea Stew 51
Baked Cod with Lemon and Herbs 51
Turkey and Vegetable Skewers 52
Asian-Inspired Lettuce Wraps 53
Eggplant and Tomato Bake 54
Shrimp and Avocado Salad 54
Spinach and Mushroom Frittata 55
Coconut Curry with Vegetables 56
Almond-Crusted Tilapia 57
Roasted Beet and Arugula Salad 57
Herb-Roasted Chicken with Vegetables 58
Mediterranean Chickpea Salad 58
Spaghetti Squash Pad Thai 59
Lentil and Vegetable Shepherd's Pie 60
Kale and Quinoa Power Bowl 61
Veggie-Packed Stuffed Bell Peppers 62
Garlic and Herb Roasted Mushrooms 63
Chicken and Avocado Salad 63

VEGETARIAN & VEGAN OPTIONS ... 64

- Cauliflower and Chickpea Tacos ... 65
- Zucchini and Tomato Gratin ... 66
- Spicy Sweet Potato and Black Bean Tacos ... 67
- Baked Tofu with Sesame Seeds ... 68
- Quinoa-Stuffed Acorn Squash ... 69
- Spicy Red Lentil Dhal ... 70
- Chickpea and Sweet Potato Curry ... 71
- Butternut Squash Soup ... 72
- Golden Milk Overnight Oats ... 73
- Avocado and Berry Salad ... 73
- Roasted Carrot and Ginger Soup ... 74
- Roasted Veggie Breakfast Bowl ... 75
- Spirulina Smoothie ... 75
- Stuffed Zucchini Boats ... 76
- Apple Cinnamon Quinoa ... 77
- Tomato Basil Frittata ... 78
- Hemp Seed Granola ... 79
- Spiced Lentil Porridge ... 80
- Mango Turmeric Smoothie ... 81
- Turmeric Cauliflower Rice ... 81

FISH AND SHELLFISH ... 82

- Lemon Herb Grilled Salmon ... 83
- Baked Cod with Tomato and Basil ... 83
- Sesame Crusted Tuna ... 84
- Miso Glazed Salmon ... 84
- Cilantro Lime Tilapia ... 85
- Tuna Avocado Salad ... 85
- Garlic Butter Shrimp ... 86
- Baked Halibut with Herbs ... 86
- Coconut Curry Shrimp ... 87
- Pesto Crusted Salmon ... 87
- Chili Lime Shrimp Skewers ... 88
- Garlic Parmesan Crusted Cod ... 89
- Lemon Dill Baked Trout ... 89
- Salmon and Avocado Sushi Rolls ... 90
- Mediterranean Baked Sardines ... 91
- Garlic Lemon Scallops ... 91
- Spicy Fish Tacos ... 92
- Thai Coconut Fish Soup ... 93
- Herb Crusted Salmon Cakes ... 94
- Garlic Ginger Shrimp Stir-Fry ... 95
- Baked Mackerel with Mustard Sauce ... 96
- Cajun Spiced Shrimp ... 96
- Salmon Nicoise Salad ... 97
- Teriyaki Glazed Salmon ... 98

Fish en Papillote 99
Spicy Tuna Poke Bowl 100
Ginger Soy Steamed Fish 101
Lemon Basil Shrimp Pasta 101
Citrus Herb Grilled Swordfish 102
Smoked Salmon and Avocado Toast 102

POULTRY & MEAT 103

Lemon Herb Chicken 104
Turmeric Chicken Thighs 104
Balsamic Glazed Turkey Meatballs 105
Garlic Rosemary Lamb Chops 106
Herb Crusted Pork Tenderloin 106
Ginger Lime Chicken Skewers 107
Cilantro Lime Turkey Burgers 108
Pesto Stuffed Chicken Breast 109
Rosemary Lemon Roast Turkey Breast 110
Spiced Moroccan Lamb Stew 111
Chicken and Vegetable Stir-Fry 112
Lemon Dill Turkey Cutlets 113
Apple Cider Vinegar Chicken 113
Lemon Garlic Shrimp and Chicken 114
Spicy Thai Basil Chicken 115
Rosemary Garlic Roast Pork Loin 116
Mustard Herb Grilled Chicken 116
Coconut Curry Chicken 117
Ginger Soy Chicken Thighs 118
Balsamic Glazed Pork Chops 119
Mediterranean Chicken 120
Paprika Lime Chicken 120
Spicy Moroccan Chicken 121
Herb Marinated Lamb Kebabs 122
Lemon Thyme Turkey Meatballs 122
Pomegranate Glazed Chicken 123
Sage and Apple Pork Chops 124
Ginger Turmeric Chicken Soup 125
Garlic Herb Roasted Chicken 126
Cilantro Lime Chicken Tacos 126

SNACKS & SWEETS 127

Coconut Macaroons 128
Baked Apple Chips 128
Avocado Chocolate Mousse 129
Golden Milk Popsicles 129
Spiced Almonds 130
Turmeric Ginger Energy Balls 130
Pumpkin Seed Brittle 131
Chia Seed Pudding 131

- Cucumber Hummus Bites 132
- Berry Yogurt Parfait 132
- Dark Chocolate Bark 133
- Turmeric Roasted Chickpeas 133
- Banana Oat Cookies 134
- Almond Butter Stuffed Dates 134
- Matcha Green Tea Energy Bars 135
- Pineapple Coconut Smoothie 135
- Cashew Coconut Bites 136
- Sweet Potato Chips 136
- Mango Chia Popsicles 137
- Carrot Cake Bites 137
- Zucchini Chips 138
- Pomegranate Yogurt Bark 138
- Spicy Pumpkin Seeds 139
- Frozen Grapes 139
- Apple Cinnamon Overnight Oats 140
- Cacao Nib Trail Mix 140
- Baked Plantain Chips 141
- Lemon Coconut Energy Balls 141
- Berry Smoothie Bowl 142
- Cinnamon Spiced Pears 142

EXERCISES TO REDUCE INFLAMMATION 143

TYPES OF EXERCISES TO INCLUDE 143
SAMPLE EXERCISE ROUTINES 144
Morning Routine: Start Your Day Right 144
Midday Movement: Break Up Your Day 144
Evening Routine: Wind Down 144
Weekend Routine: Longer Sessions 144

CONCLUSION 145

RECAP AND ENCOURAGEMENT 145
SUMMARIZE THE BOOK 146
APPENDICES 147
Allergen-Aware Labels 147
Glossary 147
Index 147

Introduction

Welcome and Purpose

Welcome to the Anti-Inflammatory Cookbook! If you're reading this, you're probably looking for a way to improve your health through what you eat, and you're in the right place. This book is for anyone who wants to reduce inflammation in their body with delicious, satisfying meals.

Inflammation is a term that gets thrown around a lot, but what does it really mean? Essentially, inflammation is your body's way of protecting itself. When you get injured or sick, your body sends out inflammatory cells to help fight off the problem and begin the healing process. This is a good thing—without it, simple injuries or infections could become very serious. However, problems arise when inflammation sticks around for too long. Chronic inflammation occurs when your body continues to send out these inflammatory cells, even when there's no immediate threat. This can lead to damage in your cells, tissues, and organs, contributing to a variety of health issues.

Chronic inflammation has been linked to many serious health conditions. For instance, it can contribute to heart disease by promoting the buildup of plaques in your arteries. It can affect your body's ability to regulate blood sugar, leading to or worsening diabetes. For those with arthritis, it can mean painful, swollen joints. Inflammatory bowel diseases like Crohn's disease and ulcerative colitis are direct results of chronic inflammation in the digestive tract. There's also evidence linking chronic inflammation to certain cancers.

This is where an anti-inflammatory diet comes in. By choosing foods that reduce inflammation and avoiding those that trigger it, you can help manage and even prevent these health issues. An anti-inflammatory diet is rich in fruits, vegetables, lean proteins, healthy fats, and whole grains. It minimizes processed foods, sugars, and unhealthy fats.

So, what can you expect from this diet? First, you may see a reduced risk of chronic diseases like heart disease, diabetes, and certain cancers. Improved digestion is another benefit, particularly for those with conditions like Crohn's disease or ulcerative colitis. If you have arthritis, you might experience less pain and better joint function. The diet can also help stabilize your blood sugar levels, which is crucial for managing diabetes. Additionally, it can promote healthy weight loss and maintenance by focusing on nutrient-dense foods that keep you full and satisfied. And finally, the vitamins and minerals found in anti-inflammatory foods can give your immune system a boost.

By adopting an anti-inflammatory diet, you're taking a big step towards better health. This cookbook will guide you through the process, providing you with a variety of recipes that are not only good for you but also delicious and easy to prepare. Here's to a healthier, inflammation-free life!

Reader's Problems and Solutions

When it comes to cookbooks, especially those focused on health and dietary changes, many readers face common frustrations. Let's take a moment to address these issues and explain how this cookbook is designed to overcome them.

One of the most frequent complaints is that recipes in other cookbooks are not Anti-Inflammatory Protocol (AIP) compliant. This can be incredibly frustrating for someone trying to follow a strict dietary plan. In this book, you'll find recipes specifically tailored to meet AIP guidelines, ensuring that every meal you prepare is not only delicious but also supports your health goals.

Another common problem is that recipes often don't taste good. It's disheartening to spend time and effort cooking a meal only to find it unappetizing. Here, we've focused on creating recipes that are not only healthy but also flavorful. We've tested and refined these recipes to make sure they taste great and will be enjoyed by everyone, not just those on a special diet.

A significant issue is that some cookbooks include ingredients that are scientifically proven to cause inflammation, such as grilled meats, certain whole grains, and beans. Our recipes avoid these problematic ingredients, focusing instead on foods known to reduce inflammation. We ensure that every ingredient contributes positively to your health, making it easier to stick to your dietary plan without worrying about inadvertently triggering inflammation.

Additionally, some readers feel left out because many healthy cookbooks seem to cater mainly to vegetarians. If you're not vegetarian, this can be off-putting. While this book includes plenty of vegetarian and vegan options, it also provides a variety of recipes featuring fish, poultry, and lean meats. This ensures that everyone, regardless of their dietary preferences, can find recipes they enjoy and that support their health.

Now, let's talk about how this cookbook stands out in a crowded market. One major advantage is the focus on easy meal planning. We provide comprehensive weekly meal plans complete with shopping lists, making it simple to plan and prepare your meals. You'll find that sticking to an anti-inflammatory diet is much more manageable when you have a clear plan and all the necessary ingredients on hand.

We also offer simple, satisfying recipes that don't require a culinary degree to execute. These recipes are designed for real people with real lives, ensuring that you can make delicious, healthy meals without spending hours in the kitchen.

Food coaching is another unique feature of this book. Alongside recipes, you'll find tips and guidance on how to make healthier food choices, understand ingredient labels, and incorporate anti-inflammatory foods into your daily routine. This holistic approach helps you make lasting changes, rather than just following a temporary diet.

We've ensured that our recipes cater to a variety of dietary needs, including vegan, gluten-free, and dairy-free options. This inclusivity means that no matter your dietary restrictions, you can find recipes that work for you. Each recipe is clearly labeled with allergen-aware tags, making it easy to identify those that fit your specific needs.

The weekly prep plans are another standout feature. These plans are comprehensive, offering not just meal suggestions but also a detailed shopping list. This helps streamline your grocery trips and ensures you have everything you need for the week.

Finally, we've included a comprehensive food list detailing what to eat and what to avoid. This list simplifies your shopping and meal planning, helping you make informed choices. Additionally, we provide exercises to reduce inflammation, recognizing that diet and physical activity go hand in hand in managing inflammation.

In conclusion, this cookbook addresses the common frustrations many readers have with other health-focused cookbooks. By offering tasty, visually appealing, and easy-to-make recipes that cater to a variety of dietary needs, this book aims to be a helpful companion on your journey to better health.

Preparing for the Anti-Inflammatory Diet

Basics of Inflammation and Effects on the Body

Before diving into the specifics of the anti-inflammatory diet, it's important to understand the basics of inflammation and how it affects your body. This foundational knowledge will help you appreciate the significant role your diet plays in managing and reducing inflammation.

Inflammation is a natural and essential part of your body's immune response. Imagine you accidentally cut your finger. Almost immediately, your body springs into action. Blood rushes to the area, white blood cells start fighting off potential infections, and a series of chemical signals trigger the healing process. This is acute inflammation—your body's short-term response to injury or infection, and it's a good thing. It protects you and promotes healing.

However, problems arise when inflammation becomes chronic. Unlike acute inflammation, which is short-lived and resolves once the threat is eliminated, chronic inflammation lingers. Your immune system continues to release inflammatory cells even when there's no injury or infection to fight off. This prolonged state of alert can cause significant damage over time, contributing to various health issues.

Chronic inflammation can have far-reaching effects on your health. Let's explore how it impacts different parts of your body:

Cardiovascular System: Chronic inflammation is a key player in the development of heart disease. It contributes to the buildup of plaque in your arteries, a condition known as atherosclerosis. Over time, these plaques can harden and narrow your arteries, making it harder for blood to flow through. This increases the risk of heart attacks and strokes. Inflammation can also make the inner lining of your blood vessels more prone to damage, further exacerbating cardiovascular problems.

Metabolic Health: Inflammation can interfere with your body's ability to regulate blood sugar, which is crucial for preventing and managing diabetes. In people with chronic inflammation, the body's cells can become resistant to insulin, the hormone that helps control blood sugar levels. This insulin resistance can lead to higher blood sugar levels and, eventually, type 2 diabetes. Additionally, inflammation is often present in individuals with metabolic syndrome, a cluster of conditions that increase the risk of heart disease, stroke, and diabetes.

Joints and Bones: For those with arthritis, chronic inflammation is a significant source of pain and discomfort. Inflammatory arthritis, such as rheumatoid arthritis, occurs when the immune system mistakenly attacks the joints, leading to swelling, stiffness, and pain. Over time, this inflammation can cause joint damage and reduce mobility, impacting the quality of life.

Digestive System: Inflammatory bowel diseases (IBD), including Crohn's disease and ulcerative colitis, are directly related to chronic inflammation in the digestive tract. This inflammation can cause severe pain, diarrhea, fatigue, and weight loss. Managing inflammation is a crucial part of treating these conditions and improving the quality of life for those affected.

Cancer: There's growing evidence that chronic inflammation can contribute to the development of certain cancers. Inflammation can cause DNA damage and promote the growth of tumors. For example, chronic inflammation in the colon can increase the risk of colorectal cancer. By reducing inflammation, you may lower your risk of developing some types of cancer.

Overall Well-being: Beyond specific diseases, chronic inflammation can affect your overall well-being. It can cause fatigue, mood swings, and general malaise. When your body is constantly fighting off inflammation, it can leave you feeling worn out and less able to enjoy life. This is why managing inflammation through diet and lifestyle changes is so important.

In summary, understanding inflammation and its effects on your body is the first step towards making informed decisions about your diet. By adopting an anti-inflammatory diet, you can help reduce chronic inflammation, improve your overall health, and prevent a range of serious health conditions.

Preparing for a Healthy Change

Adopting an anti-inflammatory diet isn't just about changing your eating habits—it's about embracing a whole new mindset and finding the motivation to make lasting changes. To set yourself up for success, it's crucial to prepare mentally and emotionally.

First, think of this dietary change as a journey towards better health rather than a restrictive diet. It's an opportunity to nourish your body with foods that promote healing and well-being. Embrace the process and focus on the benefits you'll gain, such as increased energy, reduced pain, and improved overall health. The key is to see this as a positive transformation rather than a chore.

Understanding your personal reasons for adopting an anti-inflammatory diet can provide powerful motivation. Maybe you want to reduce chronic pain, manage a health condition, or simply feel better day-to-day. Write down your reasons and keep them somewhere you can see them. When you need a motivational boost, look at that list to remind yourself why you started this journey.

Staying positive is crucial. It's easy to get discouraged if you encounter setbacks or if progress seems slow. Remember, change takes time. Celebrate your successes, no matter how small, and use them as fuel to keep going. If you slip up, don't dwell on it—acknowledge it, learn from it, and move forward. Focus on what you've achieved and the positive changes you're making, rather than any occasional missteps.

Support from friends, family, or even online communities can make a big difference. Sharing your journey with others provides encouragement, advice, and a sense of accountability. You don't have to do this alone, and having a support system can make the transition smoother and more enjoyable.

Setting realistic and achievable goals is also crucial for long-term success. Unrealistic expectations can lead to frustration and burnout, so it's important to be practical about what you can achieve and how quickly.

Start with small, manageable changes rather than trying to overhaul your entire diet overnight. For instance, begin by incorporating more anti-inflammatory foods into your meals and gradually reduce your intake of inflammatory foods. Small changes are easier to stick to and can build momentum over time.

When setting goals, be specific about what you want to achieve. Instead of saying, "I want to eat healthier," set a goal like, "I will include at least one serving of vegetables in every meal." Clear, specific goals are easier to track and achieve.

Give yourself time to adjust. Transitioning to an anti-inflammatory diet is a process, and it's okay to take it step by step. Listen to your body and make adjustments as needed. The goal is to create sustainable habits that will benefit you in the long run, not to follow a rigid plan that feels overwhelming.

Remember to be kind to yourself throughout this journey. It's not about perfection, but about progress and making choices that support your health and well-being. Each positive change, no matter how small, is a step towards a healthier, happier you.

By adopting a positive mindset, understanding your motivations, setting realistic goals, and seeking support, you'll be well-prepared to embrace the anti-inflammatory diet and enjoy the many benefits it brings. This is a journey towards better health, and every step you take is worth celebrating.

How an Anti-Inflammatory Diet Helps

Making the switch to an anti-inflammatory diet can have profound effects on your health and well-being. Let's explore the scientific evidence supporting this diet and hear from real people who have experienced its benefits firsthand.

The anti-inflammatory diet is backed by a growing body of scientific research. Numerous studies have shown that certain foods can reduce inflammation and improve health outcomes.

Research indicates that a diet rich in fruits, vegetables, whole grains, and healthy fats, such as those found in olive oil and fatty fish, can significantly reduce markers of inflammation in the body. These foods are packed with antioxidants and other nutrients that help fight inflammation and support overall health. For instance, omega-3 fatty acids found in fish like salmon and sardines have been shown to reduce inflammation and lower the risk of chronic diseases such as heart disease and arthritis.

One landmark study, the Mediterranean Diet Study, found that participants who followed a Mediterranean-style diet—which is similar to the anti-inflammatory diet—had lower levels of inflammation and a reduced risk of heart disease compared to those who followed a standard Western diet. The Mediterranean diet emphasizes fruits, vegetables, whole grains, nuts, seeds, and healthy fats, and limits processed foods and red meat.

Another significant piece of research published in the Journal of Internal Medicine found that diets high in anti-inflammatory foods were associated with lower risks of all-cause mortality, cardiovascular diseases, and cancer. The study highlighted the importance of incorporating a variety of anti-inflammatory foods into your diet to achieve these health benefits.

In addition to cardiovascular benefits, an anti-inflammatory diet has been shown to help with conditions like rheumatoid arthritis and inflammatory bowel disease. By reducing inflammation, individuals with these conditions often experience less pain and discomfort, and improved quality of life.

Personal Stories and Testimonials

While scientific evidence provides a strong foundation, hearing personal stories can be incredibly motivating and relatable. Here are a few testimonials from individuals who have experienced the positive effects of an anti-inflammatory diet:

Sarah's Story: Sarah, a 45-year-old mother of two, struggled with chronic joint pain for years. She was diagnosed with rheumatoid arthritis and found it challenging to manage the pain and stiffness in her joints. After reading about the benefits of an anti-inflammatory diet, Sarah decided to give it a try. Within a few weeks of cutting out processed foods and adding more fruits, vegetables, and fatty fish to her diet, she noticed a significant reduction in her joint pain. "I never thought food could make such a difference," Sarah says. "I feel more energetic, and the pain in my joints has decreased dramatically. It's been a life-changer."

John's Journey: John, a 60-year-old retiree, had been battling heart disease for several years. Despite taking medications, he struggled to keep his cholesterol and blood pressure under control. His doctor recommended trying an anti-inflammatory diet. John started eating more whole foods, like leafy greens, berries, and nuts, and cut back on red meat and sugary snacks. "My doctor was amazed at the difference," John recalls. "My cholesterol levels dropped, and my blood pressure is the best it's been in years. I feel healthier and more active."

Emily's Experience: Emily, a 30-year-old graphic designer, suffered from severe digestive issues due to Crohn's disease. She often felt fatigued and was frequently in pain. On a friend's recommendation, she started an anti-inflammatory diet. Emily noticed improvements in her symptoms within a month. "It was incredible how quickly I felt better," Emily shares. "I have more energy, and my digestive issues have calmed down. I finally feel like I have control over my health."

These personal stories illustrate the transformative power of an anti-inflammatory diet. While everyone's journey is unique, the common thread is the significant improvement in health and quality of life that can come from making mindful dietary choices.

By understanding the scientific evidence and hearing from those who have walked this path, you can feel more confident and motivated to embrace the anti-inflammatory diet. It's a powerful tool for improving your health and well-being, backed by research and real-life experiences.

Understanding Allergies, Intolerances, and Sensitivities

To get the most out of an anti-inflammatory diet, it's important to understand the differences between allergies, intolerances, and sensitivities, as well as common inflammatory triggers. This knowledge helps you make informed choices about what to include and avoid in your diet.

Allergies occur when your immune system mistakenly identifies a harmless substance, such as a particular food or pollen, as a threat. In response, it releases chemicals like histamines to defend against this perceived threat. Common symptoms of allergies include hives, itching, swelling, difficulty breathing, and even anaphylaxis, which can be life-threatening. Food allergies, for example, can be triggered by nuts, shellfish, dairy, and eggs. Unlike intolerances and sensitivities, allergies typically cause immediate and severe reactions.

Intolerances are generally less severe than allergies and do not involve the immune system. Instead, they occur when your body has difficulty digesting certain substances. A common example is lactose intolerance, where the body lacks the enzyme lactase needed to break down lactose in dairy products. Symptoms of intolerances can include bloating, gas, diarrhea, and stomach cramps. These symptoms usually appear gradually and can be dose-dependent, meaning the more of the offending food you consume, the worse the symptoms.

Sensitivities are less understood than allergies and intolerances but can still cause significant discomfort. They involve a reaction to certain foods that doesn't trigger the immune system in the same way as allergies. Symptoms can vary widely and might include headaches, fatigue, joint pain, or digestive issues. Unlike allergies, which usually cause immediate reactions, sensitivities can cause delayed symptoms, making it harder to pinpoint the trigger.

Foods to Avoid

Knowing which foods to avoid is a crucial step in managing inflammation through your diet. Certain foods can trigger inflammatory responses in the body, leading to various health issues. Here's a detailed list of these foods and why they are problematic.

Processed Foods: Processed foods are often packed with unhealthy ingredients. This includes fast food, packaged snacks, and ready-to-eat meals. They usually contain high levels of refined sugars, unhealthy fats, and artificial additives, all of which can trigger inflammation in the body. Regular consumption of these foods can contribute to chronic inflammation, increasing the risk of diseases like heart disease, diabetes, and obesity. Processed foods often lack essential nutrients and fiber, which are vital for maintaining a healthy immune system and reducing inflammation.

Refined Carbohydrates: White bread, pastries, and sugary cereals are examples of refined carbohydrates. These foods cause rapid spikes in blood sugar levels, leading to increased inflammation. They lack essential nutrients and fiber, making them detrimental to your health. Consuming refined carbs regularly can also contribute to weight gain and insulin resistance, both of which are linked to inflammation. High blood sugar levels stimulate the production of inflammatory cytokines and increase oxidative stress, both of which can exacerbate chronic inflammation.

Sugar: Sugar is one of the major culprits when it comes to inflammation. Consuming too much sugar can lead to increased inflammatory markers in the body. It's not just the obvious sources like candy and soda that you need to watch out for; sugar is often hidden in sauces, dressings, and many processed foods. High sugar intake can lead to a range of health problems, including obesity, heart disease, and diabetes. Excessive sugar consumption can cause an imbalance in insulin levels, which triggers an inflammatory response and contributes to the development of insulin resistance.

Trans Fats: Trans fats are found in many fried and baked goods, such as doughnuts, cookies, and crackers. They are created through an industrial process that adds hydrogen to vegetable oil, making the oil solid at room temperature. Trans fats are known to increase inflammation and are linked to a higher risk of heart disease. They raise levels of low-density lipoprotein (LDL) cholesterol, often referred to as "bad" cholesterol, and decrease levels of high-density lipoprotein (HDL) cholesterol, or "good" cholesterol. This imbalance can lead to the buildup of plaques in arteries, causing inflammation and increasing the risk of cardiovascular diseases.

Red meats, such as beef and pork, and processed meats, like sausages and hot dogs, can be inflammatory for some people. These meats often contain high levels of saturated fats and advanced glycation end products (AGEs), which are compounds formed when meat is cooked at high temperatures. These substances can promote inflammation and are linked to increased risks of heart disease, cancer, and other chronic conditions. AGEs can trigger oxidative stress and inflammation, contributing to the aging process and the development of degenerative diseases.

Dairy Products: For those who are intolerant or sensitive to lactose or casein, a protein found in milk, dairy products can cause inflammation. Symptoms can range from digestive discomfort, such as bloating and diarrhea, to joint pain and fatigue. If you suspect that dairy might be an issue for you, try eliminating it from your diet to see if your symptoms improve. Dairy can stimulate the production of mucus and inflammatory chemicals, especially in individuals with lactose intolerance or a dairy allergy.

Alcohol: While moderate alcohol consumption, particularly red wine, can have some health benefits, excessive alcohol intake can increase inflammation. High levels of alcohol can disrupt the balance of healthy gut bacteria, leading to increased intestinal permeability and systemic inflammation. It's best to drink in moderation and choose anti-inflammatory options like red wine, which contains antioxidants. Excessive alcohol consumption can also lead to liver damage, which impairs the liver's ability to regulate inflammation and detoxify the body.

Artificial Additives and Preservatives: Many processed foods contain artificial additives and preservatives to extend shelf life and enhance flavor. Substances like MSG, food colorings, and artificial sweeteners can trigger inflammatory reactions in sensitive individuals. These additives can disrupt normal bodily functions and contribute to chronic inflammation over time. They can also affect gut health by altering the microbiome, which plays a crucial role in regulating the immune system and inflammatory responses.

By avoiding these inflammatory foods, you can help reduce your body's inflammatory response and improve your overall health. Making mindful choices about what to exclude from your diet is just as important as knowing what to include. This awareness will help you create a balanced and effective anti-inflammatory eating plan.

From the Author

Dear Reader,

Thank you for choosing this book and allowing it to be part of your journey toward better health. Writing this book has been a deeply personal and fulfilling experience for me, and I am honored to share it with you.

Health and wellness have always been passions of mine, and this book is a culmination of years of research, experimentation, and personal experience. I believe that the food we eat has a profound impact on our well-being, and that making informed, conscious choices can lead to a healthier, happier life.

As you explore the recipes and tips within these pages, my hope is that you find inspiration to nourish your body and soul. Whether you are new to an anti-inflammatory diet or looking to expand your repertoire, I've strived to create recipes that are not only nutritious but also enjoyable and satisfying.

I understand that the journey to better health can sometimes feel overwhelming, but remember that every small step you take is a victory. Be kind to yourself, and embrace the process with an open heart and mind.

If you find joy, comfort, and positive changes from these recipes, then this book has fulfilled its purpose. Please don't hesitate to reach out and share your experiences—I would love to hear from you.

Wishing you vibrant health and happiness,

Lucy Malone.

Meal Planning

Meal planning is an essential part of maintaining an anti-inflammatory diet. It helps you stay organized, ensures you have the necessary ingredients on hand, and makes it easier to stick to your dietary goals. By planning your meals in advance, you can make more informed choices about what you eat, reduce stress around mealtimes, and avoid the temptation of unhealthy, inflammatory foods.

Planning your meals also allows you to incorporate a variety of anti-inflammatory foods into your diet. This variety not only keeps your meals interesting but also ensures that you get a broad spectrum of nutrients that support overall health. Additionally, meal planning can help you save money by reducing food waste and allowing you to buy ingredients in bulk.

One of the biggest benefits of meal planning is that it helps you maintain consistency. When you have a plan in place, you're less likely to make impulsive food choices that can derail your efforts to reduce inflammation. Consistency is key to seeing long-term improvements in your health, and meal planning is a powerful tool to help you achieve that.

Using the meal plans provided in this book is straightforward and designed to make your life easier. At the beginning of each week, take some time to review the meal plan. This will give you an overview of what you'll be eating and help you prepare mentally and logistically. Look at the recipes and check if there are any ingredients or cooking methods you are unfamiliar with. Familiarizing yourself with the plan will make the execution smoother.

Each weekly meal plan comes with a detailed shopping list. Use this list to shop for all the ingredients you'll need for the week. Having everything on hand at the beginning of the week prevents last-minute trips to the store and reduces the temptation to stray from your plan.

If possible, set aside some time at the beginning of the week to do some prep work. This might include washing and chopping vegetables, marinating proteins, or cooking grains. Preparing ingredients in advance can save you time during the week and make it easier to put together meals quickly.

Each day's plan includes specific meals for breakfast, lunch, dinner, and snacks. Follow these guides to ensure you're eating balanced, anti-inflammatory meals throughout the day. If you need to adjust portions or ingredients based on your dietary needs or preferences, feel free to do so while keeping the principles of the anti-inflammatory diet in mind.

Life can be unpredictable, and sometimes your plans might need to change. If you find yourself unable to follow the meal plan exactly as written, don't stress. The goal is to make the best possible choices given your circumstances. Use the recipes and guidelines as a flexible framework rather than a rigid set of rules.

By embracing meal planning, you can make your journey towards an anti-inflammatory diet more manageable and enjoyable. With a bit of preparation and organization, you'll find it easier to stick to your dietary goals and reap the benefits of reduced inflammation and improved health.

Sample Weekly Meal Plans

Following an anti-inflammatory diet can seem daunting at first, but having a structured meal plan can make it much easier. Here, you'll find a series of sample weekly meal plans designed to help you incorporate anti-inflammatory foods into your daily routine. These plans are flexible and can be adjusted based on your personal preferences and needs. Each week also includes a detailed shopping list to streamline your grocery trips.

Week 1: Introduction to Anti-Inflammatory Eating

Monday

Breakfast:	Overnight oats with blueberries and chia seeds.
Lunch:	Quinoa salad with mixed greens, cherry tomatoes, avocado, and a lemon-tahini dressing.
Dinner:	Baked salmon with roasted Brussels sprouts and sweet potatoes.
Snacks:	Apple slices with almond butter, a handful of walnuts.

Tuesday

Breakfast:	Smoothie with spinach, banana, almond milk, and flax seeds.
Lunch:	Lentil soup with a side of mixed greens and olive oil vinaigrette.
Dinner:	Grilled chicken breast with a quinoa and vegetable stir-fry.
Snacks:	Carrot sticks with hummus, a small handful of pumpkin seeds.

Wednesday

Breakfast:	Greek yogurt with honey, walnuts, and fresh strawberries.
Lunch:	Chickpea and cucumber salad with feta and a balsamic dressing.
Dinner:	Turkey meatballs with zucchini noodles and marinara sauce.
Snacks:	Celery sticks with almond butter, a piece of dark chocolate.

Thursday

Breakfast:	Avocado toast on whole-grain bread with a sprinkle of chia seeds.
Lunch:	Black bean and corn salad with lime dressing and cilantro.
Dinner:	Shrimp stir-fry with bell peppers, broccoli, and brown rice.
Snacks:	Sliced pear with cottage cheese, a small handful of almonds.

Friday

Breakfast:	Smoothie bowl with mixed berries, granola, and a drizzle of honey.
Lunch:	Sweet potato and kale salad with tahini dressing.
Dinner:	Grilled tuna steak with a side of quinoa and steamed asparagus.
Snacks:	Cherry tomatoes with mozzarella, a handful of pistachios.

Saturday

Breakfast: Chia pudding with mango and coconut flakes.
Lunch: Mediterranean wrap with hummus, roasted veggies, and spinach.
Dinner: Lemon garlic chicken with roasted root vegetables.
Snacks: Red bell pepper slices with guacamole, a small handful of cashews.

Sunday

Breakfast: Scrambled eggs with spinach, tomatoes, and a slice of whole-grain toast.
Lunch: Roasted beet and arugula salad with goat cheese and walnuts.
Dinner: Stuffed bell peppers with ground turkey, brown rice, and black beans.
Snacks: Fresh berries with Greek yogurt, a few squares of dark chocolate.

Shopping List for Week 1

Blueberries
Chia seeds
Quinoa
Mixed greens
Cherry tomatoes
Avocados
Lemons
Tahini
Salmon
Brussels sprouts
Sweet potatoes
Apples
Almond butter
Walnuts
Spinach
Bananas
Almond milk
Flax seeds
Lentils
Olive oil
Chicken breast
Carrots
Hummus
Pumpkin seeds
Greek yogurt
Honey
Strawberries
Chickpeas
Cucumbers
Feta cheese
Balsamic vinegar
Ground turkey

Zucchini
Marinara sauce
Celery
Whole-grain bread
Black beans
Corn
Bell peppers
Broccoli
Brown rice
Pears
Cottage cheese
Almonds
Mixed berries
Granola
Tuna steak
Asparagus
Cherry tomatoes
Mozzarella
Pistachios
Mango
Coconut flakes
Hummus
Red bell peppers
Cashews
Eggs
Tomatoes
Whole-grain toast
Beets
Arugula
Goat cheese

Week 2: Building on Basics

Monday

Breakfast: Overnight oats with chia seeds, almond milk, and fresh berries.
Lunch: Spinach and lentil salad with a lemon-olive oil dressing.
Dinner: Baked cod with sautéed kale and sweet potato fries.
Snacks: Apple slices with almond butter, roasted chickpeas.

Tuesday

Breakfast: Smoothie with kale, pineapple, coconut water, and flax seeds.
Lunch: Quinoa and black bean bowl with avocado and salsa.
Dinner: Chicken and vegetable kebabs with brown rice.
Snacks: Carrot sticks with hummus, a handful of sunflower seeds.

Wednesday

Breakfast: Greek yogurt with honey, sliced almonds, and fresh peaches.
Lunch: Tuna salad with mixed greens, cherry tomatoes, and a vinaigrette.
Dinner: Turkey chili with kidney beans and bell peppers.
Snacks: Celery sticks with peanut butter, dark chocolate-covered almonds.

Thursday

Breakfast: Avocado smoothie with banana, spinach, and almond milk.
Lunch: Roasted vegetable and farro salad with feta.
Dinner: Grilled salmon with quinoa and steamed broccoli.
Snacks: Sliced cucumber with tzatziki, a small handful of walnuts.

Friday

Breakfast: Smoothie bowl with mixed berries, chia seeds, and granola.
Lunch: Chickpea curry with basmati rice.
Dinner: Lemon herb chicken with roasted Brussels sprouts and brown rice.
Snacks: Cherry tomatoes with mozzarella, a handful of pistachios.

Saturday

Breakfast: Chia pudding with almond milk, vanilla, and fresh raspberries.
Lunch: Mediterranean quinoa salad with olives, cucumber, and cherry tomatoes.
Dinner: Shrimp and vegetable stir-fry with jasmine rice.
Snacks: Bell pepper slices with guacamole, a small handful of pecans.

Sunday

Breakfast: Scrambled tofu with spinach, mushrooms, and whole-grain toast.
Lunch: Roasted beet and arugula salad with goat cheese and walnuts.
Dinner: Stuffed bell peppers with quinoa, black beans, and corn.
Snacks: Fresh blueberries with Greek yogurt, a few squares of dark chocolate.

Shopping List for Week 2

Chia seeds
Almond milk
Fresh berries
Spinach
Lentils
Lemons
Olive oil
Cod
Kale
Sweet potatoes
Pineapple

Coconut water
Flax seeds
Avocado
Salsa
Chicken breast
Brown rice
Sunflower seeds
Peaches
Almonds
Tuna
Kidney beans
Peanut butter
Dark chocolate-covered almonds
Farro
Feta cheese
Tzatziki
Cucumber
Walnuts
Tofu
Mushrooms
Jasmine rice
Raspberries
Olives
Pecans
Basmati rice

Week 3: Expanding Your Repertoire

Monday

Breakfast: Overnight oats with almond milk, chia seeds, and sliced strawberries.
Lunch: Mixed greens with roasted sweet potatoes, black beans, and avocado dressing.
Dinner: Baked halibut with roasted cauliflower and wild rice.
Snacks: Sliced apple with cashew butter, roasted edamame.

Tuesday

Breakfast: Smoothie with spinach, mango, coconut water, and chia seeds.
Lunch: Lentil and vegetable stew with whole-grain bread.
Dinner: Grilled chicken thighs with quinoa pilaf and steamed green beans.
Snacks: Carrot sticks with almond butter, a handful of pumpkin seeds.

Wednesday

Breakfast: Greek yogurt with honey, pistachios, and blueberries.
Lunch: Falafel wrap with hummus, cucumber, and mixed greens.
Dinner: Beef stir-fry with bell peppers, snap peas, and brown rice.
Snacks: Celery sticks with sunflower seed butter, dark chocolate almonds.

Thursday

Breakfast: Avocado toast on whole-grain bread with a sprinkle of hemp seeds.
Lunch: Chickpea and avocado salad with lime dressing and cilantro.
Dinner: Grilled trout with roasted sweet potatoes and asparagus.
Snacks: Sliced pear with cottage cheese, a handful of almonds.

Friday

Breakfast: Smoothie bowl with mixed berries, granola, and a drizzle of almond butter.
Lunch: Kale and quinoa salad with tahini dressing and pomegranate seeds.
Dinner: Grilled lamb chops with a side of quinoa and steamed broccoli.
Snacks: Cherry tomatoes with goat cheese, a handful of walnuts.

Saturday

Breakfast: Chia pudding with coconut milk, vanilla, and sliced kiwi.
Lunch: Roasted vegetable wrap with hummus and spinach.
Dinner: Lemon rosemary chicken with roasted carrots and brown rice.
Snacks: Bell pepper slices with tzatziki, a small handful of cashews.

Sunday

Breakfast: Scrambled eggs with tomatoes, basil, and a slice of whole-grain toast.
Lunch: Spinach and beet salad with goat cheese and walnuts.
Dinner: Stuffed zucchini boats with ground turkey, quinoa, and marinara sauce.
Snacks: Fresh raspberries with Greek yogurt, a few squares of dark chocolate.

Shopping List for Week 3

Almond milk
Strawberries
Avocado
Cauliflower
Wild rice
Edamame
Mango
Whole-grain bread
Chicken thighs
Quinoa
Green beans
Snap peas
Bell peppers
Beef
Hemp seeds
Trout
Pomegranate seeds
Lamb chops

Granola
Coconut milk
Kiwi
Hummus
Cashews
Basil
Tomatoes
Zucchini
Ground turkey
Marinara sauce

Week 4: Maintaining and Enjoying Variety

Monday

Breakfast: Overnight oats with chia seeds, almond milk, and sliced peaches.
Lunch: Mixed greens with roasted butternut squash, chickpeas, and tahini dressing.
Dinner: Baked sea bass with roasted Brussels sprouts and wild rice.
Snacks: Sliced apple with almond butter, roasted chickpeas.

Tuesday

Breakfast: Smoothie with kale, pineapple, coconut water, and chia seeds.
Lunch: Quinoa and black bean bowl with avocado and salsa.
Dinner: Chicken and vegetable kebabs with brown rice.
Snacks: Carrot sticks with hummus, a handful of sunflower seeds.

Wednesday

Breakfast: Greek yogurt with honey, sliced almonds, and fresh blueberries.
Lunch: Tuna salad with mixed greens, cherry tomatoes, and a vinaigrette.
Dinner: Turkey chili with kidney beans and bell peppers.
Snacks: Celery sticks with peanut butter, dark chocolate-covered almonds.

Thursday

Breakfast: Avocado smoothie with banana, spinach, and almond milk.
Lunch: Roasted vegetable and farro salad with feta.
Dinner: Grilled salmon with quinoa and steamed broccoli.
Snacks: Sliced cucumber with tzatziki, a small handful of walnuts.

Friday

Breakfast: Smoothie bowl with mixed berries, chia seeds, and granola.
Lunch: Chickpea curry with basmati rice.
Dinner: Lemon herb chicken with roasted Brussels sprouts and brown rice.
Snacks: Cherry tomatoes with mozzarella, a handful of pistachios.

Saturday

Breakfast: Chia pudding with almond milk, vanilla, and fresh raspberries.
Lunch: Mediterranean quinoa salad with olives, cucumber, and cherry tomatoes.
Dinner: Shrimp and vegetable stir-fry with jasmine rice.
Snacks: Bell pepper slices with guacamole, a small handful of pecans.

Sunday

Breakfast: Scrambled tofu with spinach, mushrooms, and whole-grain toast.
Lunch: Roasted beet and arugula salad with goat cheese and walnuts.
Dinner: Stuffed bell peppers with quinoa, black beans, and corn.
Snacks: Fresh blueberries with Greek yogurt, a few squares of dark chocolate.

Shopping List for Week 4

Chia seeds
Peaches
Butternut squash
Sea bass
Pineapple
Avocado
Salsa
Sunflower seeds
Blueberries
Tuna
Kidney beans
Farro
Feta cheese
Cucumber
Tzatziki
Walnuts
Basmati rice
Pistachios
Raspberries
Olives
Shrimp
Jasmine rice
Pecans
Tofu
Mushrooms
Corn

These sample weekly meal plans are designed to help you ease into an anti-inflammatory diet, build on the basics, expand your repertoire, and finally maintain and enjoy a variety of delicious and nutritious meals. Adjust them to fit your preferences and lifestyle, and enjoy the journey towards better health.

Breakfast & Brunch

Starting your day with a nutritious, anti-inflammatory breakfast sets a positive tone for the rest of the day

Turmeric Oatmeal with Berries

Yield: 2 servings **Prep Time:** 5 minutes
Cook Time: 10 minutes

Ingredients
- 1 cup rolled oats
- 2 cups almond milk (or any plant-based milk)
- 1 teaspoon ground turmeric
- 1 tablespoon chia seeds
- 1 teaspoon cinnamon
- 1 cup mixed berries (blueberries, strawberries, raspberries)
- 1 tablespoon honey (optional)
- 1 teaspoon vanilla extract
- Pinch of black pepper (enhances the absorption of turmeric)
- Optional toppings: nuts, seeds, additional berries

Directions
1. Prepare the Oats: In a medium saucepan, combine the rolled oats and almond milk. Bring to a gentle boil over medium heat.
2. Add Turmeric and Chia Seeds: Stir in the ground turmeric, chia seeds, cinnamon, and black pepper. Reduce the heat to low and simmer for about 5-7 minutes, stirring occasionally until the oats are cooked and the mixture is creamy.
3. Add Vanilla Extract: Stir in the vanilla extract and remove from heat.
4. Serve: Divide the oatmeal into two bowls. Top each bowl with the mixed berries and drizzle with honey if desired.
5. Optional Toppings: Add additional toppings like nuts, seeds, or more berries for extra flavor and texture.

Nutritional Information (per serving)
- Calories: 250
- Protein: 6g
- Carbohydrates: 45g
- Dietary Fiber: 10g
- Sugars: 15g
- Fat: 5g
- Saturated Fat: 0.5g
- Sodium: 150mg
- Potassium: 450mg
- Vitamin C: 20% of Daily Value
- Calcium: 20% of Daily Value
- Iron: 15% of Daily Value

Avocado Toast with Cherry Tomatoes

Yield: 2 servings **Prep Time:** 5 minutes
Cook Time: 5 minutes

Ingredients
- 2 slices whole grain bread
- 1 ripe avocado
- 1 cup cherry tomatoes, halved
- 1 tablespoon flax seeds
- 1 tablespoon lemon juice
- Salt and pepper to taste
- Optional: a pinch of red pepper flakes for a spicy kick

Directions
1. Toast the Bread: Toast the whole grain bread slices to your desired level of crispiness.
2. Prepare the Avocado: While the bread is toasting, cut the avocado in half, remove the pit, and scoop the flesh into a bowl. Mash the avocado with a fork until smooth. Mix in the lemon juice, salt, and pepper.
3. Assemble the Toast: Spread the mashed avocado evenly over the toasted bread slices.
4. Add Tomatoes: Top each slice with the halved cherry tomatoes.
5. Sprinkle Flax Seeds: Sprinkle the flax seeds over the top for added crunch and nutrition.
6. Serve: Optionally, sprinkle with red pepper flakes for a bit of heat. Serve immediately.

Nutritional Information (per serving)
- Calories: 250
- Protein: 6g
- Carbohydrates: 28g
- Dietary Fiber: 10g
- Sugars: 3g
- Fat: 16g
- Saturated Fat: 2g
- Sodium: 150mg
- Potassium: 700mg
- Vitamin A: 10% of Daily Value
- Vitamin C: 25% of Daily Value
- Calcium: 6% of Daily Value
- Iron: 10% of Daily Value

Veggie Omelette

Yield: 2 servings **Prep Time:** 10 minutes
Cook Time: 10 minutes

Ingredients
- 4 large eggs
- 1/4 cup unsweetened almond milk (or any plant-based milk)
- 1 cup fresh spinach, chopped
- 1/2 red bell pepper, diced
- 1/2 yellow bell pepper, diced
- 1 small red onion, finely chopped
- 1 medium tomato, diced
- 1 tablespoon olive oil
- Salt and pepper to taste
- Optional: a pinch of red pepper flakes for a spicy kick

Directions
1. Prepare the Vegetables: Wash and chop the spinach, bell peppers, onion, and tomato.
2. Whisk the Eggs: In a bowl, whisk the eggs with the almond milk, salt, and pepper until well combined.
3. Sauté the Vegetables: Heat the olive oil in a non-stick skillet over medium heat. Add the onion and bell peppers and sauté for about 3-4 minutes until they start to soften. Add the spinach and tomato and cook for another 2 minutes until the spinach is wilted and the tomato is slightly softened.
4. Cook the Omelette: Pour the egg mixture over the vegetables in the skillet. Cook without stirring for about 3-4 minutes, or until the eggs start to set around the edges.
5. Fold the Omelette: Carefully fold the omelette in half using a spatula. Continue to cook for another 1-2 minutes until the eggs are fully set and cooked through.
6. Serve: Divide the omelette into two servings and serve immediately.

Nutritional Information (per serving)
- Calories: 200
- Protein: 14g
- Carbohydrates: 8g
- Dietary Fiber: 2g
- Sugars: 4g
- Fat: 12g
- Saturated Fat: 3g
- Sodium: 200mg
- Potassium: 450mg
- Vitamin A: 60% of Daily Value
- Vitamin C: 100% of Daily Value
- Calcium: 10% of Daily Value
- Iron: 15% of Daily Value

Sweet Potato Hash

Yield: 2 servings **Prep Time:** 10 minutes
Cook Time: 20 minutes

Ingredients
- 2 medium sweet potatoes, peeled and diced
- 1 red bell pepper, diced
- 1 yellow bell pepper, diced
- 1 small red onion, diced
- 2 cups fresh spinach
- 2 tablespoons olive oil
- 1 teaspoon ground turmeric
- 1 teaspoon paprika
- Salt and pepper to taste
- Optional: 1 avocado, sliced (for serving)

Directions
1. Prepare the Sweet Potatoes: Peel and dice the sweet potatoes into small, even cubes.
2. Heat the Oil: In a large skillet, heat the olive oil over medium heat.
3. Cook the Sweet Potatoes: Add the diced sweet potatoes to the skillet. Cook, stirring occasionally, for about 10 minutes or until they start to soften and brown.
4. Add Vegetables: Add the diced bell peppers and red onion to the skillet. Cook for another 5-7 minutes until the vegetables are tender.
5. Season: Stir in the ground turmeric, paprika, salt, and pepper. Cook for another 2 minutes, allowing the spices to blend.
6. Add Spinach: Add the fresh spinach and cook until wilted, about 1-2 minutes.
7. Serve: Divide the sweet potato hash into two bowls. Optionally, top with sliced avocado and serve immediately.

Nutritional Information (per serving)
- Calories: 250
- Protein: 4g
- Carbohydrates: 40g
- Dietary Fiber: 8g
- Sugars: 12g
- Fat: 10g
- Saturated Fat: 1.5g
- Sodium: 150mg
- Potassium: 800mg
- Vitamin A: 450% of Daily Value
- Vitamin C: 150% of Daily Value
- Calcium: 10% of Daily Value
- Iron: 10% of Daily Value

Green Smoothie Bowl

Yield: 2 servings **Prep Time:** 10 minutes
Cook Time: None

Ingredients
- 2 cups fresh spinach
- 1 ripe banana
- 1/2 ripe avocado
- 1 cup unsweetened almond milk (or any plant-based milk)
- 1 tablespoon chia seeds
- 1/2 cup granola (gluten-free if needed)
- Fresh fruits for topping (e.g., berries, sliced kiwi, mango)
- Optional: a drizzle of honey or maple syrup for extra sweetness

Directions
1. Blend the Smoothie: In a blender, combine the spinach, banana, avocado, and almond milk. Blend until smooth and creamy.
2. Adjust Consistency: If the smoothie is too thick, add a little more almond milk until you reach your desired consistency.
3. Serve: Pour the smoothie into two bowls.
4. Add Toppings: Top each bowl with granola, chia seeds, and fresh fruits. Optionally, drizzle with honey or maple syrup for extra sweetness.
5. Enjoy: Serve immediately for the best texture and flavor.

Nutritional Information (per serving)
- Calories: 300
- Protein: 7g
- Carbohydrates: 40g
- Dietary Fiber: 10g
- Sugars: 12g
- Fat: 14g
- Saturated Fat: 2g
- Sodium: 130mg
- Potassium: 850mg
- Vitamin A: 150% of Daily Value
- Vitamin C: 80% of Daily Value
- Calcium: 25% of Daily Value
- Iron: 20% of Daily Value

Quinoa Breakfast Bowl

Yield: 2 servings **Prep Time:** 10 minutes
Cook Time: 15 minutes

Ingredients
- 1 cup quinoa
- 2 cups unsweetened almond milk (or any plant-based milk)
- 1 tablespoon maple syrup or honey (optional)
- 1 teaspoon vanilla extract
- 1/2 teaspoon ground cinnamon
- 1/4 cup mixed nuts (e.g., almonds, walnuts, pecans), chopped
- 1/4 cup mixed seeds (e.g., chia seeds, flaxseeds, pumpkin seeds)
- 1 cup fresh fruits (e.g., berries, sliced banana, kiwi)
- Optional: a sprinkle of shredded coconut

Directions
1. Rinse Quinoa: Rinse the quinoa thoroughly under cold water to remove any bitterness.
2. Cook Quinoa: In a medium saucepan, combine the quinoa and almond milk. Bring to a boil over medium heat, then reduce the heat to low, cover, and simmer for about 15 minutes, or until the quinoa is cooked and the liquid is absorbed.
3. Flavor the Quinoa: Remove from heat and stir in the maple syrup or honey (if using), vanilla extract, and ground cinnamon.
4. Serve: Divide the quinoa mixture into two bowls.
5. Add Toppings: Top each bowl with mixed nuts, seeds, and fresh fruits. Optionally, sprinkle with shredded coconut.
6. Enjoy: Serve warm or chilled.

Nutritional Information (per serving)
- Calories: 350
- Protein: 10g
- Carbohydrates: 45g
- Dietary Fiber: 8g
- Sugars: 12g
- Fat: 14g
- Saturated Fat: 1.5g
- Sodium: 60mg
- Potassium: 550mg
- Vitamin A: 6% of Daily Value
- Vitamin C: 15% of Daily Value
- Calcium: 25% of Daily Value
- Iron: 20% of Daily Value

Berry Smoothie

Yield: 2 servings **Prep Time:** 5 minutes
Cook Time: None

Ingredients
- 1 cup mixed berries (e.g., blueberries, strawberries, raspberries, blackberries)
- 1 cup fresh spinach
- 1 1/2 cups coconut water
- 1 ripe banana (optional for added sweetness and creaminess)
- 1 tablespoon chia seeds (optional for added nutrition)

Directions
1. Prepare Ingredients: Wash the berries and spinach thoroughly. Peel the banana if using.
2. Blend the Smoothie: In a blender, combine the mixed berries, spinach, coconut water, and banana (if using). Blend until smooth and creamy.
3. Adjust Consistency: If the smoothie is too thick, add a little more coconut water until you reach your desired consistency.
4. Serve: Pour the smoothie into two glasses.
5. Add Toppings: Optionally, sprinkle chia seeds on top for added nutrition.
6. Enjoy: Serve immediately for the best texture and flavor.

Nutritional Information (per serving)
- Calories: 120
- Protein: 2g
- Carbohydrates: 28g
- Dietary Fiber: 6g
- Sugars: 15g
- Fat: 1g
- Saturated Fat: 0g
- Sodium: 60mg
- Potassium: 400mg
- Vitamin A: 50% of Daily Value
- Vitamin C: 100% of Daily Value
- Calcium: 8% of Daily Value
- Iron: 6% of Daily Value

Coconut Yogurt with Fresh Fruit

Yield: 2 servings **Prep Time:** 10 minutes
Cook Time: None

Ingredients
- 2 cups dairy-free coconut yogurt
- 1 cup mixed fresh fruits (e.g., berries, sliced kiwi, mango, banana)
- 1/4 cup mixed nuts (e.g., almonds, walnuts, pecans), chopped
- 1 tablespoon chia seeds
- 1 tablespoon honey or maple syrup (optional)
- 1 teaspoon vanilla extract (optional)

Directions
1. Prepare the Fruits: Wash and slice the fresh fruits as needed.
2. Flavor the Yogurt: In a medium bowl, mix the coconut yogurt with honey or maple syrup and vanilla extract if using.
3. Assemble the Bowls: Divide the flavored coconut yogurt into two bowls.
4. Add Fruits and Nuts: Top each bowl with the mixed fresh fruits and chopped nuts.
5. Sprinkle Chia Seeds: Sprinkle the chia seeds evenly over the bowls.
6. Serve: Serve immediately.

Nutritional Information (per serving)
- Calories: 250
- Protein: 4g
- Carbohydrates: 28g
- Dietary Fiber: 6g
- Sugars: 18g
- Fat: 14g
- Saturated Fat: 10g
- Sodium: 30mg
- Potassium: 400mg
- Vitamin A: 6% of Daily Value
- Vitamin C: 60% of Daily Value
- Calcium: 15% of Daily Value
- Iron: 10% of Daily Value

Almond Flour Pancakes

Yield: 8 pancakes **Prep Time:** 10 minutes
Cook Time: 15 minutes

Ingredients
For the Pancakes
- 1 1/2 cups almond flour
- 1/4 cup tapioca flour (or arrowroot flour)
- 1 teaspoon baking powder
- 1/4 teaspoon salt
- 3 large eggs
- 1/2 cup unsweetened almond milk (or any plant-based milk)
- 1 tablespoon maple syrup (optional)
- 1 teaspoon vanilla extract
- 2 tablespoons coconut oil (for cooking)

For the Berry Compote
- 1 cup mixed berries (e.g., blueberries, strawberries, raspberries)
- 1 tablespoon lemon juice
- 1 tablespoon maple syrup or honey
- 1/4 cup water

Directions
For the Pancakes
1. Prepare the Batter: In a large bowl, whisk together the almond flour, tapioca flour, baking powder, and salt. In another bowl, whisk together the eggs, almond milk, maple syrup (if using), and vanilla extract. Combine the wet and dry ingredients and mix until smooth.
2. Heat the Skillet: Heat a non-stick skillet or griddle over medium heat and add a little coconut oil.
3. Cook the Pancakes: Pour 1/4 cup of batter onto the skillet for each pancake. Cook for about 2-3 minutes until bubbles form on the surface, then flip and cook for another 2-3 minutes until golden brown. Repeat with the remaining batter, adding more coconut oil as needed.

For the Berry Compote
1. Cook the Berries: In a small saucepan, combine the mixed berries, lemon juice, maple syrup or honey, and water. Bring to a gentle boil over medium heat.
2. Simmer: Reduce the heat and simmer for about 10 minutes, stirring occasionally, until the berries have broken down and the compote has thickened.
3. Serve: Remove from heat and let cool slightly.

To Serve
1. Plate the Pancakes: Stack the pancakes on plates and spoon the berry compote over the top.
2. Optional Toppings: Add additional toppings like fresh berries, nuts, or a drizzle of maple syrup if desired.

Nutritional Information (per serving, 2 pancakes with compote)
- Calories: 300
- Protein: 10g
- Carbohydrates: 20g
- Dietary Fiber: 6g
- Sugars: 10g
- Fat: 20g
- Saturated Fat: 6g
- Sodium: 250mg
- Potassium: 150mg
- Vitamin A: 4% of Daily Value
- Vitamin C: 20% of Daily Value
- Calcium: 15% of Daily Value
- Iron: 10% of Daily Value

Papaya Boat

Yield: 2 servings **Prep Time:** 10 minutes
Cook Time: None

Ingredients
- 1 ripe papaya
- 1 cup coconut yogurt (dairy-free)
- 1/2 cup mixed fresh fruits (e.g., berries, kiwi, banana, mango)
- 1 tablespoon chia seeds (optional)
- 1 tablespoon shredded coconut (optional)
- 1 tablespoon nuts or seeds (optional)
- Drizzle of honey or maple syrup (optional)

Directions
1. Prepare the Papaya: Cut the papaya in half lengthwise. Scoop out the seeds and discard them.
2. Fill with Yogurt: Divide the coconut yogurt evenly between the two papaya halves, filling the cavities.
3. Add Fresh Fruits: Top each papaya half with the mixed fresh fruits.
4. Optional Toppings: Sprinkle chia seeds, shredded coconut, and nuts or seeds over the fruits. Drizzle with honey or maple syrup if desired.
5. Serve: Serve immediately with a spoon.

Nutritional Information (per serving)
- Calories: 200
- Protein: 3g
- Carbohydrates: 35g
- Dietary Fiber: 6g
- Sugars: 20g
- Fat: 8g
- Saturated Fat: 6g
- Sodium: 20mg
- Potassium: 500mg
- Vitamin A: 60% of Daily Value
- Vitamin C: 150% of Daily Value
- Calcium: 10% of Daily Value
- Iron: 6% of Daily Value

Turmeric Scrambled Eggs

Yield: 2 servings **Prep Time:** 5 minutes
Cook Time: 10 minutes

Ingredients
- 4 large eggs
- 1/4 cup unsweetened almond milk (or any plant-based milk)
- 1/2 teaspoon ground turmeric
- 1/4 teaspoon salt
- 1/4 teaspoon black pepper
- 1 tablespoon olive oil
- 1 small red onion, finely chopped
- 2 cups fresh spinach, chopped
- Optional: a pinch of red pepper flakes for a spicy kick

Directions
1. Whisk the Eggs: In a medium bowl, whisk together the eggs, almond milk, ground turmeric, salt, and black pepper until well combined.
2. Sauté the Onions: In a non-stick skillet, heat the olive oil over medium heat. Add the chopped red onion and sauté for about 3-4 minutes until the onions are soft and translucent.
3. Add the Spinach: Add the chopped spinach to the skillet and cook for another 2 minutes until the spinach is wilted.
4. Cook the Eggs: Pour the egg mixture into the skillet with the onions and spinach. Let the eggs sit for about 30 seconds, then gently stir and scramble until the eggs are just set, about 3-4 minutes.
5. Serve: Divide the scrambled eggs into two servings. Optionally, sprinkle with red pepper flakes for a bit of heat.

Nutritional Information (per serving)
- Calories: 180
- Protein: 12g
- Carbohydrates: 6g
- Dietary Fiber: 2g
- Sugars: 2g
- Fat: 12g
- Saturated Fat: 3g
- Sodium: 300mg
- Potassium: 450mg
- Vitamin A: 70% of Daily Value
- Vitamin C: 25% of Daily Value
- Calcium: 10% of Daily Value
- Iron: 15% of Daily Value

Buckwheat Porridge

Yield: 2 servings **Prep Time:** 5 minutes
Cook Time: 15 minutes

Ingredients
- 1 cup buckwheat groats
- 2 cups unsweetened almond milk (or any plant-based milk)
- 1 tablespoon maple syrup or honey (optional)
- 1 teaspoon vanilla extract
- 1 teaspoon ground cinnamon
- 1 cup mixed berries (e.g., blueberries, strawberries, raspberries)
- 1/4 cup mixed nuts (e.g., almonds, walnuts, pecans), chopped
- Optional toppings: chia seeds, shredded coconut

Directions
1. Rinse the Buckwheat: Rinse the buckwheat groats thoroughly under cold water to remove any dust or impurities.
2. Cook the Buckwheat: In a medium saucepan, combine the buckwheat groats and almond milk. Bring to a gentle boil over medium heat.
3. Simmer: Reduce the heat to low and simmer for about 12-15 minutes, stirring occasionally, until the buckwheat is tender and has absorbed most of the liquid.
4. Add Flavorings: Stir in the maple syrup or honey (if using), vanilla extract, and ground cinnamon. Cook for another 2 minutes, until the flavors are well combined.
5. Serve: Divide the buckwheat porridge into two bowls. Top each bowl with mixed berries and chopped nuts.
6. Optional Toppings: Add additional toppings like chia seeds or shredded coconut if desired.

Nutritional Information (per serving)
- Calories: 300
- Protein: 8g
- Carbohydrates: 45g
- Dietary Fiber: 8g
- Sugars: 10g
- Fat: 12g
- Saturated Fat: 1.5g
- Sodium: 60mg
- Potassium: 500mg
- Vitamin A: 4% of Daily Value
- Vitamin C: 20% of Daily Value
- Calcium: 20% of Daily Value
- Iron: 15% of Daily Value

Zucchini Fritters

Yield: 4 servings (8 fritters) **Prep Time:** 15 minutes
Cook Time: 15 minutes

Ingredients
- 2 medium zucchinis, grated
- 1 teaspoon salt
- 1/2 cup almond flour
- 2 large eggs, beaten
- 2 cloves garlic, minced
- 1/4 cup chopped green onions
- 1/4 teaspoon black pepper
- 1/4 teaspoon paprika (optional)
- 2 tablespoons olive oil (for frying)

Directions
1. Prepare the Zucchini: Place the grated zucchini in a colander and sprinkle with salt. Let it sit for 10 minutes to draw out excess moisture. After 10 minutes, use a clean kitchen towel or cheesecloth to squeeze out as much liquid as possible.
2. Mix Ingredients: In a large bowl, combine the grated zucchini, almond flour, beaten eggs, minced garlic, chopped green onions, black pepper, and paprika (if using). Mix well until all ingredients are thoroughly combined.
3. Heat the Oil: Heat the olive oil in a large non-stick skillet over medium heat.
4. Form the Fritters: Scoop about 1/4 cup of the zucchini mixture and shape it into a patty. Place the patty in the hot skillet. Repeat with the remaining mixture, making sure not to overcrowd the skillet.
5. Cook the Fritters: Cook the fritters for about 3-4 minutes on each side, or until they are golden brown and crispy. Adjust the heat as necessary to avoid burning.
6. Serve: Transfer the cooked fritters to a paper towel-lined plate to drain any excess oil. Serve warm.

Nutritional Information (per serving)
- Calories: 150
- Protein: 6g
- Carbohydrates: 6g
- Dietary Fiber: 2g
- Sugars: 2g
- Fat: 11g
- Saturated Fat: 2g
- Sodium: 300mg
- Potassium: 350mg
- Vitamin A: 6% of Daily Value
- Vitamin C: 20% of Daily Value
- Calcium: 6% of Daily Value
- Iron: 8% of Daily Value

Acai Bowl

Yield: 2 servings **Prep Time:** 10 minutes
Cook Time: None

Ingredients
- 1 (100g) packet of frozen acai puree
- 1 ripe banana
- 1/2 cup unsweetened almond milk (or any plant-based milk)
- 1 tablespoon chia seeds (optional)
- 1/2 cup granola (gluten-free if needed)
- 1 cup mixed fresh fruits (e.g., berries, sliced kiwi, mango, banana)
- Optional toppings: shredded coconut, nuts, seeds, honey or maple syrup

Directions
1. Prepare the Acai Mixture: In a blender, combine the frozen acai puree, banana, almond milk, and chia seeds (if using). Blend until smooth and creamy. If the mixture is too thick, add a little more almond milk until you reach your desired consistency.
2. Serve: Pour the acai mixture into two bowls.
3. Add Toppings: Top each bowl with granola and mixed fresh fruits. Optionally, add shredded coconut, nuts, seeds, or a drizzle of honey or maple syrup for extra flavor.
4. Enjoy: Serve immediately.

Nutritional Information (per serving)
- Calories: 250
- Protein: 5g
- Carbohydrates: 40g
- Dietary Fiber: 8g
- Sugars: 20g
- Fat: 9g
- Saturated Fat: 2g
- Sodium: 50mg
- Potassium: 500mg
- Vitamin A: 4% of Daily Value
- Vitamin C: 30% of Daily Value
- Calcium: 15% of Daily Value
- Iron: 10% of Daily Value

Cauliflower Breakfast Skillet

Yield: 2 servings **Prep Time:** 10 min. **Cook Time:** 15 min.

Ingredients
- 1 small head of cauliflower, grated or 3 cups cauliflower rice
- 1 red bell pepper, diced
- 1 green bell pepper, diced
- 1 small red onion, finely chopped
- 2 cups fresh spinach, chopped
- 2 cloves garlic, minced
- 2 tablespoons olive oil
- 1 teaspoon ground turmeric
- 1/2 teaspoon paprika
- Salt and pepper to taste
- Optional: a pinch of red pepper flakes for a spicy kick
- Optional: 2 eggs (for added protein, can be poached or fried and served on top)

Directions
1. Prepare the Cauliflower: Grate the cauliflower using a box grater or pulse in a food processor until it resembles rice. Alternatively, use pre-packaged cauliflower rice.
2. Heat the Oil: In a large skillet, heat the olive oil over medium heat.
3. Sauté the Vegetables: Add the diced bell peppers and red onion to the skillet. Sauté for about 5 minutes until they start to soften.
4. Add Garlic and Spices: Stir in the minced garlic, ground turmeric, and paprika. Cook for another 1 minute until fragrant.
5. Cook the Cauliflower: Add the cauliflower rice to the skillet. Cook, stirring occasionally, for about 5-7 minutes until the cauliflower is tender.
6. Add Spinach: Stir in the chopped spinach and cook for another 2 minutes until wilted. Season with salt and pepper to taste. Add red pepper flakes if desired.
7. Optional Eggs: If adding eggs, cook them separately (poached or fried) and place them on top of the cauliflower skillet before serving.
8. Serve: Divide the cauliflower breakfast skillet into two bowls and serve immediately.

Nutritional Information (per serving without eggs)
- Calories: 180
- Protein: 5g
- Carbohydrates: 18g
- Dietary Fiber: 6g
- Sugars: 8g
- Fat: 11g
- Saturated Fat: 1.5g
- Sodium: 150mg
- Potassium: 700mg
- Vitamin A: 60% of Daily Value
- Vitamin C: 220% of Daily Value
- Calcium: 8% of Daily Value

Pumpkin Spice Smoothie

Yield: 2 servings **Prep Time:** 5 minutes **Cook Time:** None

Ingredients
- 1 cup pumpkin puree
- 1 ripe banana
- 1 1/2 cups unsweetened almond milk (or any plant-based milk)
- 1 teaspoon pumpkin pie spice
- 1 tablespoon maple syrup or honey (optional)
- 1/2 teaspoon vanilla extract (optional)
- Ice cubes (optional, for a colder smoothie)

Directions
1. Prepare Ingredients: Peel the banana and measure out the pumpkin puree.
2. Blend the Smoothie: In a blender, combine the pumpkin puree, banana, almond milk, pumpkin pie spice, maple syrup or honey (if using), and vanilla extract (if using). Blend until smooth and creamy.
3. Adjust Consistency: If the smoothie is too thick, add a little more almond milk until you reach your desired consistency. Add ice cubes if you prefer a colder smoothie.
4. Serve: Pour the smoothie into two glasses and serve immediately.

Nutritional Information (per serving)
- Calories: 120
- Protein: 2g
- Carbohydrates: 27g
- Dietary Fiber: 4g
- Sugars: 14g
- Fat: 2g
- Saturated Fat: 0g
- Sodium: 75mg
- Potassium: 450mg
- Vitamin A: 280% of Daily Value
- Vitamin C: 15% of Daily Value
- Calcium: 25% of Daily Value
- Iron: 8% of Daily Value

Stuffed Bell Peppers

Yield: 4 servings **Prep Time:** 15 minutes
Cook Time: 40 minutes

Ingredients
- 4 large bell peppers (any color)
- 1 cup quinoa, rinsed
- 1 1/2 cups water or vegetable broth
- 1 tablespoon olive oil
- 1 small red onion, finely chopped
- 2 cloves garlic, minced
- 1 (15-ounce) can black beans, rinsed and drained
- 1 cup diced tomatoes (fresh or canned)
- 1 teaspoon ground cumin
- 1 teaspoon paprika
- 1/2 teaspoon salt
- 1/4 teaspoon black pepper
- 1 cup fresh spinach, chopped
- 1/4 cup chopped fresh cilantro (optional)
- Optional toppings: avocado slices, salsa, dairy-free cheese

Directions
1. Preheat the Oven: Preheat your oven to 375°F (190°C).
2. Prepare the Bell Peppers: Cut the tops off the bell peppers and remove the seeds and membranes. Place the bell peppers upright in a baking dish.
3. Cook the Quinoa: In a medium saucepan, bring the quinoa and water or vegetable broth to a boil. Reduce heat to low, cover, and simmer for about 15 minutes, or until the quinoa is cooked and the liquid is absorbed. Fluff with a fork and set aside.
4. Sauté the Vegetables: In a large skillet, heat the olive oil over medium heat. Add the chopped red onion and sauté for about 3-4 minutes until softened. Add the minced garlic and cook for another 1 minute.
5. Mix the Filling: Add the black beans, diced tomatoes, ground cumin, paprika, salt, and black pepper to the skillet. Stir to combine and cook for about 5 minutes. Add the cooked quinoa and chopped spinach, and cook for another 2-3 minutes until the spinach is wilted. Remove from heat and stir in the chopped cilantro if using.
6. Stuff the Peppers: Spoon the quinoa and black bean mixture into each bell pepper, filling them completely.
7. Bake: Cover the baking dish with foil and bake in the preheated oven for 30 minutes. Remove the foil and bake for an additional 10 minutes, or until the peppers are tender.
8. Serve: Remove the stuffed peppers from the oven and let cool slightly. Top with optional toppings like avocado slices, salsa, or dairy-free cheese if desired. Serve immediately.

Nutritional Information (per serving)
- Calories: 250
- Protein: 10g
- Carbohydrates: 45g
- Dietary Fiber: 12g
- Sugars: 6g
- Fat: 5g
- Saturated Fat: 0.5g
- Sodium: 400mg
- Potassium: 800mg
- Vitamin A: 60% of Daily Value
- Vitamin C: 240% of Daily Value
- Calcium: 8% of Daily Value
- Iron: 20% of Daily Value

Golden Berry Smoothie

Yield: 2 servings **Prep Time:** 5 minutes
Cook Time: None

Ingredients
- 1 cup golden berries (also known as physalis or cape gooseberries)
- 1 ripe banana
- 1 1/2 cups unsweetened almond milk (or any plant-based milk)
- 1 tablespoon chia seeds (optional, for added nutrition)
- 1/2 teaspoon vanilla extract (optional)
- Ice cubes (optional, for a colder smoothie)

Directions
1. Prepare Ingredients: If using fresh golden berries, wash them thoroughly. Peel the banana.
2. Blend the Smoothie: In a blender, combine the golden berries, banana, almond milk, chia seeds (if using), and vanilla extract (if using). Blend until smooth and creamy.
3. Adjust Consistency: If the smoothie is too thick, add a little more almond milk until you reach your desired consistency. Add ice cubes if you prefer a colder smoothie.
4. Serve: Pour the smoothie into two glasses and serve immediately.

Nutritional Information (per serving)
- Calories: 130
- Protein: 2g
- Carbohydrates: 28g
- Dietary Fiber: 5g
- Sugars: 18g
- Fat: 2.5g
- Saturated Fat: 0g
- Sodium: 60mg
- Potassium: 450mg
- Vitamin A: 6% of Daily Value
- Vitamin C: 50% of Daily Value
- Calcium: 20% of Daily Value
- Iron: 6% of Daily Value

Coconut Flour Muffins

Yield: 12 muffins **Prep Time:** 10 minutes
Cook Time: 20-25 minutes

Ingredients
- 1/2 cup coconut flour
- 1/2 teaspoon baking soda
- 1/4 teaspoon salt
- 4 large eggs
- 1/2 cup unsweetened almond milk (or any plant-based milk)
- 1/4 cup coconut oil, melted
- 1/4 cup maple syrup or honey
- 1 teaspoon vanilla extract
- 1 cup fresh or frozen blueberries

Directions
1. Preheat the Oven: Preheat your oven to 350°F (175°C). Line a 12-cup muffin tin with paper liners or lightly grease it.
2. Mix Dry Ingredients: In a medium bowl, whisk together the coconut flour, baking soda, and salt.
3. Mix Wet Ingredients: In a large bowl, whisk together the eggs, almond milk, melted coconut oil, maple syrup or honey, and vanilla extract until well combined.
4. Combine Ingredients: Gradually add the dry ingredients to the wet ingredients, stirring until just combined. The batter will be thick. Gently fold in the blueberries.
5. Fill the Muffin Tin: Divide the batter evenly among the 12 muffin cups, filling each about 3/4 full.
6. Bake: Bake in the preheated oven for 20-25 minutes, or until a toothpick inserted into the center of a muffin comes out clean.
7. Cool: Allow the muffins to cool in the tin for 5 minutes before transferring them to a wire rack to cool completely.

Nutritional Information (per muffin)
- Calories: 120
- Protein: 3g
- Carbohydrates: 10g
- Dietary Fiber: 3g
- Sugars: 6g
- Fat: 8g
- Saturated Fat: 5g
- Sodium: 110mg
- Potassium: 70mg
- Vitamin A: 2% of Daily Value
- Vitamin C: 4% of Daily Value
- Calcium: 4% of Daily Value
- Iron: 4% of Daily Value

Mushroom Spinach Frittata

Yield: 4 servings **Prep Time:** 10 minutes
Cook Time: 25 minutes

Ingredients
- 8 large eggs
- 1/4 cup unsweetened almond milk (or any plant-based milk)
- 1 tablespoon olive oil
- 1 small red onion, finely chopped
- 2 cups fresh spinach, chopped
- 1 cup mushrooms, sliced
- 2 cloves garlic, minced
- 1/2 teaspoon salt
- 1/4 teaspoon black pepper
- 1/4 teaspoon ground turmeric (optional)
- 1/4 teaspoon paprika (optional)

Directions
1. Preheat the Oven: Preheat your oven to 375°F (190°C).
2. Prepare the Vegetables: Heat the olive oil in a large oven-safe skillet over medium heat. Add the chopped red onion and sauté for about 3 minutes until softened. Add the minced garlic and cook for another minute until fragrant.
3. Cook the Mushrooms and Spinach: Add the sliced mushrooms to the skillet and cook for about 5 minutes until they release their moisture and begin to brown. Add the chopped spinach and cook for another 2 minutes until wilted.
4. Whisk the Eggs: In a medium bowl, whisk together the eggs, almond milk, salt, black pepper, ground turmeric, and paprika until well combined.
5. Combine and Cook: Pour the egg mixture over the vegetables in the skillet. Stir gently to ensure the vegetables are evenly distributed. Let the mixture cook on the stovetop for about 2 minutes until the edges start to set.
6. Bake the Frittata: Transfer the skillet to the preheated oven and bake for 15-20 minutes, or until the frittata is fully set and lightly golden on top. A knife inserted into the center should come out clean.
7. Serve: Let the frittata cool for a few minutes before slicing. Serve warm or at room temperature.

Nutritional Information (per serving)
- Calories: 200
- Protein: 14g
- Carbohydrates: 5g
- Dietary Fiber: 2g
- Sugars: 2g
- Fat: 14g
- Saturated Fat: 4g
- Sodium: 300mg
- Potassium: 450mg
- Vitamin A: 40% of Daily Value
- Vitamin C: 15% of Daily Value
- Calcium: 10% of Daily Value
- Iron: 15% of Daily Value

Kale and Quinoa Salad

Yield: 4 servings **Prep Time:** 15 minutes **Cook Time:** 15 minutes

Ingredients
For the Salad
- 1 cup quinoa, rinsed
- 2 cups water or vegetable broth
- 1 bunch kale, stems removed and leaves chopped
- 1 avocado, diced
- 1/2 cup cherry tomatoes, halved
- 1/4 cup red onion, thinly sliced
- 1/4 cup sunflower seeds or pumpkin seeds

For the Lemon Vinaigrette
- 1/4 cup extra virgin olive oil
- 2 tablespoons fresh lemon juice
- 1 teaspoon Dijon mustard
- 1 teaspoon maple syrup or honey
- 1 clove garlic, minced
- Salt and pepper to taste

Directions
1. Cook the Quinoa: In a medium saucepan, bring the quinoa and water or vegetable broth to a boil. Reduce heat to low, cover, and simmer for about 15 minutes, or until the quinoa is cooked and the liquid is absorbed. Fluff with a fork and let cool.
2. Prepare the Kale: While the quinoa is cooking, place the chopped kale in a large bowl. Massage the kale with a pinch of salt for about 2-3 minutes until it becomes tender and slightly wilted.
3. Make the Vinaigrette: In a small bowl, whisk together the olive oil, lemon juice, Dijon mustard, maple syrup or honey, minced garlic, salt, and pepper until well combined.
4. Combine the Salad: Add the cooked quinoa, diced avocado, cherry tomatoes, red onion, and sunflower seeds or pumpkin seeds to the bowl with the kale. Pour the lemon vinaigrette over the salad and toss gently to combine.
5. Serve: Divide the salad into four servings and serve immediately.

Nutritional Information (per serving)
- Calories: 300
- Protein: 7g
- Carbohydrates: 27g
- Dietary Fiber: 8g
- Sugars: 4g
- Fat: 20g
- Saturated Fat: 3g
- Sodium: 150mg
- Potassium: 700mg
- Vitamin A: 200% of Daily Value
- Vitamin C: 120% of Daily Value
- Calcium: 10% of Daily Value
- Iron: 15% of Daily Value

Beetroot Smoothie

Yield: 2 servings **Prep Time:** 10 minutes **Cook Time:** 10 minutes (for cooking beetroot, if not pre-cooked)

Ingredients
- 1 cup cooked beetroot, diced (about 1 medium beet)
- 1 ripe banana
- 1 1/2 cups unsweetened almond milk (or any plant-based milk)
- 1 tablespoon chia seeds (optional, for added nutrition)
- 1/2 teaspoon vanilla extract (optional)
- Ice cubes (optional, for a colder smoothie)

Directions
1. Cook the Beetroot: If not using pre-cooked beetroot, peel and dice the beetroot. Boil or steam until tender, about 10 minutes. Let cool before using.
2. Prepare Ingredients: Peel the banana and dice the cooked beetroot if not already done.
3. Blend the Smoothie: In a blender, combine the cooked beetroot, banana, almond milk, chia seeds (if using), and vanilla extract (if using). Blend until smooth and creamy.
4. Adjust Consistency: If the smoothie is too thick, add a little more almond milk until you reach your desired consistency. Add ice cubes if you prefer a colder smoothie.
5. Serve: Pour the smoothie into two glasses and serve immediately.

Nutritional Information (per serving)
- Calories: 120
- Protein: 2g
- Carbohydrates: 26g
- Dietary Fiber: 5g
- Sugars: 15g
- Fat: 2.5g
- Saturated Fat: 0g
- Sodium: 60mg
- Potassium: 500mg
- Vitamin A: 2% of Daily Value
- Vitamin C: 15% of Daily Value
- Calcium: 20% of Daily Value
- Iron: 6% of Daily Value

Berry Chia Jam on Toast

Yield: 2 servings **Prep Time:** 5 minutes
Cook Time: 15 minutes (plus cooling time)

Ingredients
For the Berry Chia Jam:
- 1 cup mixed berries (e.g., strawberries, blueberries, raspberries)
- 1 tablespoon honey or maple syrup
- 1 tablespoon chia seeds
- 1/2 teaspoon vanilla extract (optional)

For the Toast
- 2 slices whole grain bread
- Optional toppings: additional fresh berries, nut butter

Directions
For the Berry Chia Jam
1. Cook the Berries: In a small saucepan, heat the mixed berries over medium heat. Stir occasionally and cook for about 5-10 minutes until the berries break down and become juicy.
2. Mash the Berries: Use a fork or potato masher to gently mash the berries to your desired consistency.
3. Add Sweetener and Chia Seeds: Stir in the honey or maple syrup, chia seeds, and vanilla extract (if using). Continue to cook for another 2-3 minutes until the mixture thickens.
4. Cool the Jam: Remove from heat and let the jam cool for about 10-15 minutes. It will continue to thicken as it cools. Store any leftover jam in an airtight container in the refrigerator for up to 1 week.

For the Toast
1. Toast the Bread: While the jam is cooling, toast the whole grain bread slices to your desired level of crispiness.
2. Assemble the Toast: Spread the homemade berry chia jam over the toasted bread slices.
3. Add Optional Toppings: Add additional toppings such as fresh berries or nut butter for extra flavor and nutrition.
4. Serve: Serve immediately.

Nutritional Information (per serving)
- Calories: 200
- Protein: 5g
- Carbohydrates: 34g
- Dietary Fiber: 8g
- Sugars: 12g
- Fat: 5g
- Saturated Fat: 0.5g
- Sodium: 150mg
- Potassium: 200mg
- Vitamin A: 2% of Daily Value
- Vitamin C: 30% of Daily Value
- Calcium: 10% of Daily Value
- Iron: 10% of Daily Value

Flaxseed Porridge

Yield: 2 servings **Prep Time:** 5 minutes
Cook Time: 5 minutes

Ingredients
- 1/2 cup ground flaxseeds
- 1 1/2 cups unsweetened almond milk (or any plant-based milk)
- 1 tablespoon chia seeds (optional, for added thickness)
- 1 tablespoon maple syrup or honey (optional, for sweetness)
- 1 teaspoon vanilla extract (optional)
- 1/2 teaspoon ground cinnamon
- 1/4 cup mixed nuts (e.g., almonds, walnuts, pecans), chopped
- 1/2 cup mixed berries (e.g., blueberries, strawberries, raspberries)

Directions
1. Mix Ingredients: In a medium saucepan, combine the ground flaxseeds, almond milk, chia seeds (if using), maple syrup or honey (if using), vanilla extract, and ground cinnamon. Stir well to combine.
2. Cook the Porridge: Place the saucepan over medium heat and bring the mixture to a gentle simmer. Cook for about 5 minutes, stirring frequently, until the porridge thickens to your desired consistency.
3. Serve: Divide the porridge into two bowls. Top each bowl with chopped nuts and mixed berries.
4. Optional Toppings: Add additional toppings like shredded coconut, a drizzle of nut butter, or more fruit if desired.

Nutritional Information (per serving)
- Calories: 250
- Protein: 8g
- Carbohydrates: 18g
- Dietary Fiber: 12g
- Sugars: 8g
- Fat: 18g
- Saturated Fat: 1.5g
- Sodium: 50mg
- Potassium: 300mg
- Vitamin A: 2% of Daily Value
- Vitamin C: 10% of Daily Value
- Calcium: 20% of Daily Value
- Iron: 15% of Daily Value

Blueberry Almond Smoothie

Yield: 2 servings **Prep Time:** 5 minutes
Cook Time: None

Ingredients
- 1 1/2 cups fresh or frozen blueberries
- 2 tablespoons almond butter
- 1 1/2 cups unsweetened almond milk (or any plant-based milk)
- 1 ripe banana (optional, for added sweetness and creaminess)
- 1 tablespoon chia seeds (optional, for added nutrition)
- 1/2 teaspoon vanilla extract (optional)
- Ice cubes (optional, for a colder smoothie)

Directions
1. Prepare Ingredients: If using fresh blueberries, wash them thoroughly. Peel the banana if using.
2. Blend the Smoothie: In a blender, combine the blueberries, almond butter, almond milk, banana (if using), chia seeds (if using), and vanilla extract (if using). Blend until smooth and creamy.
3. Adjust Consistency: If the smoothie is too thick, add a little more almond milk until you reach your desired consistency. Add ice cubes if you prefer a colder smoothie.
4. Serve: Pour the smoothie into two glasses and serve immediately.

Nutritional Information (per serving)
- Calories: 180
- Protein: 4g
- Carbohydrates: 24g
- Dietary Fiber: 6g
- Sugars: 12g
- Fat: 8g
- Saturated Fat: 0.5g
- Sodium: 60mg
- Potassium: 350mg
- Vitamin A: 2% of Daily Value
- Vitamin C: 20% of Daily Value
- Calcium: 20% of Daily Value
- Iron: 6% of Daily Value

Cucumber Avocado Salad

Yield: 2 servings **Prep Time:** 10 minutes
Cook Time: None

Ingredients
For the Salad
- 1 large cucumber, thinly sliced
- 1 ripe avocado, diced
- 1/4 red onion, thinly sliced
- 1/4 cup fresh cilantro, chopped (optional)

For the Lemon Dressing
- 2 tablespoons extra virgin olive oil
- 2 tablespoons fresh lemon juice
- 1 teaspoon Dijon mustard
- 1 teaspoon honey or maple syrup (optional)
- 1 clove garlic, minced
- Salt and pepper to taste

Directions
1. Prepare the Vegetables: Thinly slice the cucumber and red onion, and dice the avocado. Chop the fresh cilantro if using.
2. Make the Dressing: In a small bowl, whisk together the olive oil, lemon juice, Dijon mustard, honey or maple syrup (if using), minced garlic, salt, and pepper until well combined.
3. Combine Ingredients: In a large bowl, gently toss the cucumber, avocado, red onion, and cilantro (if using) with the lemon dressing until evenly coated.
4. Serve: Divide the salad into two servings and serve immediately.

Nutritional Information (per serving)
- Calories: 200
- Protein: 2g
- Carbohydrates: 14g
- Dietary Fiber: 7g
- Sugars: 5g
- Fat: 17g
- Saturated Fat: 2.5g
- Sodium: 50mg
- Potassium: 600mg
- Vitamin A: 6% of Daily Value
- Vitamin C: 30% of Daily Value
- Calcium: 4% of Daily Value
- Iron: 6% of Daily Value

Collard Green Wraps

Yield: 4 wraps **Prep Time:** 15 minutes
Cook Time: None

Ingredients
- 4 large collard green leaves
- 1 cup hummus
- 1 ripe avocado, sliced
- 1 red bell pepper, thinly sliced
- 1 cucumber, julienned
- 1 carrot, julienned
- 1/4 red onion, thinly sliced
- 1/4 cup fresh cilantro, chopped
- 1 tablespoon lemon juice
- Salt and pepper to taste

Directions
1. Prepare the Collard Greens: Wash the collard green leaves thoroughly. Using a sharp knife, carefully trim the thick stem at the base of each leaf, ensuring not to cut through the leaf itself. This will make the leaves easier to roll.
2. Prepare the Filling: In a medium bowl, combine the sliced avocado, red bell pepper, cucumber, carrot, red onion, and chopped cilantro. Drizzle with lemon juice and season with salt and pepper. Toss gently to combine.
3. Assemble the Wraps: Lay a collard green leaf flat on a clean surface. Spread about 1/4 cup of hummus evenly over the leaf. Place a portion of the veggie mixture in the center of the leaf.
4. Roll the Wraps: Fold in the sides of the collard green leaf, then roll it up from the bottom, burrito-style, to enclose the filling. Repeat with the remaining leaves and filling.
5. Serve: Cut each wrap in half, if desired, and serve immediately.

Nutritional Information (per wrap)
- Calories: 150
- Protein: 4g
- Carbohydrates: 16g
- Dietary Fiber: 7g
- Sugars: 4g
- Fat: 9g
- Saturated Fat: 1g
- Sodium: 220mg
- Potassium: 600mg
- Vitamin A: 110% of Daily Value
- Vitamin C: 150% of Daily Value
- Calcium: 8% of Daily Value
- Iron: 10% of Daily Value

Peach Quinoa Bowl

Yield: 2 servings **Prep Time:** 10 minutes
Cook Time: 15 minutes

Ingredients
- 1 cup quinoa, rinsed
- 2 cups water or unsweetened almond milk (or any plant-based milk)
- 2 fresh peaches, diced
- 1 tablespoon honey (optional, for sweetness)
- 1/2 teaspoon ground cinnamon
- 1/4 teaspoon vanilla extract (optional)
- 1/4 cup chopped nuts (e.g., almonds, walnuts, pecans) (optional)
- Fresh mint leaves for garnish (optional)

Directions
1. Cook the Quinoa: In a medium saucepan, bring the quinoa and water or almond milk to a boil. Reduce heat to low, cover, and simmer for about 15 minutes, or until the quinoa is cooked and the liquid is absorbed. Fluff with a fork.
2. Prepare the Peaches: While the quinoa is cooking, dice the fresh peaches into small pieces.
3. Combine Ingredients: Once the quinoa is cooked, stir in the diced peaches, ground cinnamon, honey (if using), and vanilla extract (if using). Cook for another 2-3 minutes over low heat, until the peaches are slightly softened and the flavors are well combined.
4. Serve: Divide the quinoa mixture into two bowls. Top each bowl with chopped nuts and garnish with fresh mint leaves if desired.
5. Enjoy: Serve warm.

Nutritional Information (per serving)
- Calories: 250
- Protein: 6g
- Carbohydrates: 45g
- Dietary Fiber: 6g
- Sugars: 15g
- Fat: 6g
- Saturated Fat: 0.5g
- Sodium: 30mg
- Potassium: 350mg
- Vitamin A: 4% of Daily Value
- Vitamin C: 10% of Daily Value
- Calcium: 8% of Daily Value
- Iron: 15% of Daily Value

Eggplant Breakfast Skillet

Yield: 2 servings **Prep Time:** 10 minutes
Cook Time: 20 minutes

Ingredients
- 1 medium eggplant, diced
- 1 red bell pepper, diced
- 1 yellow bell pepper, diced
- 1 small red onion, finely chopped
- 2 cloves garlic, minced
- 2 medium tomatoes, diced
- 2 tablespoons olive oil
- 1 teaspoon ground turmeric
- 1/2 teaspoon paprika
- Salt and pepper to taste
- Optional: fresh herbs (e.g., parsley, cilantro) for garnish

Directions
1. Prepare the Vegetables: Dice the eggplant, bell peppers, tomatoes, and finely chop the red onion and garlic.
2. Heat the Oil: In a large skillet, heat the olive oil over medium heat.
3. Cook the Onions and Garlic: Add the finely chopped red onion and minced garlic to the skillet. Sauté for about 3 minutes until the onions are softened and translucent.
4. Add the Eggplant: Add the diced eggplant to the skillet. Cook for about 5-7 minutes, stirring occasionally, until the eggplant starts to soften and brown.
5. Add Bell Peppers and Spices: Stir in the diced red and yellow bell peppers, ground turmeric, paprika, salt, and pepper. Cook for another 5 minutes until the bell peppers are tender.
6. Add Tomatoes: Add the diced tomatoes to the skillet. Cook for another 2-3 minutes until the tomatoes are softened and heated through.
7. Serve: Divide the eggplant breakfast skillet into two bowls. Garnish with fresh herbs if desired.
8. Enjoy: Serve immediately.

Nutritional Information (per serving)
- Calories: 200
- Protein: 3g
- Carbohydrates: 20g
- Dietary Fiber: 8g
- Sugars: 10g
- Fat: 12g
- Saturated Fat: 2g
- Sodium: 20mg
- Potassium: 600mg
- Vitamin A: 50% of Daily Value
- Vitamin C: 150% of Daily Value
- Calcium: 4% of Daily Value
- Iron: 6% of Daily Value

Turmeric Coconut Porridge

Yield: 2 servings **Prep Time:** 5 minutes
Cook Time: 10 minutes

Ingredients
- 1 cup rolled oats
- 2 cups unsweetened coconut milk (or any plant-based milk)
- 1 teaspoon ground turmeric
- 1/2 teaspoon ground cinnamon
- 1 tablespoon maple syrup or honey (optional)
- 1/2 teaspoon vanilla extract (optional)
- Pinch of black pepper (to enhance turmeric absorption)
- 1/4 cup mixed nuts (e.g., almonds, walnuts, pecans), chopped
- 2 tablespoons mixed seeds (e.g., chia seeds, flaxseeds, pumpkin seeds)

Directions
1. Prepare the Oats: In a medium saucepan, combine the rolled oats and coconut milk. Bring to a gentle boil over medium heat.
2. Add Spices and Sweetener: Stir in the ground turmeric, ground cinnamon, maple syrup or honey (if using), vanilla extract (if using), and a pinch of black pepper. Reduce the heat to low and simmer for about 5-7 minutes, stirring occasionally, until the oats are cooked and the porridge is creamy.
3. Serve: Divide the turmeric coconut porridge into two bowls.
4. Add Toppings: Top each bowl with chopped nuts and mixed seeds.
5. Enjoy: Serve warm.

Nutritional Information (per serving)
- Calories: 300
- Protein: 7g
- Carbohydrates: 35g
- Dietary Fiber: 7g
- Sugars: 8g
- Fat: 15g
- Saturated Fat: 8g
- Sodium: 50mg
- Potassium: 350mg
- Vitamin A: 2% of Daily Value
- Vitamin C: 2% of Daily Value
- Calcium: 10% of Daily Value
- Iron: 15% of Daily Value

Lunch & Dinner Recipes

Balanced and nutritious meals are essential for maintaining an anti-inflammatory diet

Turmeric Chicken and Vegetable Stir-Fry

Yield: 4 servings, **Prep Time:** 15 minutes
Cook Time: 15 minutes

Ingredients

- 1 lb chicken breast, thinly sliced
- 1 tablespoon olive oil
- 1 teaspoon ground turmeric
- 1 teaspoon ground ginger
- 2 cloves garlic, minced
- 1 tablespoon fresh ginger, minced
- 1 red bell pepper, thinly sliced
- 1 yellow bell pepper, thinly sliced
- 1 cup broccoli florets
- 1 carrot, julienned
- 1 small red onion, thinly sliced
- 3 tablespoons tamari or soy sauce (gluten-free if needed)
- 1 tablespoon rice vinegar
- 1 tablespoon honey or maple syrup (optional)
- 1/4 teaspoon black pepper
- 1/4 cup fresh cilantro, chopped (optional)
- Cooked brown rice or quinoa, for serving

Directions

1. Prepare the Sauce: In a small bowl, combine the tamari or soy sauce, rice vinegar, honey or maple syrup (if using), ground turmeric, ground ginger, and black pepper. Mix well and set aside.
2. Cook the Chicken: In a large skillet or wok, heat the olive oil over medium-high heat. Add the sliced chicken breast and cook for 5-7 minutes, or until fully cooked and lightly browned. Remove the chicken from the skillet and set aside.
3. Stir-Fry the Vegetables: In the same skillet, add the minced garlic and fresh ginger. Cook for about 1 minute until fragrant. Add the red and yellow bell peppers, broccoli florets, julienned carrot, and red onion. Stir-fry for about 5 minutes, or until the vegetables are tender-crisp.
4. Combine Chicken and Sauce: Return the cooked chicken to the skillet. Pour the sauce over the chicken and vegetables. Stir well to coat everything evenly. Cook for another 2-3 minutes until heated through.
5. Serve: Divide the stir-fry into four servings. Garnish with chopped fresh cilantro if desired. Serve over cooked brown rice or quinoa.

Nutritional Information (per serving)

- Calories: 250
- Protein: 25g
- Carbohydrates: 20g
- Dietary Fiber: 4g
- Sugars: 6g
- Fat: 8g
- Saturated Fat: 1.5g
- Sodium: 600mg
- Potassium: 750mg
- Vitamin A: 50% of Daily Value
- Vitamin C: 150% of Daily Value
- Calcium: 6% of Daily Value
- Iron: 10% of Daily Value

Quinoa and Black Bean Salad

Yield: 4 servings **Prep Time:** 15 minutes
Cook Time: 15 minutes

Ingredients

- 1 cup quinoa, rinsed
- 2 cups water or vegetable broth
- 1 (15-ounce) can black beans, rinsed and drained
- 1 cup corn kernels (fresh, frozen, or canned)
- 1 avocado, diced
- 1 red bell pepper, diced
- 1/4 red onion, finely chopped
- 1/4 cup fresh cilantro, chopped
- 1/4 cup extra virgin olive oil
- 3 tablespoons fresh lime juice (about 2 limes)
- 1 teaspoon lime zest
- 1 clove garlic, minced
- 1 teaspoon ground cumin
- 1/2 teaspoon ground turmeric
- 1/2 teaspoon salt
- 1/4 teaspoon black pepper

Directions

1. Cook the Quinoa: In a medium saucepan, combine the rinsed quinoa and water or vegetable broth. Bring to a boil over medium-high heat. Reduce the heat to low, cover, and simmer for about 15 minutes, or until the quinoa is cooked and the liquid is absorbed. Fluff with a fork and let it cool slightly.
2. Prepare the Dressing: In a small bowl, whisk together the olive oil, fresh lime juice, lime zest, minced garlic, ground cumin, ground turmeric, salt, and black pepper until well combined.
3. Mix the Salad: In a large bowl, combine the cooked quinoa, black beans, corn kernels, diced avocado, red bell pepper, red onion, and chopped cilantro.
4. Add the Dressing: Pour the cilantro-lime dressing over the salad and toss gently to combine, ensuring all ingredients are evenly coated.
5. Serve: Divide the salad into four servings and serve immediately, or refrigerate for up to 2 days.

Nutritional Information (per serving)

- Calories: 320
- Protein: 9g
- Carbohydrates: 38g
- Dietary Fiber: 10g
- Sugars: 3g
- Fat: 17g
- Saturated Fat: 2.5g
- Sodium: 400mg
- Potassium: 650mg
- Vitamin A: 20% of Daily Value
- Vitamin C: 60% of Daily Value
- Calcium: 6% of Daily Value
- Iron: 15% of Daily Value

Baked Salmon with Asparagus

Yield: 4 servings **Prep Time:** 10 minutes
Cook Time: 20 minutes

Ingredients

- 4 salmon fillets (about 6 ounces each)
- 1 bunch asparagus, trimmed
- 2 tablespoons olive oil
- 1 lemon, thinly sliced
- 2 tablespoons fresh dill, chopped (or 1 tablespoon dried dill)
- 2 cloves garlic, minced
- Salt and pepper to taste
- Lemon wedges, for serving

Directions

1. Preheat the Oven: Preheat your oven to 400°F (200°C). Line a baking sheet with parchment paper or lightly grease it with olive oil.
2. Prepare the Asparagus: Place the trimmed asparagus on one side of the prepared baking sheet. Drizzle with 1 tablespoon of olive oil and season with salt and pepper. Toss to coat evenly.
3. Prepare the Salmon: Place the salmon fillets on the other side of the baking sheet. Drizzle with the remaining 1 tablespoon of olive oil. Season the salmon fillets with salt, pepper, and minced garlic. Arrange lemon slices on top of the salmon fillets and sprinkle with fresh or dried dill.
4. Bake: Bake in the preheated oven for 15-20 minutes, or until the salmon is cooked through and flakes easily with a fork, and the asparagus is tender.
5. Serve: Divide the salmon fillets and roasted asparagus among four plates. Serve with additional lemon wedges.

Nutritional Information (per serving)

- Calories: 350
- Protein: 30g
- Carbohydrates: 5g
- Dietary Fiber: 2g
- Sugars: 2g
- Fat: 22g
- Saturated Fat: 4g
- Sodium: 120mg
- Potassium: 800mg
- Vitamin A: 20% of Daily Value
- Vitamin C: 30% of Daily Value
- Calcium: 6% of Daily Value
- Iron: 15% of Daily Value

Cauliflower Rice Stir-Fry

Yield: 4 servings **Prep Time:** 15 minutes
Cook Time: 10 minutes

Ingredients

- 1 large head of cauliflower, grated into rice-sized pieces (about 4 cups cauliflower rice)
- 1 tablespoon olive oil
- 1 red bell pepper, diced
- 1 yellow bell pepper, diced
- 1 cup snap peas, trimmed and halved
- 1 cup carrots, julienned
- 1 cup broccoli florets
- 3 green onions, sliced
- 2 cloves garlic, minced
- 1 tablespoon fresh ginger, minced

For the Tamari-Ginger Sauce

- 1/4 cup tamari (gluten-free soy sauce)
- 1 tablespoon rice vinegar
- 1 tablespoon sesame oil
- 1 tablespoon honey or maple syrup (optional)
- 1/2 teaspoon ground turmeric
- 1/4 teaspoon black pepper
- 1/4 teaspoon red pepper flakes (optional)

Directions

1. Prepare the Cauliflower Rice: Grate the cauliflower using a box grater or pulse in a food processor until it resembles rice. Set aside.
2. Prepare the Sauce: In a small bowl, whisk together the tamari, rice vinegar, sesame oil, honey or maple syrup (if using), ground turmeric, black pepper, and red pepper flakes (if using). Set aside.
3. Heat the Oil: In a large skillet or wok, heat the olive oil over medium-high heat.
4. Cook the Vegetables: Add the minced garlic and fresh ginger to the skillet and sauté for about 1 minute until fragrant. Add the red and yellow bell peppers, snap peas, carrots, and broccoli florets. Stir-fry for about 5 minutes until the vegetables are tender-crisp.
5. Add the Cauliflower Rice: Add the cauliflower rice to the skillet and stir well to combine. Cook for another 3-4 minutes until the cauliflower is tender.
6. Add the Sauce: Pour the tamari-ginger sauce over the vegetable mixture and stir well to coat evenly. Cook for another 1-2 minutes until heated through.
7. Serve: Divide the cauliflower rice stir-fry into four servings. Garnish with sliced green onions and serve immediately.

Nutritional Information (per serving)

- Calories: 150
- Protein: 4g
- Carbohydrates: 20g
- Dietary Fiber: 6g
- Sugars: 8g
- Fat: 6g
- Saturated Fat: 1g
- Sodium: 700mg
- Potassium: 600mg
- Vitamin A: 100% of Daily Value
- Vitamin C: 150% of Daily Value
- Calcium: 6% of Daily Value
- Iron: 10% of Daily Value

Lentil and Spinach Soup

Yield: 4 servings **Prep Time:** 15 minutes
Cook Time: 30 minutes

Ingredients
- 1 cup dried green or brown lentils, rinsed and drained
- 1 tablespoon olive oil
- 1 large onion, chopped
- 2 cloves garlic, minced
- 2 carrots, diced
- 2 celery stalks, diced
- 1 (14.5-ounce) can diced tomatoes
- 6 cups vegetable broth
- 2 teaspoons ground cumin
- 1 teaspoon ground turmeric
- 1 teaspoon paprika
- 1/2 teaspoon ground black pepper
- 1/2 teaspoon salt (or to taste)
- 4 cups fresh spinach, chopped
- 1/4 cup fresh parsley, chopped (optional)
- Juice of 1 lemon

Directions
1. Heat the Oil: In a large pot, heat the olive oil over medium heat. Add the chopped onion and sauté for about 5 minutes until softened.
2. Add Vegetables: Add the minced garlic, diced carrots, and diced celery. Cook for another 5 minutes until the vegetables are tender.
3. Add Lentils and Spices: Stir in the rinsed lentils, ground cumin, ground turmeric, paprika, black pepper, and salt. Cook for about 1 minute until the spices are fragrant.
4. Add Broth and Tomatoes: Pour in the vegetable broth and add the diced tomatoes with their juice. Bring the mixture to a boil.
5. Simmer: Reduce the heat to low and let the soup simmer for about 20-25 minutes, or until the lentils are tender.
6. Add Spinach: Stir in the chopped spinach and cook for another 2-3 minutes until the spinach is wilted.
7. Finish with Lemon and Parsley: Stir in the lemon juice and chopped parsley (if using). Adjust the seasoning with more salt and pepper if needed.
8. Serve: Ladle the soup into bowls and serve hot.

Nutritional Information (per serving)
- Calories: 250
- Protein: 12g
- Carbohydrates: 40g
- Dietary Fiber: 15g
- Sugars: 8g
- Fat: 5g
- Saturated Fat: 0.5g
- Sodium: 600mg
- Potassium: 900mg
- Vitamin A: 100% of Daily Value
- Vitamin C: 40% of Daily Value
- Calcium: 10% of Daily Value
- Iron: 25% of Daily Value

Zucchini Noodles with Pesto

Yield: 4 servings **Prep Time:** 15 minutes
Cook Time: 5 minutes

Ingredients
For the Zucchini Noodles
- 4 medium zucchinis, spiralized
- 1 tablespoon olive oil
- Salt and pepper to taste

For the Basil Pesto
- 2 cups fresh basil leaves, packed
- 1/2 cup pine nuts (or walnuts)
- 1/2 cup extra virgin olive oil
- 1/4 cup nutritional yeast (or Parmesan cheese if not vegan)
- 2 cloves garlic, minced
- Juice of 1 lemon
- Salt and pepper to taste

Directions
1. Prepare the Pesto: In a food processor, combine the fresh basil leaves, pine nuts, nutritional yeast (or Parmesan cheese), minced garlic, and lemon juice. Pulse until the ingredients are finely chopped. With the food processor running, gradually add the olive oil in a steady stream until the pesto is smooth and creamy. Season with salt and pepper to taste.
2. Prepare the Zucchini Noodles: Spiralize the zucchinis to create noodles. If you don't have a spiralizer, you can use a vegetable peeler to create thin strips.
3. Cook the Zucchini Noodles: In a large skillet, heat 1 tablespoon of olive oil over medium heat. Add the spiralized zucchini noodles and sauté for about 2-3 minutes until they are just tender but still firm. Season with salt and pepper to taste.
4. Toss with Pesto: Remove the skillet from heat and add the prepared basil pesto to the zucchini noodles. Toss until the noodles are evenly coated with the pesto.
5. Serve: Divide the zucchini noodles with pesto among four plates. Serve immediately.

Nutritional Information (per serving)
- Calories: 250
- Protein: 5g
- Carbohydrates: 8g
- Dietary Fiber: 3g
- Sugars: 4g
- Fat: 22g
- Saturated Fat: 3g
- Sodium: 150mg
- Potassium: 600mg
- Vitamin A: 20% of Daily Value
- Vitamin C: 50% of Daily Value
- Calcium: 8% of Daily Value
- Iron: 15% of Daily Value

Miso Soup with Tofu and Seaweed

Yield: 4 servings **Prep Time:** 10 minutes
Cook Time: 10 minutes

Ingredients
- 4 cups water
- 1/4 cup miso paste (white or yellow)
- 1 cup tofu, cubed (firm or silken)
- 1/4 cup dried wakame seaweed
- 1/4 cup green onions, sliced
- 1/2 cup shiitake mushrooms, sliced (optional)
- 1 tablespoon tamari or soy sauce (gluten-free if needed)
- 1 teaspoon grated ginger (optional)
- 1 teaspoon sesame oil (optional)

Directions
1. Prepare the Seaweed: In a small bowl, soak the dried wakame seaweed in warm water for about 5 minutes until it rehydrates and expands. Drain and set aside.
2. Heat the Water: In a medium saucepan, bring the water to a gentle simmer over medium heat.
3. Add Miso Paste: In a small bowl, whisk together the miso paste with a ladleful of the hot water until it is smooth and dissolved. Then, add this mixture back into the saucepan. Stir well to combine.
4. Add Tofu and Mushrooms: Add the cubed tofu and sliced shiitake mushrooms (if using) to the pot. Simmer for about 3-4 minutes until the mushrooms are tender.
5. Add Seaweed and Tamari: Stir in the rehydrated wakame seaweed and tamari or soy sauce. Simmer for another 1-2 minutes.
6. Finish with Green Onions and Ginger: Stir in the sliced green onions and grated ginger (if using). Remove from heat and add a drizzle of sesame oil if desired.
7. Serve: Ladle the miso soup into bowls and serve immediately.

Nutritional Information (per serving)
- Calories: 80
- Protein: 6g
- Carbohydrates: 6g
- Dietary Fiber: 2g
- Sugars: 2g
- Fat: 4g
- Saturated Fat: 0.5g
- Sodium: 700mg
- Potassium: 250mg
- Vitamin A: 10% of Daily Value
- Vitamin C: 4% of Daily Value
- Calcium: 10% of Daily Value
- Iron: 8% of Daily Value

Greek Salad with Grilled Chicken

Yield: 4 servings **Prep Time:** 20 minutes
Cook Time: 15 minutes

Ingredients
For the Grilled Chicken
- 2 boneless, skinless chicken breasts
- 2 tablespoons olive oil
- 1 tablespoon lemon juice
- 1 teaspoon dried oregano
- 1 teaspoon garlic powder
- Salt and pepper to taste

For the Salad
- 6 cups mixed greens (e.g., romaine, spinach, arugula)
- 1 cucumber, sliced
- 1 cup cherry tomatoes, halved
- 1/2 red onion, thinly sliced
- 1/2 cup Kalamata olives, pitted
- 1/2 cup feta cheese, crumbled
- 1/4 cup fresh parsley, chopped (optional)

For the Dressing
- 1/4 cup extra virgin olive oil
- 2 tablespoons red wine vinegar
- 1 tablespoon lemon juice
- 1 teaspoon dried oregano
- 1 clove garlic, minced
- Salt and pepper to taste

Directions
1. Marinate the Chicken: In a small bowl, mix the olive oil, lemon juice, dried oregano, garlic powder, salt, and pepper. Place the chicken breasts in a resealable plastic bag or a shallow dish and pour the marinade over them. Let marinate for at least 15 minutes.
2. Grill the Chicken: Preheat the grill to medium-high heat. Grill the chicken breasts for about 6-7 minutes per side, or until fully cooked and the internal temperature reaches 165°F (75°C). Remove from the grill and let rest for a few minutes before slicing.
3. Prepare the Dressing: In a small bowl, whisk together the olive oil, red wine vinegar, lemon juice, dried oregano, minced garlic, salt, and pepper until well combined.
4. Assemble the Salad: In a large bowl, combine the mixed greens, sliced cucumber, cherry tomatoes, red onion, Kalamata olives, feta cheese, and chopped parsley (if using). Toss gently to combine.
5. Add Chicken and Dressing: Top the salad with the sliced grilled chicken. Drizzle the dressing over the salad and toss gently to coat.
6. Serve: Divide the salad into four servings and serve immediately.

Nutritional Information (per serving)
- Calories: 350
- Protein: 25g
- Carbohydrates: 10g
- Dietary Fiber: 4g
- Sugars: 4g
- Fat: 25g
- Saturated Fat: 7g
- Sodium: 700mg
- Potassium: 600mg
- Vitamin A: 60% of Daily Value
- Vitamin C: 30% of Daily Value
- Calcium: 20% of Daily Value
- Iron: 10% of Daily Value

Spaghetti Squash with Marinara Sauce

Yield: 4 servings **Prep Time:** 15 minutes
Cook Time: 45 minutes

Ingredients
For the Spaghetti Squash
- 1 large spaghetti squash
- 2 tablespoons olive oil
- Salt and pepper to taste

For the Marinara Sauce
- 2 tablespoons olive oil
- 1 large onion, finely chopped
- 3 cloves garlic, minced
- 1 (28-ounce) can crushed tomatoes
- 1 (14.5-ounce) can diced tomatoes
- 2 tablespoons tomato paste
- 1 teaspoon dried oregano
- 1 teaspoon dried basil
- 1/2 teaspoon dried thyme
- 1/4 teaspoon red pepper flakes (optional)
- Salt and pepper to taste
- 1/4 cup fresh basil leaves, chopped

Directions
1. Preheat the Oven: Preheat your oven to 400°F (200°C). Line a baking sheet with parchment paper.
2. Prepare the Spaghetti Squash: Cut the spaghetti squash in half lengthwise and scoop out the seeds. Drizzle the inside of each half with 1 tablespoon of olive oil and season with salt and pepper. Place the squash halves cut-side down on the prepared baking sheet.
3. Roast the Squash: Roast the spaghetti squash in the preheated oven for 40-45 minutes, or until the squash is tender and easily pierced with a fork. Remove from the oven and let cool slightly.
4. Prepare the Marinara Sauce: While the squash is roasting, heat 2 tablespoons of olive oil in a large skillet over medium heat. Add the finely chopped onion and sauté for about 5 minutes until softened. Add the minced garlic and cook for another 1-2 minutes until fragrant.
5. Add Tomatoes and Herbs: Stir in the crushed tomatoes, diced tomatoes, and tomato paste. Add the dried oregano, dried basil, dried thyme, red pepper flakes (if using), salt, and pepper. Bring the sauce to a simmer and let it cook for about 20 minutes, stirring occasionally, until thickened and flavorful.
6. Finish the Squash: Once the spaghetti squash is cool enough to handle, use a fork to scrape out the strands of squash into a large bowl. Discard the skins.
7. Combine and Serve: Divide the spaghetti squash among four plates. Top each serving with the homemade marinara sauce. Garnish with chopped fresh basil leaves.

Nutritional Information (per serving)
- Calories: 200
- Protein: 4g
- Carbohydrates: 30g
- Dietary Fiber: 7g
- Sugars: 12g
- Fat: 9g
- Saturated Fat: 1.5g
- Sodium: 600mg
- Potassium: 1000mg
- Vitamin A: 15% of Daily Value
- Vitamin C: 35% of Daily Value
- Calcium: 10% of Daily Value
- Iron: 15% of Daily Value

Roasted Brussels Sprouts and Sweet Potatoes

Yield: 4 servings **Prep Time:** 10 minutes
Cook Time: 30 minutes

Ingredients
- 1 pound Brussels sprouts, trimmed and halved
- 2 medium sweet potatoes, peeled and diced
- 3 tablespoons olive oil
- 1 teaspoon ground turmeric
- 1 teaspoon ground cumin
- 1/2 teaspoon paprika
- 1/2 teaspoon garlic powder
- Salt and pepper to taste
- Optional: 1 tablespoon balsamic vinegar for drizzling

Directions
1. Preheat the Oven: Preheat your oven to 425°F (220°C). Line a baking sheet with parchment paper.
2. Prepare the Vegetables: In a large bowl, combine the halved Brussels sprouts and diced sweet potatoes.
3. Season the Vegetables: Drizzle the olive oil over the vegetables. Add the ground turmeric, ground cumin, paprika, garlic powder, salt, and pepper. Toss to coat the vegetables evenly.
4. Roast the Vegetables: Spread the seasoned vegetables in a single layer on the prepared baking sheet. Roast in the preheated oven for 25-30 minutes, stirring halfway through, until the vegetables are tender and caramelized.
5. Serve: Remove from the oven and transfer to a serving dish. If desired, drizzle with balsamic vinegar before serving.

Nutritional Information (per serving)
- Calories: 200
- Protein: 4g
- Carbohydrates: 30g
- Dietary Fiber: 7g
- Sugars: 7g
- Fat: 9g
- Saturated Fat: 1.5g
- Sodium: 100mg
- Potassium: 700mg
- Vitamin A: 400% of Daily Value
- Vitamin C: 120% of Daily Value
- Calcium: 6% of Daily Value
- Iron: 10% of Daily Value

Cabbage and Carrot Slaw with Tahini Dressing

Yield: 4 servings **Prep Time:** 15 minutes
Cook Time: None

Ingredients
For the Slaw
- 4 cups shredded cabbage (green, red, or a mix)
- 2 large carrots, shredded
- 1/4 cup chopped fresh cilantro (optional)
- 1/4 cup chopped green onions

For the Tahini Dressing
- 1/4 cup tahini
- 2 tablespoons fresh lemon juice
- 2 tablespoons water (more as needed)
- 1 tablespoon olive oil
- 1 tablespoon apple cider vinegar
- 1 tablespoon maple syrup or honey
- 1 clove garlic, minced
- 1/2 teaspoon ground cumin
- Salt and pepper to taste

Directions
1. Prepare the Vegetables: In a large bowl, combine the shredded cabbage, shredded carrots, chopped cilantro (if using), and chopped green onions.
2. Make the Dressing: In a small bowl, whisk together the tahini, fresh lemon juice, water, olive oil, apple cider vinegar, maple syrup or honey, minced garlic, ground cumin, salt, and pepper. Adjust the consistency by adding more water if needed, until the dressing is smooth and creamy.
3. Toss the Slaw: Pour the tahini dressing over the cabbage and carrot mixture. Toss well to combine, ensuring all the vegetables are evenly coated with the dressing.
4. Serve: Divide the slaw into four servings and serve immediately, or refrigerate for up to 2 days.

Nutritional Information (per serving)
- Calories: 150
- Protein: 3g
- Carbohydrates: 15g
- Dietary Fiber: 5g
- Sugars: 7g
- Fat: 9g
- Saturated Fat: 1.5g
- Sodium: 100mg
- Potassium: 500mg
- Vitamin A: 100% of Daily Value
- Vitamin C: 60% of Daily Value
- Calcium: 6% of Daily Value
- Iron: 8% of Daily Value

Grilled Portobello Mushrooms

Yield: 4 servings **Prep Time:** 15 minutes (plus marinating time) **Cook Time:** 15 minutes

Ingredients
For the Grilled Portobello Mushrooms
- 4 large portobello mushrooms, stems removed
- 1/4 cup balsamic vinegar
- 2 tablespoons olive oil
- 2 cloves garlic, minced
- 1 tablespoon fresh thyme leaves (or 1 teaspoon dried thyme)
- Salt and pepper to taste

For the Steamed Vegetables
- 2 cups broccoli florets
- 2 cups cauliflower florets
- 2 large carrots, sliced
- 1 tablespoon olive oil (optional)
- Salt and pepper to taste

Directions
1. Marinate the Mushrooms: In a small bowl, whisk together the balsamic vinegar, olive oil, minced garlic, thyme, salt, and pepper. Place the portobello mushrooms in a large resealable plastic bag or a shallow dish. Pour the marinade over the mushrooms, ensuring they are well coated. Seal the bag or cover the dish and marinate in the refrigerator for at least 30 minutes, preferably up to 2 hours.
2. Preheat the Grill: Preheat the grill to medium-high heat.
3. Grill the Mushrooms: Remove the mushrooms from the marinade and shake off any excess. Grill the mushrooms for about 5-7 minutes per side, or until tender and slightly charred. Baste with the remaining marinade while grilling if desired.
4. Steam the Vegetables: While the mushrooms are grilling, steam the broccoli, cauliflower, and carrots until tender, about 5-7 minutes. If you prefer, drizzle the steamed vegetables with olive oil and season with salt and pepper.
5. Serve: Place one grilled portobello mushroom on each plate. Serve with a side of steamed vegetables.

Nutritional Information (per serving)
- Calories: 180
- Protein: 4g
- Carbohydrates: 15g
- Dietary Fiber: 6g
- Sugars: 7g
- Fat: 12g
- Saturated Fat: 2g
- Sodium: 100mg
- Potassium: 800mg
- Vitamin A: 150% of Daily Value
- Vitamin C: 130% of Daily Value
- Calcium: 6% of Daily Value
- Iron: 8% of Daily Value

Moroccan Chickpea Stew

Yield: 4 servings **Prep Time:** 15 minutes
Cook Time: 30 minutes

Ingredients
- 2 tablespoons olive oil
- 1 large onion, chopped
- 3 cloves garlic, minced
- 1 tablespoon fresh ginger, minced
- 1 teaspoon ground turmeric
- 1 teaspoon ground cumin
- 1 teaspoon ground cinnamon
- 1 teaspoon ground coriander
- 1/2 teaspoon ground paprika
- 1/4 teaspoon cayenne pepper (optional)
- 1 (14.5-ounce) can diced tomatoes
- 1 (15-ounce) can chickpeas, rinsed and drained
- 2 cups vegetable broth
- 1 cup diced carrots
- 1 cup diced zucchini
- 1/2 cup dried apricots, chopped
- 1/4 cup raisins
- Salt and pepper to taste
- 1/4 cup fresh cilantro, chopped (for garnish)
- Cooked quinoa or couscous (for serving)

Directions
1. Heat the Oil: In a large pot or Dutch oven, heat the olive oil over medium heat. Add the chopped onion and sauté for about 5 minutes until softened.
2. Add Garlic and Spices: Add the minced garlic and fresh ginger and cook for another 1-2 minutes until fragrant. Stir in the ground turmeric, cumin, cinnamon, coriander, paprika, and cayenne pepper (if using). Cook for about 1 minute until the spices are well mixed and fragrant.
3. Add Vegetables and Chickpeas: Add the diced tomatoes (with their juice), chickpeas, vegetable broth, diced carrots, zucchini, chopped dried apricots, and raisins. Stir well to combine.
4. Simmer: Bring the mixture to a boil, then reduce the heat to low. Cover and simmer for about 20-25 minutes, or until the vegetables are tender and the flavors are well developed. Season with salt and pepper to taste.
5. Serve: Ladle the stew into bowls and garnish with chopped fresh cilantro. Serve over cooked quinoa or couscous.

Nutritional Information (per serving)
- Calories: 350
- Protein: 10g
- Carbohydrates: 55g
- Dietary Fiber: 12g
- Sugars: 18g
- Fat: 10g
- Saturated Fat: 1.5g
- Sodium: 600mg
- Potassium: 1000mg
- Vitamin A: 120% of Daily Value
- Vitamin C: 40% of Daily Value
- Calcium: 10% of Daily Value

Iron: 20% of Daily Value

Baked Cod with Lemon and Herbs

Yield: 4 servings **Prep Time:** 10 minutes
Cook Time: 15-20 minutes

Ingredients
- 4 cod fillets (about 6 ounces each)
- 2 tablespoons olive oil
- 2 lemons, thinly sliced
- 3 cloves garlic, minced
- 1 tablespoon fresh parsley, chopped
- 1 tablespoon fresh dill, chopped
- 1 tablespoon fresh thyme leaves
- Salt and pepper to taste
- Optional: Lemon wedges for serving

Directions
1. Preheat the Oven: Preheat your oven to 400°F (200°C). Line a baking sheet with parchment paper or lightly grease it.
2. Prepare the Cod: Place the cod fillets on the prepared baking sheet. Drizzle with olive oil and season with salt and pepper.
3. Add Lemon and Herbs: Sprinkle the minced garlic, chopped parsley, dill, and thyme evenly over the cod fillets. Arrange the lemon slices on top of and around the fillets.
4. Bake: Bake in the preheated oven for 15-20 minutes, or until the cod is cooked through and flakes easily with a fork.
5. Serve: Remove the cod from the oven and transfer to serving plates. Serve with additional lemon wedges if desired.

Nutritional Information (per serving)
- Calories: 200
- Protein: 30g
- Carbohydrates: 4g
- Dietary Fiber: 1g
- Sugars: 1g
- Fat: 7g
- Saturated Fat: 1g
- Sodium: 100mg
- Potassium: 800mg
- Vitamin A: 4% of Daily Value
- Vitamin C: 30% of Daily Value
- Calcium: 4% of Daily Value
- Iron: 6% of Daily Value

Turkey and Vegetable Skewers

Yield: 4 servings **Prep Time:** 20 minutes
Cook Time: 15 minutes

Ingredients
For the Skewers
- 1 lb ground turkey
- 1/4 cup breadcrumbs (gluten-free if needed)
- 1 egg, beaten
- 2 cloves garlic, minced
- 1 tablespoon fresh parsley, chopped
- 1 teaspoon ground cumin
- 1 teaspoon ground paprika
- 1/2 teaspoon salt
- 1/4 teaspoon black pepper

For the Vegetables
- 1 red bell pepper, cut into 1-inch pieces
- 1 yellow bell pepper, cut into 1-inch pieces
- 1 red onion, cut into wedges
- 1 zucchini, sliced into 1/2-inch rounds
- 1 tablespoon olive oil
- Salt and pepper to taste

Directions
1. Prepare the Turkey Mixture: In a large bowl, combine the ground turkey, breadcrumbs, beaten egg, minced garlic, chopped parsley, ground cumin, ground paprika, salt, and black pepper. Mix well until all ingredients are evenly combined.
2. Form the Meatballs: Using your hands, shape the turkey mixture into small meatballs, about 1 inch in diameter.
3. Prepare the Vegetables: In a separate bowl, toss the bell peppers, red onion, and zucchini with olive oil, salt, and pepper.
4. Thread the Skewers: Thread the turkey meatballs and mixed vegetables onto metal or soaked wooden skewers, alternating between meatballs and vegetables.
5. Preheat the Grill: Preheat your grill to medium-high heat.
6. Grill the Skewers: Place the skewers on the preheated grill. Grill for about 12-15 minutes, turning occasionally, until the turkey meatballs are cooked through and the vegetables are tender and slightly charred.
7. Serve: Remove the skewers from the grill and serve immediately.

Nutritional Information (per serving)
- Calories: 300
- Protein: 25g
- Carbohydrates: 12g
- Dietary Fiber: 3g
- Sugars: 4g
- Fat: 18g
- Saturated Fat: 4g
- Sodium: 500mg
- Potassium: 600mg
- Vitamin A: 40% of Daily Value
- Vitamin C: 100% of Daily Value
- Calcium: 6% of Daily Value
- Iron: 15% of Daily Value

Asian-Inspired Lettuce Wraps

Yield: 4 servings **Prep Time:** 15 minutes
Cook Time: 15 minutes

Ingredients

- 1 tablespoon olive oil
- 1 pound ground chicken
- 1 small onion, finely chopped
- 2 cloves garlic, minced
- 1 tablespoon fresh ginger, minced
- 1 (8-ounce) can water chestnuts, drained and chopped
- 2 tablespoons soy sauce (or tamari for gluten-free)
- 1 tablespoon hoisin sauce
- 1 tablespoon rice vinegar
- 1 teaspoon sesame oil
- 1/4 teaspoon crushed red pepper flakes (optional)
- Salt and pepper to taste
- 8 large lettuce leaves (e.g., Bibb, Romaine, or Iceberg)
- 1/4 cup green onions, sliced
- 1/4 cup fresh cilantro, chopped
- Optional: 1 tablespoon sesame seeds

Directions

1. Heat the Oil: In a large skillet, heat the olive oil over medium-high heat. Add the finely chopped onion and sauté for about 3-4 minutes until softened.
2. Cook the Chicken: Add the ground chicken to the skillet. Cook, breaking it up with a spoon, until it is browned and cooked through, about 5-7 minutes.
3. Add Garlic and Ginger: Stir in the minced garlic and fresh ginger. Cook for another 1-2 minutes until fragrant.
4. Add Water Chestnuts and Sauces: Stir in the chopped water chestnuts, soy sauce, hoisin sauce, rice vinegar, sesame oil, and crushed red pepper flakes (if using). Cook for another 2-3 minutes until the mixture is well combined and heated through. Season with salt and pepper to taste.
5. Prepare the Lettuce Wraps: Lay out the large lettuce leaves on a serving platter.
6. Assemble: Spoon the chicken mixture into the center of each lettuce leaf. Top with sliced green onions and chopped cilantro. Sprinkle with sesame seeds if desired.
7. Serve: Serve the lettuce wraps immediately, allowing each person to wrap the lettuce around the filling and enjoy.

Nutritional Information (per serving)

- Calories: 220
- Protein: 20g
- Carbohydrates: 10g
- Dietary Fiber: 2g
- Sugars: 4g
- Fat: 12g
- Saturated Fat: 2.5g
- Sodium: 600mg
- Potassium: 400mg
- Vitamin A: 10% of Daily Value
- Vitamin C: 15% of Daily Value
- Calcium: 4% of Daily Value
- Iron: 10% of Daily Value

Eggplant and Tomato Bake

Yield: 4 servings **Prep Time:** 20 minutes
Cook Time: 40 minutes

Ingredients
- 2 large eggplants, sliced into 1/4-inch rounds
- 4 large tomatoes, sliced into 1/4-inch rounds
- 3 cloves garlic, minced
- 2 tablespoons olive oil
- 1 teaspoon dried oregano
- 1 teaspoon dried basil
- 1/2 teaspoon dried thyme
- Salt and pepper to taste
- 1/4 cup fresh basil, chopped (optional, for garnish)

Directions
1. Preheat the Oven: Preheat your oven to 375°F (190°C). Lightly grease a baking dish with olive oil.
2. Prepare the Eggplant: Lay the eggplant slices on a paper towel and sprinkle with salt. Let them sit for about 10 minutes to draw out excess moisture. Pat them dry with another paper towel.
3. Layer the Vegetables: Arrange half of the eggplant slices in a single layer in the prepared baking dish. Top with half of the tomato slices. Sprinkle with half of the minced garlic, dried oregano, dried basil, dried thyme, salt, and pepper. Drizzle with 1 tablespoon of olive oil.
4. Repeat the Layers: Repeat the layering process with the remaining eggplant, tomatoes, garlic, herbs, salt, pepper, and the remaining 1 tablespoon of olive oil.
5. Bake: Cover the baking dish with aluminum foil and bake in the preheated oven for 30 minutes. Remove the foil and bake for an additional 10 minutes, or until the eggplant is tender and the top is slightly browned.
6. Garnish and Serve: Remove from the oven and let cool slightly. Garnish with chopped fresh basil if desired. Serve warm.

Nutritional Information (per serving)
- Calories: 150
- Protein: 2g
- Carbohydrates: 14g
- Dietary Fiber: 7g
- Sugars: 9g
- Fat: 10g
- Saturated Fat: 1.5g
- Sodium: 150mg
- Potassium: 700mg
- Vitamin A: 15% of Daily Value
- Vitamin C: 40% of Daily Value
- Calcium: 4% of Daily Value
- Iron: 5% of Daily Value

Shrimp and Avocado Salad

Yield: 4 servings **Prep Time:** 15 minutes
Cook Time: 5 minutes

Ingredients For the Salad
- 1 pound large shrimp, peeled and deveined
- 1 tablespoon olive oil
- Salt and pepper to taste
- 6 cups mixed greens (e.g., spinach, arugula, romaine)
- 1 large avocado, diced
- 1 cup cherry tomatoes, halved
- 1/4 red onion, thinly sliced
- 1/4 cup fresh cilantro, chopped

For the Lime Vinaigrette
- 1/4 cup extra virgin olive oil
- 3 tablespoons fresh lime juice (about 2 limes)
- 1 teaspoon lime zest
- 1 clove garlic, minced
- 1 teaspoon honey or maple syrup (optional)
- Salt and pepper to taste

Directions
1. Cook the Shrimp: In a large skillet, heat 1 tablespoon of olive oil over medium heat. Season the shrimp with salt and pepper. Add the shrimp to the skillet and cook for about 2-3 minutes per side, or until the shrimp are pink and opaque. Remove from heat and set aside to cool slightly.
2. Prepare the Lime Vinaigrette: In a small bowl, whisk together the olive oil, fresh lime juice, lime zest, minced garlic, honey or maple syrup (if using), salt, and pepper until well combined.
3. Assemble the Salad: In a large bowl, combine the mixed greens, diced avocado, cherry tomatoes, and sliced red onion. Add the cooked shrimp and gently toss to combine.
4. Dress the Salad: Drizzle the lime vinaigrette over the salad and toss gently to coat all the ingredients evenly.
5. Serve: Divide the salad into four servings and garnish with chopped fresh cilantro. Serve immediately.

Nutritional Information (per serving)
- Calories: 300
- Protein: 20g
- Carbohydrates: 12g
- Dietary Fiber: 6g
- Sugars: 3g
- Fat: 20g
- Saturated Fat: 3g
- Sodium: 300mg
- Potassium: 800mg
- Vitamin A: 70% of Daily Value
- Vitamin C: 50% of Daily Value
- Calcium: 10% of Daily Value
- Iron: 15% of Daily Value

Spinach and Mushroom Frittata

Yield: 4 servings **Prep Time:** 10 minutes
Cook Time: 25 minutes

Ingredients
- 8 large eggs
- 1/4 cup unsweetened almond milk (or any plant-based milk)
- 1 tablespoon olive oil
- 1 small onion, finely chopped
- 2 cloves garlic, minced
- 2 cups fresh spinach, chopped
- 1 cup mushrooms, sliced
- 1/2 teaspoon ground turmeric
- 1/2 teaspoon paprika
- 1/4 teaspoon salt
- 1/4 teaspoon black pepper
- Optional: 1/4 cup dairy-free cheese, shredded

Directions
1. Preheat the Oven: Preheat your oven to 375°F (190°C). Lightly grease a 9-inch oven-safe skillet or baking dish with olive oil.
2. Cook the Vegetables: In a large skillet, heat the olive oil over medium heat. Add the finely chopped onion and sauté for about 3-4 minutes until softened. Add the minced garlic and cook for another 1 minute. Add the sliced mushrooms and cook for about 5 minutes until they release their moisture and begin to brown. Stir in the chopped spinach and cook for another 2 minutes until wilted. Remove from heat.
3. Prepare the Egg Mixture: In a medium bowl, whisk together the eggs, almond milk, ground turmeric, paprika, salt, and black pepper until well combined.
4. Combine Ingredients: Add the cooked vegetables to the egg mixture and stir to combine. If using, fold in the shredded dairy-free cheese.
5. Bake the Frittata: Pour the mixture into the prepared skillet or baking dish. Smooth the top with a spatula. Bake in the preheated oven for 20-25 minutes, or until the frittata is set and lightly golden on top. A knife inserted into the center should come out clean.
6. Serve: Remove from the oven and let cool slightly. Cut into wedges and serve warm.

Nutritional Information (per serving)
- Calories: 200
- Protein: 12g
- Carbohydrates: 5g
- Dietary Fiber: 1g
- Sugars: 2g
- Fat: 15g
- Saturated Fat: 3.5g
- Sodium: 300mg
- Potassium: 450mg
- Vitamin A: 35% of Daily Value
- Vitamin C: 15% of Daily Value
- Calcium: 8% of Daily Value
- Iron: 10% of Daily Value

Coconut Curry with Vegetables

Yield: 4 servings **Prep Time:** 15 minutes
Cook Time: 25 minutes

Ingredients

- 1 tablespoon coconut oil or olive oil
- 1 block (14 ounces) firm tofu, drained and cubed
- 1 large onion, chopped
- 3 cloves garlic, minced
- 1 tablespoon fresh ginger, minced
- 1 red bell pepper, sliced
- 1 yellow bell pepper, sliced
- 1 medium zucchini, sliced
- 1 medium carrot, sliced
- 1 cup broccoli florets
- 1 (14-ounce) can coconut milk
- 1 (14.5-ounce) can diced tomatoes
- 2 tablespoons red curry paste
- 1 teaspoon ground turmeric
- 1 teaspoon ground cumin
- 1/2 teaspoon ground coriander
- 1/2 teaspoon salt (or to taste)
- 1/4 teaspoon black pepper
- 1 tablespoon soy sauce or tamari (gluten-free if needed)
- 1 tablespoon fresh lime juice
- 1/4 cup fresh cilantro, chopped (optional, for garnish)
- Cooked rice or quinoa, for serving

Directions

1. Prepare the Tofu: In a large skillet, heat the coconut oil over medium-high heat. Add the cubed tofu and cook for about 5-7 minutes, turning occasionally, until golden brown on all sides. Remove from the skillet and set aside.
2. Sauté Aromatics: In the same skillet, add the chopped onion and sauté for about 3-4 minutes until softened. Add the minced garlic and fresh ginger and cook for another 1-2 minutes until fragrant.
3. Add Vegetables: Stir in the sliced red and yellow bell peppers, zucchini, carrot, and broccoli florets. Cook for about 5 minutes until the vegetables are tender-crisp.
4. Add Spices and Curry Paste: Stir in the red curry paste, ground turmeric, ground cumin, ground coriander, salt, and black pepper. Cook for about 1 minute until the spices are well mixed and fragrant.
5. Add Liquids: Pour in the coconut milk and diced tomatoes (with their juice). Stir well to combine. Bring the mixture to a simmer and cook for about 10 minutes, allowing the flavors to meld and the sauce to thicken slightly.
6. Add Tofu and Seasonings: Return the cooked tofu to the skillet. Stir in the soy sauce or tamari and fresh lime juice. Cook for another 2-3 minutes until everything is heated through.
7. Serve: Divide the coconut curry into four servings. Garnish with chopped fresh cilantro if desired. Serve with cooked rice or quinoa.

Nutritional Information (per serving)

- Calories: 350
- Protein: 14g
- Carbohydrates: 28g
- Dietary Fiber: 7g
- Sugars: 10g
- Fat: 22g
- Saturated Fat: 15g
- Sodium: 600mg
- Potassium: 800mg
- Vitamin A: 100% of Daily Value
- Vitamin C: 150% of Daily Value
- Calcium: 15% of Daily Value
- Iron: 25% of Daily Value

Almond-Crusted Tilapia

Yield: 4 servings **Prep Time:** 15 minutes
Cook Time: 20 minutes

Ingredients
- 4 tilapia fillets (about 6 ounces each)
- 1 cup raw almonds, finely chopped or ground
- 1/4 cup almond flour
- 1/2 teaspoon garlic powder
- 1/2 teaspoon paprika
- 1/4 teaspoon salt
- 1/4 teaspoon black pepper
- 1 large egg
- 2 tablespoons water
- 2 tablespoons olive oil or melted coconut oil
- Lemon wedges, for serving
- Fresh parsley, chopped (optional, for garnish)

Directions
1. Preheat the Oven: Preheat your oven to 400°F (200°C). Line a baking sheet with parchment paper or lightly grease it.
2. Prepare the Almond Coating: In a shallow bowl, combine the finely chopped or ground almonds, almond flour, garlic powder, paprika, salt, and black pepper. Mix well.
3. Prepare the Egg Mixture: In another shallow bowl, whisk together the egg and water until well combined.
4. Coat the Tilapia: Dip each tilapia fillet into the egg mixture, allowing any excess to drip off. Then, press the fillet into the almond mixture, coating both sides evenly. Place the coated fillets on the prepared baking sheet.
5. Drizzle with Oil: Drizzle the olive oil or melted coconut oil over the top of the coated tilapia fillets.
6. Bake: Bake in the preheated oven for 15-20 minutes, or until the tilapia is cooked through and the almond coating is golden brown and crispy. The fish should easily flake with a fork.
7. Serve: Remove from the oven and let cool slightly. Serve the almond-crusted tilapia with lemon wedges and garnish with chopped fresh parsley if desired.

Nutritional Information (per serving)
- Calories: 350
- Protein: 30g
- Carbohydrates: 7g
- Dietary Fiber: 3g
- Sugars: 1g
- Fat: 22g
- Saturated Fat: 3g
- Sodium: 250mg
- Potassium: 600mg
- Vitamin A: 4% of Daily Value
- Vitamin C: 6% of Daily Value
- Calcium: 10% of Daily Value
- Iron: 15% of Daily Value

Roasted Beet and Arugula Salad

Yield: 4 servings **Prep Time:** 15 minutes
Cook Time: 45 minutes

Ingredients
- 4 medium beets, scrubbed and trimmed
- 2 tablespoons olive oil, divided
- Salt and pepper to taste
- 4 cups fresh arugula
- 1/2 cup crumbled goat cheese
- 1/2 cup walnuts, toasted and chopped
- 1/4 cup balsamic vinegar
- 1 tablespoon honey or maple syrup (optional)
- 1 teaspoon Dijon mustard

Directions
1. Preheat the Oven: Preheat your oven to 400°F (200°C). Line a baking sheet with parchment paper.
2. Roast the Beets: Rub the beets with 1 tablespoon of olive oil and season with salt and pepper. Wrap each beet in aluminum foil and place them on the prepared baking sheet. Roast in the preheated oven for 45 minutes, or until the beets are tender when pierced with a fork. Remove from the oven and let cool. Once cool, peel the beets and cut them into wedges.
3. Prepare the Dressing: In a small bowl, whisk together the balsamic vinegar, honey or maple syrup (if using), Dijon mustard, and the remaining 1 tablespoon of olive oil. Season with salt and pepper to taste.
4. Assemble the Salad: In a large bowl, combine the fresh arugula, roasted beets, crumbled goat cheese, and toasted walnuts.
5. Dress the Salad: Drizzle the balsamic dressing over the salad and toss gently to combine, ensuring the ingredients are evenly coated.
6. Serve: Divide the salad into four servings and serve immediately.

Nutritional Information (per serving)
- Calories: 250
- Protein: 7g
- Carbohydrates: 18g
- Dietary Fiber: 5g
- Sugars: 11g
- Fat: 18g
- Saturated Fat: 4g
- Sodium: 220mg
- Potassium: 500mg
- Vitamin A: 15% of Daily Value
- Vitamin C: 20% of Daily Value
- Calcium: 10% of Daily Value
- Iron: 10% of Daily Value

Herb-Roasted Chicken with Vegetables

Yield: 4 servings **Prep Time:** 20 minutes
Cook Time: 45 minutes

Ingredients
- 4 bone-in, skin-on chicken thighs
- 1 pound baby potatoes, halved
- 2 large carrots, sliced into rounds
- 1 large red onion, cut into wedges
- 1 tablespoon olive oil
- 1 tablespoon fresh rosemary, chopped
- 1 tablespoon fresh thyme, chopped
- 1 tablespoon fresh parsley, chopped
- 4 cloves garlic, minced
- 1 lemon, sliced
- Salt and pepper to taste

Directions
1. Preheat the Oven: Preheat your oven to 400°F (200°C). Lightly grease a large baking dish or sheet pan with olive oil.
2. Prepare the Vegetables: In a large bowl, combine the halved baby potatoes, sliced carrots, and red onion wedges. Drizzle with 1/2 tablespoon of olive oil, and season with half of the chopped rosemary, thyme, parsley, salt, and pepper. Toss to coat the vegetables evenly.
3. Prepare the Chicken: Pat the chicken thighs dry with paper towels. Rub each thigh with the remaining 1/2 tablespoon of olive oil. Season with the remaining herbs, minced garlic, salt, and pepper.
4. Arrange in Baking Dish: Arrange the seasoned vegetables in a single layer in the prepared baking dish or sheet pan. Place the chicken thighs on top of the vegetables. Tuck the lemon slices around the chicken and vegetables.
5. Roast: Roast in the preheated oven for about 45 minutes, or until the chicken is cooked through (internal temperature reaches 165°F or 75°C) and the vegetables are tender and golden brown. Stir the vegetables halfway through cooking for even roasting.
6. Serve: Remove from the oven and let cool slightly. Divide the chicken and vegetables among four plates and serve warm.

Nutritional Information (per serving)
- Calories: 450
- Protein: 25g
- Carbohydrates: 35g
- Dietary Fiber: 6g
- Sugars: 8g
- Fat: 22g
- Saturated Fat: 6g
- Sodium: 300mg
- Potassium: 1000mg
- Vitamin A: 100% of Daily Value
- Vitamin C: 40% of Daily Value
- Calcium: 6% of Daily Value
- Iron: 15% of Daily Value

Mediterranean Chickpea Salad

Yield: 4 servings **Prep Time:** 15 minutes
Cook Time: None

Ingredients
- 1 (15-ounce) can chickpeas, rinsed and drained
- 1 cup cherry tomatoes, halved
- 1 cucumber, diced
- 1/2 red onion, finely chopped
- 1/2 cup Kalamata olives, pitted and sliced
- 1/2 cup feta cheese, crumbled
- 1/4 cup fresh parsley, chopped

For the Dressing
- 1/4 cup extra virgin olive oil
- 2 tablespoons red wine vinegar
- 1 tablespoon fresh lemon juice
- 1 clove garlic, minced
- 1 teaspoon dried oregano
- Salt and pepper to taste

Directions
1. Prepare the Salad: In a large bowl, combine the chickpeas, cherry tomatoes, cucumber, red onion, Kalamata olives, feta cheese, and chopped parsley.
2. Make the Dressing: In a small bowl, whisk together the olive oil, red wine vinegar, fresh lemon juice, minced garlic, dried oregano, salt, and pepper until well combined.
3. Combine and Toss: Pour the dressing over the salad and toss gently to coat all the ingredients evenly.
4. Serve: Divide the salad into four servings and serve immediately. This salad can also be refrigerated for up to 2 days.

Nutritional Information (per serving)
- Calories: 250
- Protein: 8g
- Carbohydrates: 22g
- Dietary Fiber: 6g
- Sugars: 4g
- Fat: 16g
- Saturated Fat: 4g
- Sodium: 500mg
- Potassium: 450mg
- Vitamin A: 10% of Daily Value
- Vitamin C: 20% of Daily Value
- Calcium: 15% of Daily Value
- Iron: 15% of Daily Value

Spaghetti Squash Pad Thai

Yield: 4 servings **Prep Time:** 20 minutes
Cook Time: 45 minutes

Ingredients
For the Spaghetti Squash
- 1 large spaghetti squash
- 1 tablespoon olive oil
- Salt and pepper to taste

For the Pad Thai Sauce
- 1/4 cup tamari or soy sauce (gluten-free if needed)
- 2 tablespoons rice vinegar
- 2 tablespoons lime juice (about 1 lime)
- 2 tablespoons maple syrup or honey
- 1 tablespoon natural peanut butter or almond butter
- 2 cloves garlic, minced
- 1 teaspoon grated fresh ginger
- 1/4 teaspoon red pepper flakes (optional)

For the Stir-Fry
- 2 tablespoons olive oil or coconut oil
- 1 small red onion, thinly sliced
- 1 red bell pepper, thinly sliced
- 1 cup shredded carrots
- 2 cups snap peas, trimmed
- 3 green onions, sliced
- 2 eggs, lightly beaten
- 1/4 cup fresh cilantro, chopped
- 1/4 cup chopped peanuts (optional, for garnish)
- Lime wedges, for serving

Directions
1. Preheat the Oven: Preheat your oven to 400°F (200°C). Line a baking sheet with parchment paper.
2. Prepare the Spaghetti Squash: Cut the spaghetti squash in half lengthwise and scoop out the seeds. Drizzle the inside of each half with olive oil and season with salt and pepper. Place the squash halves cut-side down on the prepared baking sheet. Roast in the preheated oven for 30-35 minutes, or until the squash is tender and can be easily shredded with a fork.
3. Make the Pad Thai Sauce: While the squash is roasting, whisk together the tamari or soy sauce, rice vinegar, lime juice, maple syrup or honey, peanut butter or almond butter, minced garlic, grated ginger, and red pepper flakes (if using) in a small bowl. Set aside.
4. Stir-Fry the Vegetables: In a large skillet or wok, heat 2 tablespoons of olive oil or coconut oil over medium-high heat. Add the sliced red onion and bell pepper, and stir-fry for about 3-4 minutes until softened. Add the shredded carrots, snap peas, and green onions, and stir-fry for another 3-4 minutes until the vegetables are tender-crisp.
5. Cook the Eggs: Push the vegetables to one side of the skillet and pour the beaten eggs into the other side. Scramble the eggs until fully cooked, then mix them with the vegetables.
6. Combine and Serve: Remove the roasted spaghetti squash from the oven and use a fork to scrape out the spaghetti-like strands. Add the spaghetti squash strands to the skillet with the vegetables and eggs. Pour the Pad Thai sauce over the mixture and toss to combine until everything is evenly coated and heated through.
7. Garnish and Serve: Divide the Spaghetti Squash Pad Thai among four plates. Garnish with chopped fresh cilantro and chopped peanuts if desired. Serve with lime wedges.

Nutritional Information (per serving)
- Calories: 350
- Protein: 10g
- Carbohydrates: 40g
- Dietary Fiber: 8g
- Sugars: 12g
- Fat: 18g
- Saturated Fat: 3.5g
- Sodium: 800mg
- Potassium: 900mg
- Vitamin A: 120% of Daily Value
- Vitamin C: 100% of Daily Value
- Calcium: 10% of Daily Value
- Iron: 15% of Daily Value

Lentil and Vegetable Shepherd's Pie

Yield: 6 servings **Prep Time:** 20 minutes **Cook Time:** 45 minutes

Ingredients
For the Filling

- 1 cup dried green or brown lentils, rinsed and drained
- 2 tablespoons olive oil
- 1 large onion, chopped
- 2 cloves garlic, minced
- 2 large carrots, diced
- 1 cup frozen peas
- 1 cup frozen corn
- 1 (14.5-ounce) can diced tomatoes
- 2 tablespoons tomato paste
- 2 cups vegetable broth
- 1 teaspoon dried thyme
- 1 teaspoon dried rosemary
- 1/2 teaspoon ground paprika
- 1/2 teaspoon ground turmeric
- Salt and pepper to taste

For the Mashed Potato Topping

- 4 large potatoes, peeled and diced
- 1/4 cup unsweetened almond milk (or any plant-based milk)
- 2 tablespoons olive oil or vegan butter
- Salt and pepper to taste
- Optional: 1/4 cup nutritional yeast (for a cheesy flavor)

Directions

1. Cook the Lentils: In a medium saucepan, bring the lentils and 3 cups of water to a boil. Reduce heat to low, cover, and simmer for about 20 minutes or until the lentils are tender. Drain and set aside.
2. Prepare the Filling: In a large skillet, heat the olive oil over medium heat. Add the chopped onion and sauté for about 5 minutes until softened. Add the minced garlic and cook for another 1 minute until fragrant. Stir in the diced carrots and cook for about 5 minutes until they begin to soften.
3. Add Remaining Ingredients: Add the cooked lentils, frozen peas, frozen corn, diced tomatoes (with their juice), tomato paste, vegetable broth, dried thyme, dried rosemary, ground paprika, ground turmeric, salt, and pepper. Stir well to combine. Bring to a simmer and cook for about 10 minutes until the vegetables are tender and the filling has thickened slightly. Adjust seasoning to taste.
4. Prepare the Mashed Potato Topping: While the filling is simmering, cook the diced potatoes in a large pot of boiling water for about 15 minutes or until tender. Drain and return the potatoes to the pot. Add the almond milk, olive oil or vegan butter, salt, pepper, and nutritional yeast (if using). Mash until smooth and creamy.
5. Assemble the Shepherd's Pie: Preheat your oven to 375°F (190°C). Spread the lentil and vegetable filling evenly in a large baking dish. Spoon the mashed potatoes over the top and spread them out evenly. Use a fork to create ridges on the surface of the mashed potatoes (this helps them brown nicely).
6. Bake: Bake in the preheated oven for about 20-25 minutes, or until the top is golden brown and the filling is bubbling around the edges.
7. Serve: Remove from the oven and let cool slightly before serving.

Nutritional Information (per serving)

- Calories: 300
- Protein: 10g
- Carbohydrates: 50g
- Dietary Fiber: 12g
- Sugars: 6g
- Fat: 8g
- Saturated Fat: 1g
- Sodium: 400mg
- Potassium: 1000mg
- Vitamin A: 150% of Daily Value
- Vitamin C: 50% of Daily Value
- Calcium: 10% of Daily Value
- Iron: 25% of Daily Value

Kale and Quinoa Power Bowl

Yield: 4 servings **Prep Time:** 20 minutes
Cook Time: 30 minutes

Ingredients
For the Bowl
- 1 cup quinoa, rinsed
- 2 cups water or vegetable broth
- 1 large bunch of kale, stems removed and chopped
- 2 tablespoons olive oil
- 1 large sweet potato, peeled and diced
- 1 red bell pepper, diced
- 1 zucchini, sliced
- 1/2 teaspoon ground turmeric
- 1/2 teaspoon ground cumin
- Salt and pepper to taste

For the Tahini Dressing
- 1/4 cup tahini
- 2 tablespoons fresh lemon juice
- 2 tablespoons water (more as needed)
- 1 tablespoon olive oil
- 1 clove garlic, minced
- 1 teaspoon maple syrup or honey
- Salt and pepper to taste

Directions
1. Cook the Quinoa: In a medium saucepan, bring the quinoa and water or vegetable broth to a boil. Reduce heat to low, cover, and simmer for about 15 minutes, or until the quinoa is cooked and the liquid is absorbed. Fluff with a fork and set aside.
2. Roast the Vegetables: Preheat your oven to 400°F (200°C). Place the diced sweet potato, red bell pepper, and zucchini on a baking sheet. Drizzle with 1 tablespoon of olive oil, and season with ground turmeric, ground cumin, salt, and pepper. Toss to coat evenly. Roast in the preheated oven for about 25-30 minutes, or until the vegetables are tender and lightly browned.
3. Prepare the Kale: In a large skillet, heat the remaining 1 tablespoon of olive oil over medium heat. Add the chopped kale and sauté for about 5 minutes, or until the kale is wilted and tender. Season with salt and pepper to taste.
4. Make the Tahini Dressing: In a small bowl, whisk together the tahini, fresh lemon juice, water, olive oil, minced garlic, and maple syrup or honey until smooth and creamy. Adjust the consistency with more water if needed. Season with salt and pepper to taste.
5. Assemble the Bowls: Divide the cooked quinoa among four bowls. Top with sautéed kale, roasted sweet potato, red bell pepper, and zucchini.
6. Serve: Drizzle the tahini dressing over the bowls and serve immediately.

Nutritional Information (per serving)
- Calories: 350
- Protein: 10g
- Carbohydrates: 50g
- Dietary Fiber: 10g
- Sugars: 8g
- Fat: 14g
- Saturated Fat: 2g
- Sodium: 250mg
- Potassium: 1100mg
- Vitamin A: 400% of Daily Value
- Vitamin C: 150% of Daily Value
- Calcium: 15% of Daily Value
- Iron: 25% of Daily Value

Veggie-Packed Stuffed Bell Peppers

Yield: 4 servings **Prep Time:** 20 minutes
Cook Time: 40 minutes

Ingredients

- 4 large bell peppers (any color), tops cut off and seeds removed
- 1 cup cooked brown rice or quinoa
- 2 tablespoons olive oil
- 1 small onion, finely chopped
- 2 cloves garlic, minced
- 1 zucchini, diced
- 1 carrot, diced
- 1 cup cherry tomatoes, halved
- 1 (15-ounce) can black beans, rinsed and drained
- 1 teaspoon ground cumin
- 1 teaspoon ground paprika
- 1/2 teaspoon ground turmeric
- 1/2 teaspoon dried oregano
- Salt and pepper to taste
- 1/4 cup fresh parsley or cilantro, chopped (optional, for garnish)

Directions

1. Preheat the Oven: Preheat your oven to 375°F (190°C). Lightly grease a baking dish large enough to hold the bell peppers upright.
2. Prepare the Filling: In a large skillet, heat the olive oil over medium heat. Add the chopped onion and sauté for about 5 minutes until softened. Add the minced garlic and cook for another 1 minute until fragrant.
3. Add Vegetables: Stir in the diced zucchini, carrot, and cherry tomatoes. Cook for about 5-7 minutes until the vegetables are tender.
4. Add Rice and Beans: Stir in the cooked brown rice or quinoa, black beans, ground cumin, ground paprika, ground turmeric, dried oregano, salt, and pepper. Cook for another 2-3 minutes until everything is well combined and heated through. Adjust seasoning to taste.
5. Stuff the Peppers: Place the bell peppers in the prepared baking dish. Spoon the vegetable and rice mixture into each bell pepper, pressing down lightly to pack the filling.
6. Bake: Cover the baking dish with aluminum foil and bake in the preheated oven for 30 minutes. Remove the foil and bake for an additional 10 minutes, or until the peppers are tender and slightly browned on top.
7. Serve: Remove from the oven and let cool slightly. Garnish with chopped fresh parsley or cilantro if desired. Serve warm.

Nutritional Information (per serving)

- Calories: 300
- Protein: 8g
- Carbohydrates: 45g
- Dietary Fiber: 10g
- Sugars: 10g
- Fat: 10g
- Saturated Fat: 1.5g
- Sodium: 200mg
- Potassium: 900mg
- Vitamin A: 150% of Daily Value
- Vitamin C: 300% of Daily Value
- Calcium: 8% of Daily Value
- Iron: 20% of Daily Value

Garlic and Herb Roasted Mushrooms

Yield: 4 servings **Prep Time:** 10 minutes
Cook Time: 25 minutes

Ingredients
- 1 pound cremini or button mushrooms, cleaned and halved
- 3 tablespoons olive oil
- 4 cloves garlic, minced
- 1 tablespoon fresh rosemary, chopped
- 1 tablespoon fresh thyme, chopped
- 1 tablespoon fresh parsley, chopped (plus more for garnish)
- Salt and pepper to taste
- 1 tablespoon balsamic vinegar (optional)

Directions
1. Preheat the Oven: Preheat your oven to 400°F (200°C). Line a baking sheet with parchment paper.
2. Prepare the Mushrooms: In a large bowl, combine the halved mushrooms, olive oil, minced garlic, chopped rosemary, thyme, parsley, salt, and pepper. Toss to coat the mushrooms evenly.
3. Roast the Mushrooms: Spread the mushrooms in a single layer on the prepared baking sheet. Roast in the preheated oven for 20-25 minutes, or until the mushrooms are tender and golden brown, stirring halfway through.
4. Optional Balsamic Drizzle: If using, drizzle the roasted mushrooms with balsamic vinegar and toss to coat evenly. Return to the oven for an additional 2-3 minutes.
5. Serve: Remove from the oven and let cool slightly. Garnish with additional fresh parsley before serving.

Nutritional Information (per serving)
- Calories: 110
- Protein: 3g
- Carbohydrates: 6g
- Dietary Fiber: 2g
- Sugars: 3g
- Fat: 9g
- Saturated Fat: 1.5g
- Sodium: 150mg
- Potassium: 400mg
- Vitamin A: 4% of Daily Value
- Vitamin C: 8% of Daily Value
- Calcium: 2% of Daily Value
- Iron: 6% of Daily Value

Chicken and Avocado Salad

Yield: 4 servings **Prep Time:** 15 minutes
Cook Time: 15 minutes

Ingredients For the Salad
- 2 boneless, skinless chicken breasts
- 1 tablespoon olive oil
- Salt and pepper to taste
- 6 cups mixed greens (e.g., spinach, arugula, romaine)
- 1 large avocado, diced
- 1 cup cherry tomatoes, halved
- 1/4 red onion, thinly sliced
- 1/4 cup fresh cilantro, chopped (optional)

For the Lemon Vinaigrette
- 1/4 cup extra virgin olive oil
- 3 tablespoons fresh lemon juice (about 1 lemon)
- 1 teaspoon lemon zest
- 1 clove garlic, minced
- 1 teaspoon Dijon mustard
- Salt and pepper to taste

Directions
1. Grill the Chicken: Preheat your grill to medium-high heat. Brush the chicken breasts with olive oil and season with salt and pepper. Grill the chicken for about 6-7 minutes per side, or until fully cooked and the internal temperature reaches 165°F (75°C). Remove from the grill and let rest for a few minutes before slicing.
2. Prepare the Lemon Vinaigrette: In a small bowl, whisk together the olive oil, fresh lemon juice, lemon zest, minced garlic, Dijon mustard, salt, and pepper until well combined.
3. Assemble the Salad: In a large bowl, combine the mixed greens, diced avocado, cherry tomatoes, and sliced red onion. Toss gently to combine.
4. Add Chicken and Dressing: Top the salad with the sliced grilled chicken. Drizzle the lemon vinaigrette over the salad and toss gently to coat.
5. Serve: Divide the salad into four servings and garnish with fresh cilantro if desired. Serve immediately.

Nutritional Information (per serving)
- Calories: 350
- Protein: 25g
- Carbohydrates: 10g
- Dietary Fiber: 6g
- Sugars: 2g
- Fat: 25g
- Saturated Fat: 4g
- Sodium: 200mg
- Potassium: 900mg
- Vitamin A: 60% of Daily Value
- Vitamin C: 50% of Daily Value
- Calcium: 6% of Daily Value
- Iron: 10% of Daily Value

Vegetarian & Vegan Options

Plant-based recipes for those who prefer or need them

Cauliflower and Chickpea Tacos

Yield: 4 servings (8 tacos) **Prep Time:** 15 minutes
Cook Time: 30 minutes

Ingredients
For the Filling
- 1 medium head of cauliflower, cut into small florets
- 1 (15-ounce) can chickpeas, rinsed and drained
- 3 tablespoons olive oil
- 1 teaspoon ground cumin
- 1 teaspoon ground paprika
- 1/2 teaspoon ground turmeric
- 1/2 teaspoon ground coriander
- 1/2 teaspoon garlic powder
- 1/4 teaspoon cayenne pepper (optional)
- Salt and pepper to taste

For the Tacos
- 8 small corn tortillas
- 1 avocado, sliced
- 1/2 cup red cabbage, thinly sliced
- 1/4 cup fresh cilantro, chopped
- 1 lime, cut into wedges

For the Sauce
- 1/4 cup tahini
- 2 tablespoons fresh lemon juice
- 2 tablespoons water (more as needed)
- 1 clove garlic, minced
- Salt to taste

Directions
1. Preheat the Oven: Preheat your oven to 400°F (200°C). Line a baking sheet with parchment paper.
2. Prepare the Filling: In a large bowl, combine the cauliflower florets and chickpeas. Drizzle with olive oil and add the ground cumin, paprika, turmeric, coriander, garlic powder, cayenne pepper (if using), salt, and pepper. Toss to coat evenly.
3. Roast the Filling: Spread the cauliflower and chickpeas in a single layer on the prepared baking sheet. Roast in the preheated oven for 25-30 minutes, stirring halfway through, until the cauliflower is tender and golden brown.
4. Prepare the Sauce: In a small bowl, whisk together the tahini, fresh lemon juice, water, minced garlic, and salt until smooth and creamy. Adjust the consistency with more water if needed.
5. Warm the Tortillas: While the filling is roasting, warm the corn tortillas in a dry skillet over medium heat or wrap them in foil and warm them in the oven for a few minutes.
6. Assemble the Tacos: Divide the roasted cauliflower and chickpea mixture among the warm tortillas. Top with sliced avocado, red cabbage, and fresh cilantro. Drizzle with the tahini sauce and serve with lime wedges on the side.

Nutritional Information (per serving, 2 tacos):
- Calories: 350
- Protein: 10g
- Carbohydrates: 40g
- Dietary Fiber: 10g
- Sugars: 5g
- Fat: 18g
- Saturated Fat: 2.5g
- Sodium: 400mg
- Potassium: 800mg
- Vitamin A: 15% of Daily Value
- Vitamin C: 100% of Daily Value
- Calcium: 10% of Daily Value
- Iron: 20% of Daily Value

Zucchini and Tomato Gratin

Yield: 4 servings **Prep Time:** 20 minutes
Cook Time: 35 minutes

Ingredients
For the Gratin
- 2 large zucchinis, thinly sliced
- 4 large tomatoes, thinly sliced
- 1 small onion, finely chopped
- 3 cloves garlic, minced
- 2 tablespoons olive oil
- 1 teaspoon dried oregano
- 1 teaspoon dried basil
- 1/2 teaspoon salt
- 1/4 teaspoon black pepper

For the Topping
- 1/2 cup almond flour
- 1/4 cup nutritional yeast (or grated Parmesan cheese, if not vegan)
- 2 tablespoons chopped fresh parsley
- 2 tablespoons olive oil
- Salt and pepper to taste

Directions
1. Preheat the Oven: Preheat your oven to 375°F (190°C). Lightly grease a baking dish with olive oil.
2. Prepare the Vegetables: In a large skillet, heat 2 tablespoons of olive oil over medium heat. Add the chopped onion and sauté for about 5 minutes until softened. Add the minced garlic and cook for another 1 minute until fragrant. Remove from heat.
3. Layer the Vegetables: In the prepared baking dish, layer the sliced zucchinis and tomatoes, alternating between them. Sprinkle the sautéed onions and garlic evenly over the layers. Season with dried oregano, dried basil, salt, and black pepper.
4. Prepare the Topping: In a small bowl, combine the almond flour, nutritional yeast (or Parmesan cheese), chopped fresh parsley, olive oil, salt, and pepper. Mix well until the mixture is crumbly.
5. Add the Topping: Sprinkle the topping mixture evenly over the layered vegetables.
6. Bake: Bake in the preheated oven for 30-35 minutes, or until the vegetables are tender and the topping is golden brown.
7. Serve: Remove from the oven and let cool slightly before serving.

Nutritional Information (per serving)
- Calories: 200
- Protein: 6g
- Carbohydrates: 18g
- Dietary Fiber: 5g
- Sugars: 10g
- Fat: 14g
- Saturated Fat: 2g
- Sodium: 350mg
- Potassium: 800mg
- Vitamin A: 20% of Daily Value
- Vitamin C: 60% of Daily Value
- Calcium: 8% of Daily Value
- Iron: 10% of Daily Value

Spicy Sweet Potato and Black Bean Tacos

Yield: 4 servings **Prep Time:** 15 minutes
Cook Time: 30 minutes

Ingredients
For the Tacos
- 2 medium sweet potatoes, peeled and diced
- 1 can (15 oz) black beans, drained and rinsed
- 1 tablespoon olive oil
- 1 teaspoon ground cumin
- 1 teaspoon chili powder
- 1/2 teaspoon smoked paprika
- 1/2 teaspoon garlic powder
- 1/4 teaspoon sea salt
- 8 small corn or gluten-free tortillas
- 1 avocado, sliced
- Fresh cilantro, chopped (for garnish)

For the Salsa
- 1 cup cherry tomatoes, diced
- 1/4 red onion, finely chopped
- 1 jalapeño, seeded and minced
- 1/4 cup fresh cilantro, chopped
- Juice of 1 lime
- Sea salt, to taste

Directions
1. Preheat the Oven: Preheat your oven to 400°F (200°C).
2. Prepare the Sweet Potatoes: In a large bowl, toss the diced sweet potatoes with olive oil, cumin, chili powder, smoked paprika, garlic powder, and sea salt until evenly coated. Spread the sweet potatoes on a baking sheet in a single layer and roast for 25-30 minutes, or until tender and slightly crispy, stirring halfway through.
3. Prepare the Salsa: In a small bowl, combine the diced cherry tomatoes, red onion, jalapeño, cilantro, lime juice, and sea salt. Mix well and set aside.
4. Warm the Tortillas: While the sweet potatoes are roasting, warm the tortillas in a dry skillet over medium heat for about 30 seconds on each side, or until pliable.
5. Assemble the Tacos: Fill each tortilla with a generous portion of roasted sweet potatoes and black beans. Top with avocado slices and a spoonful of fresh salsa. Garnish with chopped cilantro.
6. Serve: Serve the tacos immediately with additional lime wedges on the side if desired.

Nutritional Information (per serving)
- Calories: 340 kcal
- Total Fat: 11 g
- Saturated Fat: 1.5 g
- Cholesterol: 0 mg
- Sodium: 420 mg
- Total Carbohydrates: 54 g
- Dietary Fiber: 14 g
- Sugars: 6 g
- Protein: 9 g

Baked Tofu with Sesame Seeds

Yield: 4 servings **Prep Time:** 15 minutes (plus marinating time) **Cook Time:** 30 minutes

Ingredients

- 1 block (14 ounces) firm or extra-firm tofu, drained and pressed
- 2 tablespoons soy sauce or tamari (gluten-free if needed)
- 1 tablespoon rice vinegar
- 1 tablespoon sesame oil
- 1 tablespoon maple syrup or honey
- 2 cloves garlic, minced
- 1 teaspoon fresh ginger, minced
- 2 tablespoons sesame seeds
- 1 tablespoon olive oil
- Optional: sliced green onions and fresh cilantro for garnish

Directions

1. Prepare the Tofu: Cut the pressed tofu into 1/2-inch thick slices. Place the tofu slices in a shallow dish or resealable plastic bag.
2. Make the Marinade: In a small bowl, whisk together the soy sauce or tamari, rice vinegar, sesame oil, maple syrup or honey, minced garlic, and fresh ginger.
3. Marinate the Tofu: Pour the marinade over the tofu slices, ensuring they are well coated. Marinate in the refrigerator for at least 30 minutes, preferably up to 2 hours, turning the tofu occasionally to ensure even marinating.
4. Preheat the Oven: Preheat your oven to 375°F (190°C). Line a baking sheet with parchment paper.
5. Coat with Sesame Seeds: Remove the tofu slices from the marinade and place them on the prepared baking sheet. Sprinkle both sides of the tofu slices with sesame seeds, pressing gently to adhere.
6. Bake: Drizzle the tofu slices with olive oil. Bake in the preheated oven for 25-30 minutes, turning halfway through, until the tofu is golden brown and crispy on the edges.
7. Serve: Remove from the oven and let cool slightly. Garnish with sliced green onions and fresh cilantro if desired. Serve warm.

Nutritional Information (per serving)

- Calories: 200
- Protein: 12g
- Carbohydrates: 8g
- Dietary Fiber: 2g
- Sugars: 3g
- Fat: 14g
- Saturated Fat: 2g
- Sodium: 400mg
- Potassium: 200mg
- Vitamin A: 2% of Daily Value
- Vitamin C: 4% of Daily Value
- Calcium: 20% of Daily Value
- Iron: 15% of Daily Value

Quinoa-Stuffed Acorn Squash

Yield: 4 servings **Prep Time:** 20 minutes **Cook Time:** 50 minutes

Ingredients

- 2 medium acorn squashes, halved and seeds removed
- 2 tablespoons olive oil
- Salt and pepper to taste
- 1 cup quinoa, rinsed
- 2 cups vegetable broth or water
- 1/2 cup dried cranberries
- 1/2 cup chopped pecans or walnuts
- 1 small onion, finely chopped
- 2 cloves garlic, minced
- 1 teaspoon ground cumin
- 1/2 teaspoon ground cinnamon
- 1/4 teaspoon ground turmeric
- 1/4 cup fresh parsley, chopped (optional, for garnish)

Directions

1. Preheat the Oven: Preheat your oven to 400°F (200°C). Line a baking sheet with parchment paper.
2. Prepare the Squash: Brush the cut sides of the acorn squash halves with 1 tablespoon of olive oil and season with salt and pepper. Place the squash halves cut side down on the prepared baking sheet. Roast in the preheated oven for 40-45 minutes, or until the flesh is tender and easily pierced with a fork.
3. Cook the Quinoa: While the squash is roasting, bring the vegetable broth or water to a boil in a medium saucepan. Add the rinsed quinoa, reduce heat to low, cover, and simmer for about 15 minutes, or until the quinoa is cooked and the liquid is absorbed. Remove from heat and fluff with a fork.
4. Prepare the Filling: In a large skillet, heat the remaining 1 tablespoon of olive oil over medium heat. Add the chopped onion and sauté for about 5 minutes until softened. Add the minced garlic, ground cumin, ground cinnamon, and ground turmeric, and cook for another 1-2 minutes until fragrant.
5. Combine Ingredients: Add the cooked quinoa, dried cranberries, and chopped nuts to the skillet. Stir to combine and cook for another 2-3 minutes until everything is heated through. Season with salt and pepper to taste.
6. Stuff the Squash: Remove the roasted squash from the oven and let cool slightly. Fill each squash half with the quinoa mixture, pressing down lightly to pack the filling.
7. Serve: Garnish with chopped fresh parsley if desired. Serve warm.

Nutritional Information (per serving)

- Calories: 350
- Protein: 7g
- Carbohydrates: 50g
- Dietary Fiber: 8g
- Sugars: 15g
- Fat: 14g
- Saturated Fat: 1.5g
- Sodium: 250mg
- Potassium: 900mg
- Vitamin A: 30% of Daily Value
- Vitamin C: 35% of Daily Value
- Calcium: 10% of Daily Value
- Iron: 20% of Daily Value

Spicy Red Lentil Dhal

Yield: 4 servings **Prep Time:** 10 minutes
Cook Time: 30 minutes

Ingredients

- 1 cup red lentils, rinsed and drained
- 1 tablespoon coconut oil or olive oil
- 1 large onion, finely chopped
- 3 cloves garlic, minced
- 1 tablespoon fresh ginger, minced
- 1-2 red chilies, finely chopped (adjust to taste)
- 1 teaspoon ground turmeric
- 1 teaspoon ground cumin
- 1 teaspoon ground coriander
- 1 teaspoon ground paprika
- 1 (14.5-ounce) can diced tomatoes
- 4 cups vegetable broth or water
- 1/2 teaspoon salt (or to taste)
- 1/4 teaspoon black pepper
- 1/4 cup fresh cilantro, chopped (optional, for garnish)
- Cooked steamed rice or quinoa, for serving

Directions

1. Heat the Oil: In a large pot, heat the coconut oil or olive oil over medium heat. Add the finely chopped onion and sauté for about 5 minutes until softened.
2. Add Garlic, Ginger, and Chilies: Stir in the minced garlic, fresh ginger, and chopped red chilies. Cook for another 1-2 minutes until fragrant.
3. Add Spices: Add the ground turmeric, ground cumin, ground coriander, and ground paprika. Cook for about 1 minute, stirring constantly, until the spices are well mixed and fragrant.
4. Add Lentils and Tomatoes: Stir in the red lentils and diced tomatoes. Cook for another 2-3 minutes, stirring occasionally.
5. Add Broth and Simmer: Pour in the vegetable broth or water. Bring the mixture to a boil, then reduce the heat to low and let it simmer for about 20-25 minutes, or until the lentils are tender and the dhal has thickened. Stir occasionally to prevent sticking.
6. Season and Serve: Season with salt and black pepper to taste. Serve the spicy red lentil dhal over cooked steamed rice or quinoa. Garnish with chopped fresh cilantro if desired.

Nutritional Information (per serving)

- Calories: 250
- Protein: 12g
- Carbohydrates: 40g
- Dietary Fiber: 12g
- Sugars: 6g
- Fat: 5g
- Saturated Fat: 2g
- Sodium: 600mg
- Potassium: 700mg
- Vitamin A: 20% of Daily Value
- Vitamin C: 25% of Daily Value
- Calcium: 6% of Daily Value
- Iron: 20% of Daily Value

Chickpea and Sweet Potato Curry

Yield: 4 servings **Prep Time:** 15 minutes
Cook Time: 30 minutes

Ingredients
- 1 tablespoon coconut oil or olive oil
- 1 large onion, chopped
- 3 cloves garlic, minced
- 1 tablespoon fresh ginger, minced
- 2 large sweet potatoes, peeled and diced
- 1 (15-ounce) can chickpeas, rinsed and drained
- 1 (14.5-ounce) can diced tomatoes
- 1 (14-ounce) can coconut milk
- 1 tablespoon curry powder
- 1 teaspoon ground turmeric
- 1 teaspoon ground cumin
- 1/2 teaspoon ground coriander
- 1/2 teaspoon ground cinnamon
- 1/4 teaspoon cayenne pepper (optional)
- Salt and pepper to taste
- 1 cup fresh spinach, chopped
- 1/4 cup fresh cilantro, chopped (optional, for garnish)
- Cooked rice or quinoa, for serving

Directions
1. Heat the Oil: In a large pot, heat the coconut oil or olive oil over medium heat. Add the chopped onion and sauté for about 5 minutes until softened.
2. Add Garlic and Ginger: Stir in the minced garlic and fresh ginger. Cook for another 1-2 minutes until fragrant.
3. Add Spices: Add the curry powder, ground turmeric, ground cumin, ground coriander, ground cinnamon, and cayenne pepper (if using). Cook for about 1 minute, stirring constantly, until the spices are well mixed and fragrant.
4. Add Sweet Potatoes and Chickpeas: Stir in the diced sweet potatoes and chickpeas. Cook for about 5 minutes, stirring occasionally.
5. Add Tomatoes and Coconut Milk: Pour in the diced tomatoes (with their juice) and coconut milk. Bring the mixture to a boil, then reduce the heat to low and let it simmer for about 20 minutes, or until the sweet potatoes are tender.
6. Add Spinach: Stir in the chopped spinach and cook for another 2-3 minutes until wilted. Season with salt and pepper to taste.
7. Serve: Serve the chickpea and sweet potato curry over cooked rice or quinoa. Garnish with chopped fresh cilantro if desired.

Nutritional Information (per serving)
- Calories: 400
- Protein: 10g
- Carbohydrates: 60g
- Dietary Fiber: 12g
- Sugars: 10g
- Fat: 16g
- Saturated Fat: 10g
- Sodium: 600mg
- Potassium: 1000mg
- Vitamin A: 300% of Daily Value
- Vitamin C: 50% of Daily Value
- Calcium: 10% of Daily Value
- Iron: 20% of Daily Value

Butternut Squash Soup

Yield: 4 servings **Prep Time:** 15 minutes
Cook Time: 45 minutes

Ingredients

- 1 large butternut squash, peeled, seeded, and cubed
- 2 tablespoons olive oil
- Salt and pepper to taste
- 1 large onion, chopped
- 3 cloves garlic, minced
- 1 tablespoon fresh ginger, minced
- 1 teaspoon ground turmeric
- 1/2 teaspoon ground cumin
- 1/2 teaspoon ground cinnamon
- 4 cups vegetable broth
- 1 (14-ounce) can coconut milk
- 2 tablespoons maple syrup or honey (optional)
- 1 tablespoon fresh lime juice
- Fresh cilantro, chopped (optional, for garnish)

Directions

1. Preheat the Oven: Preheat your oven to 400°F (200°C). Line a baking sheet with parchment paper.
2. Roast the Butternut Squash: Place the cubed butternut squash on the prepared baking sheet. Drizzle with 1 tablespoon of olive oil and season with salt and pepper. Toss to coat evenly. Roast in the preheated oven for 25-30 minutes, or until the squash is tender and lightly browned.
3. Cook the Onion and Garlic: In a large pot, heat the remaining 1 tablespoon of olive oil over medium heat. Add the chopped onion and sauté for about 5 minutes until softened. Add the minced garlic and fresh ginger, and cook for another 1-2 minutes until fragrant.
4. Add Spices and Broth: Stir in the ground turmeric, ground cumin, and ground cinnamon. Cook for about 1 minute, stirring constantly, until the spices are well mixed and fragrant. Add the roasted butternut squash and vegetable broth. Bring to a boil, then reduce the heat and let it simmer for about 10 minutes.
5. Blend the Soup: Using an immersion blender, blend the soup until smooth and creamy. Alternatively, carefully transfer the soup in batches to a blender and blend until smooth. Return the blended soup to the pot.
6. Add Coconut Milk and Seasonings: Stir in the coconut milk, maple syrup or honey (if using), and fresh lime juice. Simmer for another 5 minutes until heated through. Adjust seasoning with more salt and pepper if needed.
7. Serve: Ladle the soup into bowls and garnish with chopped fresh cilantro if desired. Serve warm.

Nutritional Information (per serving)

- Calories: 300
- Protein: 4g
- Carbohydrates: 35g
- Dietary Fiber: 8g
- Sugars: 10g
- Fat: 18g
- Saturated Fat: 12g
- Sodium: 600mg
- Potassium: 1000mg
- Vitamin A: 400% of Daily Value
- Vitamin C: 50% of Daily Value
- Calcium: 10% of Daily Value
- Iron: 15% of Daily Value

Golden Milk Overnight Oats

Yield: 2 servings **Prep Time:** 10 minutes
Cook Time: None (overnight soak)

Ingredients
- 1 cup rolled oats
- 1 1/2 cups unsweetened almond milk (or any plant-based milk)
- 1 tablespoon chia seeds
- 1 tablespoon maple syrup or honey (optional, for sweetness)
- 1 teaspoon ground turmeric
- 1/2 teaspoon ground cinnamon
- 1/4 teaspoon ground ginger
- 1/4 teaspoon vanilla extract
- Pinch of black pepper (enhances absorption of turmeric)
- Fresh fruit, nuts, and seeds for topping (optional)

Directions
1. Combine Ingredients: In a medium bowl or a jar, combine the rolled oats, almond milk, chia seeds, maple syrup or honey (if using), ground turmeric, ground cinnamon, ground ginger, vanilla extract, and a pinch of black pepper.
2. Mix Well: Stir well to ensure all the ingredients are thoroughly mixed. Make sure the oats and chia seeds are fully submerged in the liquid.
3. Refrigerate: Cover the bowl or jar with a lid or plastic wrap and refrigerate overnight, or for at least 6 hours.
4. Serve: In the morning, give the oats a good stir. If the mixture is too thick, add a little more almond milk to reach your desired consistency. Divide the oats into two servings and top with fresh fruit, nuts, and seeds if desired.

Nutritional Information (per serving)
- Calories: 250
- Protein: 6g
- Carbohydrates: 40g
- Dietary Fiber: 8g
- Sugars: 8g
- Fat: 8g
- Saturated Fat: 1g
- Sodium: 150mg
- Potassium: 300mg
- Vitamin A: 2% of Daily Value
- Vitamin C: 0% of Daily Value
- Calcium: 25% of Daily Value
- Iron: 15% of Daily Value

Avocado and Berry Salad

Yield: 4 servings **Prep Time:** 15 minutes
Cook Time: None

Ingredients
- 4 cups mixed salad greens (e.g., spinach, arugula, or mixed greens)
- 1 ripe avocado, diced
- 1 cup mixed berries (e.g., strawberries, blueberries, raspberries)
- 1/4 cup red onion, thinly sliced
- 1/4 cup walnuts or almonds, chopped
- 1/4 cup vegan feta cheese (optional)

For the Balsamic Glaze
- 1/2 cup balsamic vinegar
- 1 tablespoon maple syrup or honey

Directions
1. Prepare the Balsamic Glaze: In a small saucepan, combine the balsamic vinegar and maple syrup or honey. Bring to a boil over medium heat, then reduce the heat to low and simmer for about 10-15 minutes, or until the mixture has reduced by half and has a syrupy consistency. Remove from heat and let cool.
2. Assemble the Salad: In a large salad bowl, combine the mixed salad greens, diced avocado, mixed berries, red onion, and chopped walnuts or almonds. If using, add the vegan feta cheese.
3. Drizzle with Balsamic Glaze: Drizzle the cooled balsamic glaze over the salad and toss gently to combine.
4. Serve: Divide the salad into four servings and serve immediately.

Nutritional Information (per serving)
- Calories: 200
- Protein: 3g
- Carbohydrates: 20g
- Dietary Fiber: 8g
- Sugars: 10g
- Fat: 14g
- Saturated Fat: 2g
- Sodium: 100mg
- Potassium: 500mg
- Vitamin A: 20% of Daily Value
- Vitamin C: 70% of Daily Value
- Calcium: 6% of Daily Value
- Iron: 8% of Daily Value

Roasted Carrot and Ginger Soup

Yield: 4 servings **Prep Time:** 15 minutes
Cook Time: 45 minutes

Ingredients
- 1.5 pounds carrots, peeled and chopped
- 1 large onion, chopped
- 3 cloves garlic, minced
- 1 tablespoon fresh ginger, minced
- 2 tablespoons olive oil
- Salt and pepper to taste
- 4 cups vegetable broth
- 1 cup coconut milk (optional for extra creaminess)
- 1 teaspoon ground turmeric
- 1 teaspoon ground cumin
- 1/2 teaspoon ground coriander
- 1/4 teaspoon cayenne pepper (optional)
- 1 tablespoon fresh lemon juice
- Fresh cilantro or parsley, chopped (optional for garnish)

Directions
1. Preheat the Oven: Preheat your oven to 400°F (200°C). Line a baking sheet with parchment paper.
2. Roast the Vegetables: Place the chopped carrots and onion on the prepared baking sheet. Drizzle with olive oil, and season with salt and pepper. Toss to coat evenly. Roast in the preheated oven for 25-30 minutes, or until the carrots are tender and lightly browned.
3. Prepare the Soup Base: In a large pot, heat a bit of olive oil over medium heat. Add the minced garlic and fresh ginger. Cook for about 1-2 minutes until fragrant. Add the roasted carrots and onion to the pot.
4. Add Spices and Broth: Stir in the ground turmeric, ground cumin, and ground coriander. Cook for about 1 minute to toast the spices. Pour in the vegetable broth and bring the mixture to a boil. Reduce the heat and let it simmer for about 15 minutes to allow the flavors to meld.
5. Blend the Soup: Using an immersion blender, blend the soup until smooth and creamy. Alternatively, carefully transfer the soup in batches to a blender and blend until smooth. Return the blended soup to the pot.
6. Add Coconut Milk and Lemon Juice: Stir in the coconut milk (if using) and fresh lemon juice. Simmer for another 5 minutes until heated through. Adjust seasoning with more salt and pepper if needed.
7. Serve: Ladle the soup into bowls and garnish with chopped fresh cilantro or parsley. Serve warm.

Nutritional Information (per serving)
- Calories: 180
- Protein: 3g
- Carbohydrates: 24g
- Dietary Fiber: 6g
- Sugars: 10g
- Fat: 9g
- Saturated Fat: 4g
- Sodium: 400mg
- Potassium: 800mg
- Vitamin A: 450% of Daily Value
- Vitamin C: 20% of Daily Value
- Calcium: 6% of Daily Value
- Iron: 10% of Daily Value

Roasted Veggie Breakfast Bowl

Yield: 4 servings **Prep Time:** 15 minutes
Cook Time: 30 minutes

Ingredients
- 2 large sweet potatoes, peeled and diced
- 2 bell peppers (any color), diced
- 1 red onion, diced
- 3 tablespoons olive oil
- 1 teaspoon ground cumin
- 1 teaspoon ground paprika
- 1/2 teaspoon ground turmeric
- Salt and pepper to taste
- 1 avocado, sliced
- 1/4 cup fresh cilantro, chopped (optional, for garnish)
- 1 tablespoon fresh lime juice (optional, for garnish)

Directions
1. Preheat the Oven: Preheat your oven to 425°F (220°C). Line a baking sheet with parchment paper.
2. Prepare the Vegetables: In a large bowl, combine the diced sweet potatoes, bell peppers, and red onion. Drizzle with olive oil and sprinkle with ground cumin, ground paprika, ground turmeric, salt, and pepper. Toss to coat the vegetables evenly.
3. Roast the Vegetables: Spread the vegetables in a single layer on the prepared baking sheet. Roast in the preheated oven for 25-30 minutes, stirring halfway through, until the vegetables are tender and lightly browned.
4. Assemble the Bowls: Divide the roasted vegetables among four bowls. Top each bowl with sliced avocado.
5. Garnish: Garnish with chopped fresh cilantro and a squeeze of fresh lime juice if desired.
6. Serve: Serve warm and enjoy!

Nutritional Information (per serving)
- Calories: 300
- Protein: 4g
- Carbohydrates: 40g
- Dietary Fiber: 10g
- Sugars: 10g
- Fat: 15g
- Saturated Fat: 2g
- Sodium: 200mg
- Potassium: 900mg
- Vitamin A: 400% of Daily Value
- Vitamin C: 100% of Daily Value
- Calcium: 8% of Daily Value
- Iron: 10% of Daily Value

Spirulina Smoothie

Yield: 2 servings **Prep Time:** 5 minutes
Cook Time: None

Ingredients
- 1 teaspoon spirulina powder
- 2 ripe bananas
- 2 cups fresh spinach
- 2 cups coconut water
- 1 tablespoon chia seeds (optional)
- 1 tablespoon fresh lemon juice (optional, for added flavor)

Directions
1. Prepare the Ingredients: Peel the bananas and roughly chop them.
2. Blend the Smoothie: In a blender, combine the spirulina powder, chopped bananas, fresh spinach, coconut water, chia seeds (if using), and fresh lemon juice (if using). Blend until smooth and creamy.
3. Serve: Pour the smoothie into two glasses and serve immediately.

Nutritional Information (per serving)
- Calories: 150
- Protein: 3g
- Carbohydrates: 35g
- Dietary Fiber: 5g
- Sugars: 20g
- Fat: 1g
- Saturated Fat: 0g
- Sodium: 100mg
- Potassium: 700mg
- Vitamin A: 60% of Daily Value
- Vitamin C: 30% of Daily Value
- Calcium: 6% of Daily Value
- Iron: 10% of Daily Value

Stuffed Zucchini Boats

Yield: 4 servings **Prep Time:** 20 minutes
Cook Time: 30 minutes

Ingredients

- 4 large zucchinis, halved lengthwise and seeds scooped out
- 1 tablespoon olive oil
- 1 onion, finely chopped
- 2 cloves garlic, minced
- 1 red bell pepper, finely chopped
- 1 cup cherry tomatoes, halved
- 1 (15-ounce) can black beans, rinsed and drained
- 1 teaspoon ground cumin
- 1 teaspoon ground paprika
- 1/2 teaspoon ground turmeric
- Salt and pepper to taste
- 1/4 cup fresh cilantro, chopped (optional for garnish)
- 1/4 cup nutritional yeast or vegan cheese (optional for topping)

Directions

1. Preheat the Oven: Preheat your oven to 375°F (190°C). Line a baking sheet with parchment paper.
2. Prepare the Zucchini: Halve the zucchinis lengthwise and scoop out the seeds to create boats. Place the zucchini halves on the prepared baking sheet.
3. Cook the Vegetables: In a large skillet, heat the olive oil over medium heat. Add the chopped onion and sauté for about 5 minutes until softened. Add the minced garlic and cook for another 1-2 minutes until fragrant.
4. Add the Filling Ingredients: Stir in the chopped red bell pepper, cherry tomatoes, black beans, ground cumin, ground paprika, ground turmeric, salt, and pepper. Cook for about 5-7 minutes until the vegetables are tender and the flavors are well combined.
5. Stuff the Zucchini: Spoon the vegetable mixture into the zucchini boats, pressing down lightly to pack the filling.
6. Bake: If using, sprinkle nutritional yeast or vegan cheese over the top of each zucchini boat. Bake in the preheated oven for 20-25 minutes, or until the zucchinis are tender and the tops are lightly browned.
7. Serve: Remove from the oven and let cool slightly. Garnish with chopped fresh cilantro if desired. Serve warm.

Nutritional Information (per serving)

- Calories: 200
- Protein: 7g
- Carbohydrates: 30g
- Dietary Fiber: 8g
- Sugars: 10g
- Fat: 6g
- Saturated Fat: 1g
- Sodium: 300mg
- Potassium: 900mg
- Vitamin A: 50% of Daily Value
- Vitamin C: 90% of Daily Value
- Calcium: 10% of Daily Value
- Iron: 15% of Daily Value

Apple Cinnamon Quinoa

Yield: 4 servings **Prep Time:** 10 minutes
Cook Time: 20 minutes

Ingredients

- 1 cup quinoa, rinsed
- 2 cups water or unsweetened almond milk
- 2 large apples, peeled, cored, and diced
- 1 tablespoon coconut oil or olive oil
- 2 tablespoons maple syrup or honey (optional for sweetness)
- 1 teaspoon ground cinnamon
- 1/2 teaspoon ground nutmeg
- 1/4 teaspoon ground ginger
- 1/4 cup chopped walnuts or pecans (optional)
- 1/4 cup dried cranberries or raisins (optional)
- 1 teaspoon vanilla extract
- Pinch of salt

Directions

1. Cook the Quinoa: In a medium saucepan, bring the water or almond milk to a boil. Add the rinsed quinoa, reduce the heat to low, cover, and simmer for about 15 minutes, or until the quinoa is cooked and the liquid is absorbed. Fluff with a fork and set aside.
2. Cook the Apples: In a large skillet, heat the coconut oil or olive oil over medium heat. Add the diced apples, ground cinnamon, ground nutmeg, and ground ginger. Cook for about 5-7 minutes until the apples are tender and fragrant.
3. Combine and Sweeten: Stir the cooked quinoa into the skillet with the apples. Add the maple syrup or honey (if using), vanilla extract, and a pinch of salt. Stir to combine and cook for another 2-3 minutes until everything is heated through.
4. Add Optional Ingredients: If using, stir in the chopped walnuts or pecans and dried cranberries or raisins.
5. Serve: Divide the apple cinnamon quinoa among four bowls. Serve warm.

Nutritional Information (per serving)

- Calories: 250
- Protein: 5g
- Carbohydrates: 40g
- Dietary Fiber: 6g
- Sugars: 15g
- Fat: 8g
- Saturated Fat: 3g
- Sodium: 50mg
- Potassium: 300mg
- Vitamin A: 2% of Daily Value
- Vitamin C: 10% of Daily Value
- Calcium: 6% of Daily Value
- Iron: 10% of Daily Value

Tomato Basil Frittata

Yield: 4 servings **Prep Time:** 10 minutes
Cook Time: 25 minutes

Ingredients

- 8 large eggs (or equivalent egg substitute for vegan option, such as chickpea flour or tofu scramble)
- 1/4 cup unsweetened almond milk (or any plant-based milk)
- 1 tablespoon olive oil
- 1 small onion, finely chopped
- 2 cloves garlic, minced
- 2 cups cherry tomatoes, halved
- 1/4 cup fresh basil, chopped
- Salt and pepper to taste
- 1/4 cup nutritional yeast (optional, for a cheesy flavor in vegan option)
- 1/4 teaspoon turmeric (optional, for color in vegan option)

Directions

1. Preheat the Oven: Preheat your oven to 375°F (190°C). Lightly grease a baking dish or ovenproof skillet with olive oil.
2. Prepare the Vegan Egg Substitute (if using): For a chickpea flour base, mix 1 cup chickpea flour with 1 cup water, 1/4 cup nutritional yeast, and 1/4 teaspoon turmeric until smooth. For tofu scramble, blend 14 ounces of silken tofu with 1/4 cup nutritional yeast and 1/4 teaspoon turmeric until smooth.
3. Cook the Vegetables: In a large skillet, heat the olive oil over medium heat. Add the chopped onion and sauté for about 5 minutes until softened. Add the minced garlic and cook for another 1 minute until fragrant. Stir in the cherry tomatoes and cook for another 2-3 minutes until they begin to soften.
4. Mix the Eggs: In a large bowl, whisk the eggs (or prepared vegan egg substitute) with the almond milk. Season with salt and pepper.
5. Combine and Cook: Pour the egg mixture into the skillet with the cooked vegetables. Stir in the chopped basil. Cook for about 2-3 minutes, stirring gently to combine everything.
6. Bake: Transfer the skillet to the preheated oven (or transfer the mixture to the prepared baking dish if not using an ovenproof skillet). Bake for 20-25 minutes, or until the frittata is set and golden brown on top.
7. Serve: Remove from the oven and let cool slightly. Slice into wedges and serve warm.

Nutritional Information (per serving)

- Calories: 200
- Protein: 12g
- Carbohydrates: 6g
- Dietary Fiber: 1g
- Sugars: 3g
- Fat: 14g
- Saturated Fat: 3.5g
- Sodium: 150mg
- Potassium: 300mg
- Vitamin A: 15% of Daily Value
- Vitamin C: 20% of Daily Value
- Calcium: 10% of Daily Value
- Iron: 10% of Daily Value

Hemp Seed Granola

Yield: 8 servings **Prep Time:** 10 minutes **Cook Time:** 25 minutes

Ingredients

- 2 cups rolled oats
- 1/2 cup hemp seeds
- 1/2 cup chopped nuts (e.g., almonds, walnuts, pecans)
- 1/2 cup dried fruits (e.g., cranberries, raisins, apricots), chopped
- 1/4 cup pumpkin seeds
- 1/4 cup sunflower seeds
- 1/4 cup shredded coconut (optional)
- 1/4 cup coconut oil or olive oil, melted
- 1/4 cup maple syrup or honey
- 1 teaspoon vanilla extract
- 1 teaspoon ground cinnamon
- 1/2 teaspoon ground ginger
- 1/4 teaspoon salt

Directions

1. Preheat the Oven: Preheat your oven to 325°F (165°C). Line a baking sheet with parchment paper.
2. Mix the Dry Ingredients: In a large bowl, combine the rolled oats, hemp seeds, chopped nuts, dried fruits, pumpkin seeds, sunflower seeds, and shredded coconut (if using).
3. Mix the Wet Ingredients: In a small bowl, whisk together the melted coconut oil or olive oil, maple syrup or honey, vanilla extract, ground cinnamon, ground ginger, and salt until well combined.
4. Combine and Coat: Pour the wet mixture over the dry ingredients. Stir well to ensure that all the dry ingredients are evenly coated.
5. Bake: Spread the granola mixture evenly on the prepared baking sheet. Bake in the preheated oven for 20-25 minutes, stirring halfway through, until the granola is golden brown and fragrant.
6. Cool and Store: Remove from the oven and let cool completely on the baking sheet. The granola will become crisp as it cools. Once cooled, transfer to an airtight container for storage.

Nutritional Information (per serving)

- Calories: 250
- Protein: 6g
- Carbohydrates: 30g
- Dietary Fiber: 5g
- Sugars: 12g
- Fat: 14g
- Saturated Fat: 5g
- Sodium: 80mg
- Potassium: 200mg
- Vitamin A: 0% of Daily Value
- Vitamin C: 1% of Daily Value
- Calcium: 4% of Daily Value
- Iron: 10% of Daily Value

Spiced Lentil Porridge

Yield: 4 servings **Prep Time:** 10 minutes
Cook Time: 30 minutes

Ingredients

- 1 cup red lentils, rinsed and drained
- 4 cups water or vegetable broth
- 1 tablespoon coconut oil or olive oil
- 1 large onion, finely chopped
- 2 cloves garlic, minced
- 1 tablespoon fresh ginger, minced
- 1 teaspoon ground turmeric
- 1 teaspoon ground cumin
- 1/2 teaspoon ground cinnamon
- 1/4 teaspoon ground cardamom
- 1/4 teaspoon ground black pepper
- Salt to taste
- 1/2 cup coconut milk (optional, for creaminess)
- 1/4 cup fresh cilantro, chopped (optional, for garnish)
- 1/4 cup raisins or dried apricots, chopped (optional, for garnish)
- 1 cup coconut yogurt (or any plant-based yogurt), for topping

Directions

1. Prepare the Lentils: In a medium saucepan, combine the rinsed red lentils and water or vegetable broth. Bring to a boil over medium-high heat, then reduce the heat to low and let it simmer for about 20 minutes, or until the lentils are tender and the mixture has thickened. Stir occasionally to prevent sticking.
2. Cook the Aromatics: While the lentils are cooking, heat the coconut oil or olive oil in a large skillet over medium heat. Add the chopped onion and sauté for about 5 minutes until softened. Add the minced garlic and fresh ginger, and cook for another 1-2 minutes until fragrant.
3. Add the Spices: Stir in the ground turmeric, ground cumin, ground cinnamon, ground cardamom, and ground black pepper. Cook for about 1 minute, stirring constantly, until the spices are well mixed and fragrant.
4. Combine and Simmer: Add the cooked lentils to the skillet with the spices and aromatics. Stir well to combine. If using, add the coconut milk for extra creaminess. Simmer for another 5-10 minutes, stirring occasionally, until the flavors are well combined. Season with salt to taste.
5. Serve: Divide the spiced lentil porridge among four bowls. Top each serving with a dollop of coconut yogurt. Garnish with chopped fresh cilantro and raisins or dried apricots if desired. Serve warm.

Nutritional Information (per serving)

- Calories: 250
- Protein: 10g
- Carbohydrates: 35g
- Dietary Fiber: 10g
- Sugars: 8g
- Fat: 8g
- Saturated Fat: 5g
- Sodium: 300mg
- Potassium: 500mg
- Vitamin A: 2% of Daily Value
- Vitamin C: 10% of Daily Value
- Calcium: 6% of Daily Value
- Iron: 20% of Daily Value

Mango Turmeric Smoothie

Yield: 2 servings **Prep Time:** 5 minutes
Cook Time: None

Ingredients

- 1 large mango, peeled and diced (or 1 cup frozen mango chunks)
- 1 cup coconut milk (unsweetened)
- 1/2 teaspoon ground turmeric
- 1/2 teaspoon fresh ginger, grated (optional)
- 1 tablespoon chia seeds (optional)
- 1 tablespoon fresh lime juice
- 1-2 teaspoons maple syrup or honey (optional, for sweetness)
- Ice cubes (optional, for a thicker smoothie)

Directions

1. Prepare the Ingredients: If using a fresh mango, peel and dice it. If using frozen mango chunks, you can use them directly from the freezer.
2. Blend the Smoothie: In a blender, combine the diced mango, coconut milk, ground turmeric, grated fresh ginger (if using), chia seeds (if using), fresh lime juice, and maple syrup or honey (if using). Add ice cubes if desired.
3. Blend Until Smooth: Blend on high speed until smooth and creamy. If the smoothie is too thick, you can add more coconut milk to reach your desired consistency.
4. Serve: Pour the smoothie into two glasses and serve immediately.

Nutritional Information (per serving)

- Calories: 150
- Protein: 2g
- Carbohydrates: 20g
- Dietary Fiber: 4g
- Sugars: 15g
- Fat: 7g
- Saturated Fat: 6g
- Sodium: 20mg
- Potassium: 300mg
- Vitamin A: 25% of Daily Value
- Vitamin C: 60% of Daily Value
- Calcium: 2% of Daily Value
- Iron: 6% of Daily Value

Turmeric Cauliflower Rice

Yield: 4 servings **Prep Time:** 10 minutes
Cook Time: 10 minutes

Ingredients

- 1 medium head of cauliflower, riced
- 1 tablespoon coconut oil or olive oil
- 3 cloves garlic, minced
- 1 teaspoon ground turmeric
- 1/2 teaspoon ground cumin
- 1/2 teaspoon ground coriander
- Salt and pepper to taste
- 1/4 cup fresh cilantro, chopped
- 1 tablespoon lemon juice
- 2 tablespoons water (optional for steaming)

Directions

1. Rice the Cauliflower: Wash and dry the cauliflower. Remove the leaves and cut into florets. Pulse the florets in a food processor until they resemble rice grains. Alternatively, grate the cauliflower using a box grater.
2. Sauté Garlic and Spices: Heat the coconut oil or olive oil in a large skillet over medium heat. Add the minced garlic and sauté for about 1 minute until fragrant.
3. Add Cauliflower Rice: Add the riced cauliflower to the skillet and stir to combine with the garlic.
4. Season and Cook: Stir in the turmeric, cumin, coriander, salt, and pepper. Cook for 5-7 minutes, stirring occasionally, until the cauliflower is tender but not mushy. If you prefer a softer texture, add 2 tablespoons of water, cover the skillet, and steam for an additional 2-3 minutes.
5. Finish with Herbs and Lemon: Remove from heat and stir in the chopped cilantro and lemon juice.
6. Serve: Serve warm as a side dish or base for other meals.

Nutritional Information (Per Serving)

- Calories: 70
- Total Fat: 4g
- Saturated Fat: 2g
- Cholesterol: 0mg
- Sodium: 60mg
- Total Carbohydrates: 7g
- Dietary Fiber: 3g
- Sugars: 2g
- Protein: 3g

Fish and Shellfish

Omega-3 rich seafood dishes

Lemon Herb Grilled Salmon

Yield: 4 servings **Prep Time:** 15 minutes (plus 30 minutes marinating time) **Cook Time:** 10 minutes

Ingredients
- 4 salmon fillets (about 6 ounces each)
- 2 tablespoons olive oil
- 2 tablespoons fresh lemon juice
- 1 teaspoon lemon zest
- 3 cloves garlic, minced
- 1 tablespoon fresh parsley, chopped
- 1 tablespoon fresh dill, chopped
- 1 tablespoon fresh thyme, chopped
- Salt and pepper to taste
- Lemon slices (optional, for garnish)
- Fresh parsley or dill (optional, for garnish)

Directions
1. Prepare the Marinade: In a small bowl, whisk together the olive oil, fresh lemon juice, lemon zest, minced garlic, chopped parsley, chopped dill, chopped thyme, salt, and pepper.
2. Marinate the Salmon: Place the salmon fillets in a shallow dish or resealable plastic bag. Pour the marinade over the salmon, ensuring that each fillet is well coated. Marinate in the refrigerator for at least 30 minutes, or up to 2 hours.
3. Preheat the Grill: Preheat your grill to medium-high heat. Lightly oil the grill grates to prevent sticking.
4. Grill the Salmon: Remove the salmon fillets from the marinade and place them on the preheated grill. Grill for about 4-5 minutes per side, or until the salmon is cooked through and flakes easily with a fork.
5. Serve: Remove the salmon from the grill and let rest for a few minutes. Garnish with lemon slices and fresh parsley or dill if desired. Serve warm.

Nutritional Information (per serving)
- Calories: 350
- Protein: 30g
- Carbohydrates: 2g
- Dietary Fiber: 0g
- Sugars: 0g
- Fat: 24g
- Saturated Fat: 4g
- Sodium: 220mg
- Potassium: 750mg
- Vitamin A: 8% of Daily Value
- Vitamin C: 20% of Daily Value
- Calcium: 4% of Daily Value
- Iron: 8% of Daily Value

Baked Cod with Tomato and Basil

Yield: 4 servings **Prep Time:** 10 minutes **Cook Time:** 20 minutes

Ingredients
- 4 cod fillets (about 6 ounces each)
- 2 tablespoons olive oil
- 3 cloves garlic, minced
- 4 large tomatoes, diced
- 1/4 cup fresh basil leaves, chopped
- 1 teaspoon dried oregano
- Salt and pepper to taste
- Lemon wedges (optional, for serving)
- Fresh basil leaves (optional, for garnish)

Directions
1. Preheat the Oven: Preheat your oven to 400°F (200°C). Lightly grease a baking dish with olive oil.
2. Prepare the Tomato Basil Mixture: In a medium bowl, combine the diced tomatoes, minced garlic, chopped fresh basil, dried oregano, olive oil, salt, and pepper. Mix well.
3. Arrange the Cod Fillets: Place the cod fillets in the prepared baking dish. Spoon the tomato basil mixture evenly over the top of each fillet.
4. Bake: Bake in the preheated oven for 15-20 minutes, or until the cod is cooked through and flakes easily with a fork.
5. Serve: Remove from the oven and let rest for a few minutes. Garnish with fresh basil leaves and serve with lemon wedges if desired.

Nutritional Information (per serving)
- Calories: 200
- Protein: 30g
- Carbohydrates: 5g
- Dietary Fiber: 1g
- Sugars: 3g
- Fat: 6g
- Saturated Fat: 1g
- Sodium: 150mg
- Potassium: 700mg
- Vitamin A: 10% of Daily Value
- Vitamin C: 30% of Daily Value
- Calcium: 6% of Daily Value
- Iron: 10% of Daily Value

Sesame Crusted Tuna

Yield: 4 servings **Prep Time:** 15 minutes
Cook Time: 10 minutes

Ingredients
- 4 tuna steaks (about 6 ounces each)
- 1/4 cup soy sauce or tamari (gluten-free if needed)
- 1 tablespoon fresh lemon juice
- 1 tablespoon fresh ginger, grated
- 2 cloves garlic, minced
- 1/2 cup white sesame seeds
- 1/4 cup black sesame seeds
- 2 tablespoons olive oil
- Salt and pepper to taste
- Lemon wedges (optional, for serving)
- Fresh cilantro or green onions (optional, for garnish)

Directions
1. Marinate the Tuna: In a shallow dish, combine the soy sauce or tamari, fresh lemon juice, grated ginger, and minced garlic. Add the tuna steaks and marinate for 10 minutes, turning once to ensure they are well coated.
2. Prepare the Sesame Seeds: In a shallow bowl, combine the white and black sesame seeds.
3. Coat the Tuna: Remove the tuna steaks from the marinade and pat them dry with paper towels. Season with salt and pepper. Press each tuna steak into the sesame seeds, coating both sides evenly.
4. Heat the Oil: In a large skillet, heat the olive oil over medium-high heat.
5. Sear the Tuna: Add the sesame-crusted tuna steaks to the skillet. Sear for about 2-3 minutes on each side for medium-rare, or until the desired level of doneness is reached. Be careful not to overcook, as tuna can become dry.
6. Serve: Remove from heat and let rest for a few minutes. Garnish with lemon wedges and fresh cilantro or green onions if desired. Serve warm.

Nutritional Information (per serving)
- Calories: 350
- Protein: 35g
- Carbohydrates: 6g
- Dietary Fiber: 2g
- Sugars: 0g
- Fat: 20g
- Saturated Fat: 3g
- Sodium: 600mg
- Potassium: 700mg
- Vitamin A: 4% of Daily Value
- Vitamin C: 6% of Daily Value
- Calcium: 20% of Daily Value
- Iron: 25% of Daily Value

Miso Glazed Salmon

Yield: 4 servings **Prep Time:** 10 minutes (plus 30 minutes marinating time) **Cook Time:** 15 minutes

Ingredients
- 4 salmon fillets (about 6 ounces each)
- 3 tablespoons white miso paste
- 2 tablespoons rice vinegar
- 2 tablespoons mirin (sweet rice wine)
- 1 tablespoon soy sauce or tamari (gluten-free if needed)
- 1 tablespoon maple syrup or honey
- 1 teaspoon fresh ginger, grated
- 2 cloves garlic, minced
- 1 tablespoon sesame oil
- 1 teaspoon sesame seeds (optional, for garnish)
- 2 green onions, thinly sliced (optional, for garnish)

Directions
1. Prepare the Marinade: In a small bowl, whisk together the white miso paste, rice vinegar, mirin, soy sauce or tamari, maple syrup or honey, grated ginger, minced garlic, and sesame oil until smooth.
2. Marinate the Salmon: Place the salmon fillets in a shallow dish or resealable plastic bag. Pour the miso marinade over the salmon, ensuring that each fillet is well coated. Marinate in the refrigerator for at least 30 minutes, or up to 2 hours.
3. Preheat the Oven: Preheat your oven to 400°F (200°C). Line a baking sheet with parchment paper.
4. Bake the Salmon: Remove the salmon fillets from the marinade and place them on the prepared baking sheet. Bake in the preheated oven for 12-15 minutes, or until the salmon is cooked through and flakes easily with a fork.
5. Serve: Remove from the oven and let rest for a few minutes. Garnish with sesame seeds and sliced green onions if desired. Serve warm.

Nutritional Information (per serving)
- Calories: 350
- Protein: 30g
- Carbohydrates: 10g
- Dietary Fiber: 0g
- Sugars: 7g
- Fat: 20g
- Saturated Fat: 4g
- Sodium: 700mg
- Potassium: 800mg
- Vitamin A: 4% of Daily Value
- Vitamin C: 2% of Daily Value
- Calcium: 6% of Daily Value
- Iron: 8% of Daily Value

Cilantro Lime Tilapia

Yield: 4 servings **Prep Time:** 10 minutes
Cook Time: 15 minutes

Ingredients
- 4 tilapia fillets (about 6 ounces each)
- 2 tablespoons olive oil
- 2 cloves garlic, minced
- Zest and juice of 2 limes
- 1/4 cup fresh cilantro, chopped
- Salt and pepper to taste
- Lime wedges (optional, for serving)
- Fresh cilantro leaves (optional, for garnish)

Directions
1. Preheat the Oven: Preheat your oven to 375°F (190°C). Lightly grease a baking dish with olive oil.
2. Prepare the Marinade: In a small bowl, combine the olive oil, minced garlic, lime zest, lime juice, and chopped cilantro. Mix well.
3. Marinate the Tilapia: Place the tilapia fillets in the prepared baking dish. Pour the marinade over the fillets, ensuring they are well coated. Season with salt and pepper to taste.
4. Bake: Bake in the preheated oven for 12-15 minutes, or until the tilapia is cooked through and flakes easily with a fork.
5. Serve: Remove from the oven and let rest for a few minutes. Garnish with fresh cilantro leaves and serve with lime wedges if desired. Serve warm.

Nutritional Information (per serving)
- Calories: 200
- Protein: 30g
- Carbohydrates: 2g
- Dietary Fiber: 0g
- Sugars: 0g
- Fat: 8g
- Saturated Fat: 1g
- Sodium: 150mg
- Potassium: 500mg
- Vitamin A: 4% of Daily Value
- Vitamin C: 20% of Daily Value
- Calcium: 4% of Daily Value
- Iron: 6% of Daily Value

Tuna Avocado Salad

Yield: 4 servings **Prep Time:** 15 minutes
Cook Time: None

Ingredients
- 2 cans (5 ounces each) tuna in water, drained
- 1 large avocado, diced
- 6 cups mixed salad greens (e.g., spinach, arugula, or mixed greens)
- 1/2 cup cherry tomatoes, halved
- 1/4 cup red onion, thinly sliced
- 1/4 cup cucumber, diced
- 1/4 cup fresh cilantro, chopped (optional)

For the Lemon Vinaigrette
- 1/4 cup extra virgin olive oil
- 2 tablespoons fresh lemon juice
- 1 teaspoon Dijon mustard
- 1 teaspoon honey or maple syrup
- 1 clove garlic, minced
- Salt and pepper to taste

Directions
1. Prepare the Vinaigrette: In a small bowl, whisk together the olive oil, fresh lemon juice, Dijon mustard, honey or maple syrup, minced garlic, salt, and pepper until well combined. Set aside.
2. Assemble the Salad: In a large salad bowl, combine the mixed salad greens, cherry tomatoes, red onion, cucumber, and fresh cilantro (if using).
3. Add Tuna and Avocado: Gently fold in the drained tuna and diced avocado.
4. Dress the Salad: Drizzle the lemon vinaigrette over the salad and toss gently to combine, ensuring all the ingredients are evenly coated with the dressing.
5. Serve: Divide the salad among four plates and serve immediately.

Nutritional Information (per serving)
- Calories: 300
- Protein: 20g
- Carbohydrates: 10g
- Dietary Fiber: 5g
- Sugars: 3g
- Fat: 20g
- Saturated Fat: 3g
- Sodium: 300mg
- Potassium: 800mg
- Vitamin A: 35% of Daily Value
- Vitamin C: 40% of Daily Value
- Calcium: 6% of Daily Value
- Iron: 10% of Daily Value

Garlic Butter Shrimp

Yield: 4 servings **Prep Time:** 10 minutes
Cook Time: 10 minutes

Ingredients
- 1 pound large shrimp, peeled and deveined
- 3 tablespoons olive oil or ghee (clarified butter)
- 4 cloves garlic, minced
- 1/4 cup fresh parsley, chopped
- Juice of 1 lemon
- Salt and pepper to taste
- Lemon wedges (optional, for serving)

Directions
1. Prepare the Shrimp: Pat the shrimp dry with paper towels and season with salt and pepper.
2. Heat the Oil: In a large skillet, heat the olive oil or ghee over medium-high heat.
3. Cook the Garlic: Add the minced garlic to the skillet and sauté for about 1 minute until fragrant.
4. Sauté the Shrimp: Add the shrimp to the skillet in a single layer. Cook for about 2-3 minutes on each side, or until the shrimp are pink and opaque.
5. Add Lemon and Parsley: Squeeze the lemon juice over the shrimp and sprinkle with chopped fresh parsley. Toss to combine and cook for an additional 1-2 minutes until everything is heated through.
6. Serve: Remove from heat and transfer the shrimp to a serving dish. Garnish with lemon wedges if desired. Serve immediately.

Nutritional Information (per serving)
- Calories: 200
- Protein: 23g
- Carbohydrates: 2g
- Dietary Fiber: 0g
- Sugars: 0g
- Fat: 12g
- Saturated Fat: 3g
- Sodium: 400mg
- Potassium: 200mg
- Vitamin A: 10% of Daily Value
- Vitamin C: 20% of Daily Value
- Calcium: 15% of Daily Value
- Iron: 10% of Daily Value

Baked Halibut with Herbs

Yield: 4 servings **Prep Time:** 10 minutes
Cook Time: 20 minutes

Ingredients
- 4 halibut fillets (about 6 ounces each)
- 2 tablespoons olive oil
- 3 cloves garlic, minced
- 1 tablespoon fresh parsley, chopped
- 1 tablespoon fresh dill, chopped
- 1 tablespoon fresh thyme, chopped
- 1 teaspoon lemon zest
- 1 tablespoon fresh lemon juice
- Salt and pepper to taste
- Lemon wedges (optional, for serving)

Directions
1. Preheat the Oven: Preheat your oven to 400°F (200°C). Lightly grease a baking dish with olive oil.
2. Prepare the Herb Mixture: In a small bowl, combine the minced garlic, chopped parsley, chopped dill, chopped thyme, lemon zest, and fresh lemon juice. Mix well.
3. Season the Halibut: Place the halibut fillets in the prepared baking dish. Drizzle with olive oil and season with salt and pepper.
4. Add the Herb Mixture: Spoon the herb mixture evenly over the halibut fillets, pressing gently to adhere.
5. Bake: Bake in the preheated oven for 15-20 minutes, or until the halibut is cooked through and flakes easily with a fork.
6. Serve: Remove from the oven and let rest for a few minutes. Serve with lemon wedges if desired. Serve warm.

Nutritional Information (per serving)
- Calories: 220
- Protein: 30g
- Carbohydrates: 2g
- Dietary Fiber: 0g
- Sugars: 0g
- Fat: 10g
- Saturated Fat: 1.5g
- Sodium: 150mg
- Potassium: 700mg
- Vitamin A: 6% of Daily Value
- Vitamin C: 15% of Daily Value
- Calcium: 4% of Daily Value
- Iron: 6% of Daily Value

Coconut Curry Shrimp

Yield: 4 servings **Prep Time:** 10 minutes
Cook Time: 20 minutes

Ingredients
- 1 pound large shrimp, peeled and deveined
- 2 tablespoons coconut oil or olive oil
- 1 large onion, chopped
- 3 cloves garlic, minced
- 1 tablespoon fresh ginger, minced
- 1 tablespoon curry powder
- 1 teaspoon ground turmeric
- 1/2 teaspoon ground cumin
- 1/2 teaspoon ground coriander
- 1 (14-ounce) can coconut milk (full fat or light)
- 1 (14.5-ounce) can diced tomatoes
- 1 tablespoon lime juice
- Salt and pepper to taste
- 1/4 cup fresh cilantro, chopped (optional for garnish)
- Cooked rice or quinoa, for serving

Directions
1. Heat the Oil: In a large skillet, heat the coconut oil or olive oil over medium heat. Add the chopped onion and sauté for about 5 minutes until softened.
2. Add Aromatics: Stir in the minced garlic and fresh ginger. Cook for another 1-2 minutes until fragrant.
3. Add Spices: Add the curry powder, ground turmeric, ground cumin, and ground coriander. Cook for about 1 minute, stirring constantly, until the spices are well mixed and fragrant.
4. Add Liquids: Pour in the coconut milk and diced tomatoes (with their juice). Bring the mixture to a simmer and cook for about 5 minutes, allowing the flavors to meld.
5. Cook the Shrimp: Add the shrimp to the skillet and cook for about 5-7 minutes, or until the shrimp are pink and opaque.
6. Season and Serve: Stir in the lime juice and season with salt and pepper to taste. Garnish with chopped fresh cilantro if desired. Serve over cooked rice or quinoa.

Nutritional Information (per serving)
- Calories: 300
- Protein: 25g
- Carbohydrates: 10g
- Dietary Fiber: 2g
- Sugars: 4g
- Fat: 18g
- Saturated Fat: 12g
- Sodium: 500mg
- Potassium: 600mg
- Vitamin A: 10% of Daily Value
- Vitamin C: 20% of Daily Value
- Calcium: 15% of Daily Value
- Iron: 25% of Daily Value

Pesto Crusted Salmon

Yield: 4 servings **Prep Time:** 15 minutes
Cook Time: 15 minutes

Ingredients
- 4 salmon fillets (about 6 ounces each)
- 1 cup fresh basil leaves
- 1/4 cup pine nuts (or walnuts for a budget-friendly option)
- 2 cloves garlic
- 1/4 cup nutritional yeast (or grated Parmesan cheese if not vegan)
- 1/4 cup extra virgin olive oil
- 1 tablespoon fresh lemon juice
- Salt and pepper to taste
- Lemon wedges (optional, for serving)

Directions
1. Preheat the Oven: Preheat your oven to 400°F (200°C). Line a baking sheet with parchment paper.
2. Prepare the Pesto: In a food processor, combine the fresh basil leaves, pine nuts, garlic, nutritional yeast (or Parmesan cheese), and fresh lemon juice. Pulse until finely chopped. With the processor running, gradually add the olive oil until the mixture is smooth and creamy. Season with salt and pepper to taste.
3. Prepare the Salmon: Place the salmon fillets on the prepared baking sheet. Spread the pesto mixture evenly over the top of each fillet.
4. Bake: Bake in the preheated oven for 12-15 minutes, or until the salmon is cooked through and flakes easily with a fork.
5. Serve: Remove from the oven and let rest for a few minutes. Serve with lemon wedges if desired. Serve warm.

Nutritional Information (per serving)
- Calories: 400
- Protein: 30g
- Carbohydrates: 4g
- Dietary Fiber: 1g
- Sugars: 0g
- Fat: 30g
- Saturated Fat: 5g
- Sodium: 180mg
- Potassium: 800mg
- Vitamin A: 20% of Daily Value
- Vitamin C: 15% of Daily Value
- Calcium: 6% of Daily Value
- Iron: 10% of Daily Value

Chili Lime Shrimp Skewers

Yield: 4 servings **Prep Time:** 15 minutes (plus 30 minutes marinating time) **Cook Time:** 10 minutes

Ingredients
- 1 pound large shrimp, peeled and deveined
- 2 tablespoons olive oil
- 2 tablespoons fresh lime juice
- 1 teaspoon lime zest
- 2 cloves garlic, minced
- 1 teaspoon chili powder
- 1/2 teaspoon ground cumin
- 1/2 teaspoon paprika
- 1/4 teaspoon cayenne pepper (optional, for extra heat)
- Salt and pepper to taste
- Fresh cilantro, chopped (optional, for garnish)
- Lime wedges (optional, for serving)
- Skewers (if using wooden skewers, soak them in water for 30 minutes before use)

Directions
1. Prepare the Marinade: In a large bowl, combine the olive oil, fresh lime juice, lime zest, minced garlic, chili powder, ground cumin, paprika, cayenne pepper (if using), salt, and pepper. Mix well.
2. Marinate the Shrimp: Add the shrimp to the marinade, tossing to coat evenly. Cover and refrigerate for at least 30 minutes, allowing the flavors to meld.
3. Preheat the Grill: Preheat your grill to medium-high heat. Lightly oil the grill grates to prevent sticking.
4. Prepare the Skewers: Thread the marinated shrimp onto the skewers, ensuring they are evenly spaced.
5. Grill the Shrimp: Place the shrimp skewers on the preheated grill. Cook for about 2-3 minutes per side, or until the shrimp are pink and opaque.
6. Serve: Remove the shrimp skewers from the grill and let rest for a few minutes. Garnish with chopped fresh cilantro and serve with lime wedges if desired. Serve warm.

Nutritional Information (per serving)
- Calories: 200
- Protein: 25g
- Carbohydrates: 2g
- Dietary Fiber: 0g
- Sugars: 0g
- Fat: 10g
- Saturated Fat: 1.5g
- Sodium: 400mg
- Potassium: 250mg
- Vitamin A: 10% of Daily Value
- Vitamin C: 20% of Daily Value
- Calcium: 15% of Daily Value
- Iron: 10% of Daily Value

Garlic Parmesan Crusted Cod

Yield: 4 servings **Prep Time:** 15 minutes
Cook Time: 15 minutes

Ingredients
- 4 cod fillets (about 6 ounces each)
- 1/2 cup grated Parmesan cheese
- 1/4 cup almond flour
- 3 cloves garlic, minced
- 2 tablespoons fresh parsley, chopped
- 1 teaspoon lemon zest
- 1/2 teaspoon paprika
- Salt and pepper to taste
- 2 tablespoons olive oil
- Lemon wedges (optional, for serving)

Directions
1. Preheat the Oven: Preheat your oven to 400°F (200°C). Line a baking sheet with parchment paper or lightly grease it with olive oil.
2. Prepare the Crust: In a small bowl, combine the grated Parmesan cheese, almond flour, minced garlic, chopped parsley, lemon zest, paprika, salt, and pepper. Mix well.
3. Prepare the Cod Fillets: Pat the cod fillets dry with paper towels. Drizzle each fillet with olive oil and season with salt and pepper.
4. Crust the Cod Fillets: Press the Parmesan mixture onto the top of each cod fillet, ensuring they are well coated.
5. Bake: Place the cod fillets on the prepared baking sheet. Bake in the preheated oven for 12-15 minutes, or until the cod is cooked through and the crust is golden brown and crispy.
6. Serve: Remove from the oven and let rest for a few minutes. Serve with lemon wedges if desired. Serve warm.

Nutritional Information (per serving)
- Calories: 300
- Protein: 35g
- Carbohydrates: 3g
- Dietary Fiber: 1g
- Sugars: 0g
- Fat: 15g
- Saturated Fat: 4g
- Sodium: 450mg
- Potassium: 700mg
- Vitamin A: 10% of Daily Value
- Vitamin C: 8% of Daily Value
- Calcium: 20% of Daily Value
- Iron: 10% of Daily Value

Lemon Dill Baked Trout

Yield: 4 servings **Prep Time:** 10 minutes
Cook Time: 20 minutes

Ingredients
- 4 trout fillets (about 6 ounces each)
- 2 tablespoons olive oil
- 2 cloves garlic, minced
- 1 lemon, thinly sliced
- 2 tablespoons fresh lemon juice
- 1/4 cup fresh dill, chopped
- Salt and pepper to taste
- Lemon wedges (optional, for serving)

Directions
1. Preheat the Oven: Preheat your oven to 375°F (190°C). Lightly grease a baking dish with olive oil.
2. Prepare the Trout Fillets: Place the trout fillets in the prepared baking dish. Drizzle with olive oil and fresh lemon juice. Sprinkle with minced garlic, chopped fresh dill, salt, and pepper.
3. Add Lemon Slices: Place the thinly sliced lemon over the trout fillets.
4. Bake: Bake in the preheated oven for 15-20 minutes, or until the trout is cooked through and flakes easily with a fork.
5. Serve: Remove from the oven and let rest for a few minutes. Serve with lemon wedges if desired. Serve warm.

Nutritional Information (per serving)
- Calories: 250
- Protein: 28g
- Carbohydrates: 2g
- Dietary Fiber: 1g
- Sugars: 0g
- Fat: 14g
- Saturated Fat: 2.5g
- Sodium: 300mg
- Potassium: 700mg
- Vitamin A: 10% of Daily Value
- Vitamin C: 25% of Daily Value
- Calcium: 6% of Daily Value
- Iron: 8% of Daily Value

Salmon and Avocado Sushi Rolls

Yield: 4 servings (makes about 8 rolls) **Prep Time:** 20 minutes **Cook Time:** 15 minutes (for rice)

Ingredients
- 1 1/2 cups sushi rice
- 2 cups water
- 1/4 cup rice vinegar
- 1 tablespoon sugar
- 1 teaspoon salt
- 8 sheets nori (seaweed)
- 1/2 pound fresh salmon, thinly sliced
- 2 ripe avocados, thinly sliced
- 1 cucumber, julienned
- Soy sauce or tamari (gluten-free if needed), for serving
- Pickled ginger, for serving (optional)
- Wasabi, for serving (optional)

Directions
1. Prepare the Sushi Rice: Rinse the sushi rice under cold water until the water runs clear. Combine the rice and water in a rice cooker and cook according to the manufacturer's instructions. Alternatively, cook the rice in a saucepan by bringing it to a boil, then reducing the heat to low and simmering, covered, for 15 minutes.
In a small bowl, mix the rice vinegar, sugar, and salt until dissolved. Once the rice is cooked, transfer it to a large bowl and gently fold in the vinegar mixture. Let the rice cool to room temperature.
2. Prepare the Ingredients: While the rice is cooling, thinly slice the salmon and avocado. Julienne the cucumber.
3. Assemble the Sushi Rolls: Place a bamboo sushi mat on a flat surface and cover it with plastic wrap. Lay a sheet of nori on the mat, shiny side down.
Wet your hands with water to prevent sticking. Spread a thin, even layer of sushi rice over the nori, leaving about 1 inch at the top edge. Arrange a few slices of salmon, avocado, and cucumber in a line along the bottom edge of the rice.
4. Roll the Sushi: Using the bamboo mat, carefully roll the sushi away from you, pressing gently to shape the roll. Moisten the top edge of the nori with water to seal the roll.
Repeat with the remaining ingredients to make more rolls.
5. Slice and Serve: Using a sharp knife, slice each roll into 6-8 pieces. Serve the sushi rolls with soy sauce or tamari, pickled ginger, and wasabi if desired.

Nutritional Information (per serving)
- Calories: 350
- Protein: 15g
- Carbohydrates: 45g
- Dietary Fiber: 6g
- Sugars: 3g
- Fat: 15g
- Saturated Fat: 2g
- Sodium: 400mg
- Potassium: 600mg
- Vitamin A: 10% of Daily Value
- Vitamin C: 15% of Daily Value
- Calcium: 4% of Daily Value
- Iron: 8% of Daily Value

Mediterranean Baked Sardines

Yield: 4 servings **Prep Time:** 15 minutes
Cook Time: 20 minutes

Ingredients
- 1 pound fresh sardines, cleaned and gutted
- 2 tablespoons olive oil
- 1 cup cherry tomatoes, halved
- 1/2 cup Kalamata olives, pitted and halved
- 1 small red onion, thinly sliced
- 3 cloves garlic, minced
- 1 tablespoon fresh lemon juice
- 1 teaspoon lemon zest
- 1 teaspoon dried oregano
- 1 teaspoon dried thyme
- Salt and pepper to taste
- Fresh parsley, chopped (optional, for garnish)
- Lemon wedges (optional, for serving)

Directions
1. Preheat the Oven: Preheat your oven to 400°F (200°C). Lightly grease a baking dish with olive oil.
2. Prepare the Sardines: Place the cleaned sardines in the prepared baking dish. Drizzle with olive oil and fresh lemon juice, and season with salt and pepper.
3. Add the Vegetables and Herbs: Arrange the cherry tomatoes, Kalamata olives, and sliced red onion around the sardines. Sprinkle the minced garlic, lemon zest, dried oregano, and dried thyme evenly over the dish.
4. Bake: Bake in the preheated oven for 20 minutes, or until the sardines are cooked through and the vegetables are tender.
5. Serve: Remove from the oven and let rest for a few minutes. Garnish with chopped fresh parsley and serve with lemon wedges if desired. Serve warm.

Nutritional Information (per serving)
- Calories: 250
- Protein: 20g
- Carbohydrates: 6g
- Dietary Fiber: 2g
- Sugars: 3g
- Fat: 16g
- Saturated Fat: 2.5g
- Sodium: 500mg
- Potassium: 600mg
- Vitamin A: 10% of Daily Value
- Vitamin C: 20% of Daily Value
- Calcium: 15% of Daily Value
- Iron: 10% of Daily Value

Garlic Lemon Scallops

Yield: 4 servings **Prep Time:** 10 minutes
Cook Time: 10 minutes

Ingredients
- 1 pound large sea scallops, patted dry
- 2 tablespoons olive oil
- 3 cloves garlic, minced
- 1/4 cup fresh lemon juice
- 1 teaspoon lemon zest
- 2 tablespoons unsalted butter (or ghee for dairy-free)
- Salt and pepper to taste
- 2 tablespoons fresh parsley, chopped (optional, for garnish)
- Lemon wedges (optional, for serving)

Directions
1. Prepare the Scallops: Pat the scallops dry with paper towels and season both sides with salt and pepper.
2. Heat the Oil: In a large skillet, heat the olive oil over medium-high heat.
3. Sear the Scallops: Add the scallops to the skillet in a single layer, making sure not to overcrowd the pan. Sear for about 2-3 minutes on each side, or until a golden crust forms and the scallops are opaque in the center. Remove the scallops from the skillet and set aside.
4. Prepare the Sauce: In the same skillet, reduce the heat to medium and add the minced garlic. Sauté for about 1 minute until fragrant. Add the fresh lemon juice and lemon zest, stirring to combine. Cook for another 1-2 minutes.
5. Add the Butter: Stir in the unsalted butter until melted and well combined. Return the scallops to the skillet and cook for another 1-2 minutes, basting them with the sauce.
6. Serve: Remove from heat and garnish with chopped fresh parsley. Serve with lemon wedges if desired. Serve warm.

Nutritional Information (per serving)
- Calories: 200
- Protein: 20g
- Carbohydrates: 3g
- Dietary Fiber: 0g
- Sugars: 0g
- Fat: 12g
- Saturated Fat: 5g
- Sodium: 400mg
- Potassium: 300mg
- Vitamin A: 10% of Daily Value
- Vitamin C: 20% of Daily Value
- Calcium: 2% of Daily Value
- Iron: 6% of Daily Value

Spicy Fish Tacos

Yield: 4 servings **Prep Time:** 20 minutes
Cook Time: 10 minutes

Ingredients
For the Fish
- 1 pound white fish fillets (such as cod or tilapia)
- 1 tablespoon olive oil
- 1 tablespoon chili powder
- 1 teaspoon ground cumin
- 1 teaspoon paprika
- 1/2 teaspoon cayenne pepper (adjust to taste)
- 1/2 teaspoon garlic powder
- Salt and pepper to taste

For the Cabbage Slaw
- 2 cups shredded cabbage (green or red, or a mix)
- 1/4 cup fresh cilantro, chopped
- 1/4 cup fresh lime juice
- 1 tablespoon olive oil
- Salt and pepper to taste

For the Tacos
- 8 small corn tortillas
- 1 avocado, sliced
- Lime wedges (for serving)
- Fresh cilantro (optional, for garnish)

Directions
1. Prepare the Fish Marinade: In a small bowl, combine the chili powder, ground cumin, paprika, cayenne pepper, garlic powder, salt, and pepper. Rub the spice mixture evenly over the fish fillets. Drizzle with olive oil and let marinate for at least 15 minutes.
2. Prepare the Cabbage Slaw: In a large bowl, combine the shredded cabbage, chopped cilantro, fresh lime juice, olive oil, salt, and pepper. Toss well to combine. Set aside.
3. Grill the Fish: Preheat a grill or grill pan over medium-high heat. Grill the fish for about 3-4 minutes on each side, or until the fish is cooked through and flakes easily with a fork. Remove from the grill and let rest for a few minutes before flaking into large pieces.
4. Warm the Tortillas: While the fish is resting, warm the corn tortillas on the grill or in a dry skillet over medium heat for about 30 seconds on each side, or until warm and pliable.
5. Assemble the Tacos: Divide the flaked fish among the warmed tortillas. Top with slices of avocado and a generous amount of cabbage slaw. Garnish with fresh cilantro if desired.
6. Serve: Serve the tacos with lime wedges on the side.

Nutritional Information (per serving)
- Calories: 300
- Protein: 25g
- Carbohydrates: 25g
- Dietary Fiber: 8g
- Sugars: 3g
- Fat: 15g
- Saturated Fat: 2g
- Sodium: 400mg
- Potassium: 700mg
- Vitamin A: 30% of Daily Value
- Vitamin C: 60% of Daily Value
- Calcium: 8% of Daily Value
- Iron: 10% of Daily Value

Thai Coconut Fish Soup

Yield: 4 servings **Prep Time:** 15 minutes **Cook Time:** 20 minutes

Ingredients

- 1 tablespoon coconut oil or olive oil
- 1 large onion, finely chopped
- 3 cloves garlic, minced
- 1 tablespoon fresh ginger, minced
- 1-2 tablespoons red curry paste (adjust to taste)
- 4 cups vegetable or fish broth
- 1 (14-ounce) can full-fat coconut milk
- 1 pound white fish fillets (such as cod or tilapia), cut into bite-sized pieces
- 1 red bell pepper, thinly sliced
- 1 cup mushrooms, sliced
- 1 cup baby spinach
- 2 tablespoons fish sauce (optional)
- 2 tablespoons fresh lime juice
- Fresh cilantro, chopped (for garnish)
- Fresh basil leaves, chopped (for garnish)
- Lime wedges (for serving)
- Cooked rice or rice noodles (optional, for serving)

Directions

1. Heat the Oil: In a large pot, heat the coconut oil over medium heat. Add the chopped onion and sauté for about 5 minutes until softened.
2. Add Aromatics and Curry Paste: Stir in the minced garlic, fresh ginger, and red curry paste. Cook for another 1-2 minutes until fragrant.
3. Add Broth and Coconut Milk: Pour in the vegetable or fish broth and coconut milk. Bring the mixture to a simmer.
4. Cook the Vegetables and Fish: Add the fish pieces, red bell pepper, and mushrooms to the pot. Simmer gently for about 5-7 minutes, or until the fish is cooked through and the vegetables are tender.
5. Add Spinach and Seasonings: Stir in the baby spinach, fish sauce (if using), and fresh lime juice. Cook for another 1-2 minutes until the spinach is wilted. Adjust seasoning with salt and pepper if needed.
6. Serve: Ladle the soup into bowls. Garnish with chopped fresh cilantro and basil leaves. Serve with lime wedges on the side and optionally with cooked rice or rice noodles.

Nutritional Information (per serving)

- Calories: 350
- Protein: 25g
- Carbohydrates: 12g
- Dietary Fiber: 3g
- Sugars: 4g
- Fat: 22g
- Saturated Fat: 15g
- Sodium: 600mg
- Potassium: 800mg
- Vitamin A: 50% of Daily Value
- Vitamin C: 60% of Daily Value
- Calcium: 6% of Daily Value
- Iron: 15% of Daily Value

Herb Crusted Salmon Cakes

Yield: 4 servings (makes about 8 salmon cakes) **Prep Time:** 20 minutes **Cook Time:** 15 minutes

Ingredients
For the Salmon Cakes
- 1 pound cooked salmon, flaked (fresh or canned)
- 1/2 cup almond flour
- 1/4 cup finely chopped red onion
- 2 cloves garlic, minced
- 1/4 cup fresh parsley, chopped
- 1/4 cup fresh dill, chopped
- 1 tablespoon Dijon mustard
- 1 tablespoon fresh lemon juice
- 1 large egg (or flax egg for vegan option)
- Salt and pepper to taste
- 2 tablespoons olive oil or coconut oil, for frying

For the Lemon Dill Sauce
- 1/2 cup Greek yogurt or dairy-free yogurt
- 1 tablespoon fresh dill, chopped
- 1 tablespoon fresh lemon juice
- 1 teaspoon lemon zest
- Salt and pepper to taste

Directions
1. Prepare the Lemon Dill Sauce: In a small bowl, combine the Greek yogurt, fresh dill, lemon juice, lemon zest, salt, and pepper. Mix well and refrigerate until ready to serve.
2. Prepare the Salmon Cakes Mixture: In a large bowl, combine the flaked salmon, almond flour, chopped red onion, minced garlic, chopped parsley, chopped dill, Dijon mustard, lemon juice, egg (or flax egg), salt, and pepper. Mix well until all ingredients are evenly combined.
3. Form the Salmon Cakes: Using your hands, shape the mixture into 8 equal-sized patties.
4. Heat the Oil: In a large skillet, heat the olive oil or coconut oil over medium heat.
5. Cook the Salmon Cakes: Add the salmon cakes to the skillet and cook for about 3-4 minutes on each side, or until golden brown and crispy. Cook in batches if necessary to avoid overcrowding the pan.
6. Serve: Remove the salmon cakes from the skillet and let them drain on a paper towel-lined plate. Serve warm with the lemon dill sauce.

Nutritional Information (per serving)
- Calories: 320
- Protein: 25g
- Carbohydrates: 8g
- Dietary Fiber: 2g
- Sugars: 2g
- Fat: 20g
- Saturated Fat: 3g
- Sodium: 400mg
- Potassium: 700mg
- Vitamin A: 10% of Daily Value
- Vitamin C: 20% of Daily Value
- Calcium: 10% of Daily Value
- Iron: 15% of Daily Value

Garlic Ginger Shrimp Stir-Fry

Yield: 4 servings **Prep Time:** 15 minutes
Cook Time: 10 minutes

Ingredients

- 1 pound large shrimp, peeled and deveined
- 2 tablespoons olive oil or coconut oil
- 3 cloves garlic, minced
- 1 tablespoon fresh ginger, minced
- 1 red bell pepper, thinly sliced
- 1 yellow bell pepper, thinly sliced
- 1 cup snap peas
- 1 cup broccoli florets
- 1 carrot, thinly sliced
- 2 tablespoons soy sauce or tamari (gluten-free if needed)
- 1 tablespoon rice vinegar
- 1 tablespoon honey or maple syrup
- 1/4 cup green onions, chopped
- 2 tablespoons sesame seeds (optional, for garnish)
- Cooked rice or quinoa, for serving

Directions

1. Prepare the Sauce: In a small bowl, whisk together the soy sauce or tamari, rice vinegar, and honey or maple syrup. Set aside.
2. Heat the Oil: In a large skillet or wok, heat the olive oil or coconut oil over medium-high heat.
3. Cook the Shrimp: Add the shrimp to the skillet and cook for about 2-3 minutes on each side, or until they are pink and opaque. Remove the shrimp from the skillet and set aside.
4. Sauté the Aromatics: In the same skillet, add the minced garlic and fresh ginger. Sauté for about 1 minute until fragrant.
5. Stir-Fry the Vegetables: Add the sliced bell peppers, snap peas, broccoli florets, and carrot to the skillet. Stir-fry for about 5 minutes, or until the vegetables are tender-crisp.
6. Combine and Cook: Return the cooked shrimp to the skillet. Pour the prepared sauce over the shrimp and vegetables. Stir well to combine and cook for another 1-2 minutes until everything is heated through.
7. Serve: Remove from heat and garnish with chopped green onions and sesame seeds if desired. Serve over cooked rice or quinoa.

Nutritional Information (per serving)

- Calories: 250
- Protein: 25g
- Carbohydrates: 15g
- Dietary Fiber: 4g
- Sugars: 7g
- Fat: 10g
- Saturated Fat: 2g
- Sodium: 700mg
- Potassium: 400mg
- Vitamin A: 80% of Daily Value
- Vitamin C: 120% of Daily Value
- Calcium: 15% of Daily Value
- Iron: 15% of Daily Value

Baked Mackerel with Mustard Sauce

Yield: 4 servings **Prep Time:** 10 minutes
Cook Time: 20 minutes

Ingredients
- 4 mackerel fillets (about 6 ounces each)
- 2 tablespoons Dijon mustard
- 1 tablespoon whole grain mustard
- 2 tablespoons olive oil
- 2 tablespoons fresh lemon juice
- 1 teaspoon lemon zest
- 2 cloves garlic, minced
- 1 tablespoon fresh dill, chopped
- Salt and pepper to taste
- Lemon wedges (optional, for serving)

Directions
1. Preheat the Oven: Preheat your oven to 375°F (190°C). Line a baking sheet with parchment paper.
2. Prepare the Mustard Sauce: In a small bowl, combine the Dijon mustard, whole grain mustard, olive oil, fresh lemon juice, lemon zest, minced garlic, and chopped fresh dill. Mix well.
3. Prepare the Mackerel Fillets: Place the mackerel fillets on the prepared baking sheet. Season with salt and pepper.
4. Add the Sauce: Spoon the mustard sauce over the mackerel fillets, spreading it evenly to coat.
5. Bake: Bake in the preheated oven for 15-20 minutes, or until the mackerel is cooked through and flakes easily with a fork.
6. Serve: Remove from the oven and let rest for a few minutes. Serve with lemon wedges if desired. Serve warm.

Nutritional Information (per serving)
- Calories: 350
- Protein: 30g
- Carbohydrates: 2g
- Dietary Fiber: 0g
- Sugars: 1g
- Fat: 24g
- Saturated Fat: 5g
- Sodium: 400mg
- Potassium: 800mg
- Vitamin A: 6% of Daily Value
- Vitamin C: 10% of Daily Value
- Calcium: 8% of Daily Value
- Iron: 15% of Daily Value

Cajun Spiced Shrimp

Yield: 4 servings **Prep Time:** 10 minutes
Cook Time: 10 minutes

Ingredients
- 1 pound large shrimp, peeled and deveined
- 2 tablespoons olive oil
- 1 tablespoon Cajun seasoning
- 1 teaspoon paprika
- 1/2 teaspoon garlic powder
- 1/2 teaspoon onion powder
- 1/4 teaspoon cayenne pepper (optional, for extra heat)
- Salt and pepper to taste
- 2 tablespoons fresh lemon juice
- Fresh parsley, chopped (optional, for garnish)
- Lemon wedges (optional, for serving)

Directions
1. Prepare the Shrimp: In a large bowl, combine the shrimp, olive oil, Cajun seasoning, paprika, garlic powder, onion powder, cayenne pepper (if using), salt, and pepper. Toss to coat the shrimp evenly with the spices.
2. Preheat the Grill: Preheat your grill to medium-high heat. Lightly oil the grill grates to prevent sticking.
3. Grill the Shrimp: Thread the seasoned shrimp onto skewers, or place them directly on the grill. Grill for about 2-3 minutes per side, or until the shrimp are pink and opaque.
4. Add Lemon Juice: Remove the shrimp from the grill and place them in a large bowl. Drizzle with fresh lemon juice and toss to coat.
5. Serve: Garnish with chopped fresh parsley if desired. Serve with lemon wedges on the side.

Nutritional Information (per serving)
- Calories: 200
- Protein: 25g
- Carbohydrates: 2g
- Dietary Fiber: 0g
- Sugars: 0g
- Fat: 10g
- Saturated Fat: 1.5g
- Sodium: 600mg
- Potassium: 200mg
- Vitamin A: 10% of Daily Value
- Vitamin C: 15% of Daily Value
- Calcium: 15% of Daily Value
- Iron: 10% of Daily Value

Salmon Nicoise Salad

Yield: 4 servings **Prep Time:** 20 minutes
Cook Time: 20 minutes

Ingredients
For the Salad
- 1 pound salmon fillets
- 1/2 pound small potatoes, halved
- 1/2 pound green beans, trimmed
- 4 cups mixed salad greens
- 1 cup cherry tomatoes, halved
- 1/2 cup Kalamata olives, pitted
- 4 hard-boiled eggs, halved
- 1/4 cup red onion, thinly sliced

For the Dressing
- 1/4 cup extra virgin olive oil
- 2 tablespoons fresh lemon juice
- 1 tablespoon Dijon mustard
- 1 teaspoon honey or maple syrup
- 1 clove garlic, minced
- Salt and pepper to taste

Directions
1. Prepare the Salmon: Preheat the oven to 400°F (200°C). Place the salmon fillets on a baking sheet lined with parchment paper. Season with salt and pepper. Bake for 15-20 minutes, or until the salmon is cooked through and flakes easily with a fork. Remove from the oven and let cool slightly.
2. Cook the Potatoes: While the salmon is baking, place the halved potatoes in a pot of salted water. Bring to a boil and cook for about 10-12 minutes, or until tender. Drain and let cool.
3. Cook the Green Beans: In the same pot of boiling water, blanch the green beans for 2-3 minutes, or until tender-crisp. Drain and transfer to a bowl of ice water to stop the cooking process. Drain again and set aside.
4. Prepare the Dressing: In a small bowl, whisk together the olive oil, fresh lemon juice, Dijon mustard, honey or maple syrup, minced garlic, salt, and pepper until well combined.
5. Assemble the Salad: In a large salad bowl or platter, arrange the mixed salad greens. Top with the cherry tomatoes, Kalamata olives, hard-boiled eggs, red onion, cooked potatoes, and green beans. Flake the baked salmon into large pieces and add to the salad.
6. Dress the Salad: Drizzle the dressing over the salad and toss gently to combine.
7. Serve: Serve immediately and enjoy.

Nutritional Information (per serving)
- Calories: 450
- Protein: 30g
- Carbohydrates: 25g
- Dietary Fiber: 6g
- Sugars: 5g
- Fat: 28g
- Saturated Fat: 5g
- Sodium: 500mg
- Potassium: 1200mg
- Vitamin A: 35% of Daily Value
- Vitamin C: 40% of Daily Value
- Calcium: 10% of Daily Value
- Iron: 15% of Daily Value

Teriyaki Glazed Salmon

Yield: 4 servings **Prep Time:** 10 minutes **Cook Time:** 20 minutes

Ingredients

- 4 salmon fillets (about 6 ounces each)
- 2 tablespoons olive oil
- 1/4 cup low-sodium soy sauce or tamari (gluten-free if needed)
- 1/4 cup water
- 2 tablespoons honey or maple syrup
- 1 tablespoon rice vinegar
- 2 cloves garlic, minced
- 1 tablespoon fresh ginger, minced
- 1 teaspoon sesame oil
- 1 teaspoon cornstarch mixed with 1 tablespoon water (optional, for thickening)
- 2 tablespoons green onions, chopped (for garnish)
- 1 tablespoon sesame seeds (optional, for garnish)

Directions

1. Prepare the Teriyaki Sauce: In a small saucepan, combine the soy sauce or tamari, water, honey or maple syrup, rice vinegar, minced garlic, minced ginger, and sesame oil. Bring to a simmer over medium heat, stirring occasionally. If you prefer a thicker sauce, add the cornstarch mixture and cook for another 1-2 minutes until the sauce has thickened. Remove from heat and set aside.
2. Preheat the Oven: Preheat your oven to 400°F (200°C). Line a baking sheet with parchment paper or lightly grease it with olive oil.
3. Prepare the Salmon: Place the salmon fillets on the prepared baking sheet. Drizzle with olive oil and season with salt and pepper.
4. Glaze the Salmon: Brush the teriyaki sauce generously over the salmon fillets, reserving some sauce for serving.
5. Bake: Bake in the preheated oven for 15-20 minutes, or until the salmon is cooked through and flakes easily with a fork.
6. Serve: Remove from the oven and let rest for a few minutes. Garnish with chopped green onions and sesame seeds if desired. Serve warm with the reserved teriyaki sauce.

Nutritional Information (per serving)

- Calories: 350
- Protein: 30g
- Carbohydrates: 12g
- Dietary Fiber: 0g
- Sugars: 10g
- Fat: 20g
- Saturated Fat: 4g
- Sodium: 800mg
- Potassium: 800mg
- Vitamin A: 4% of Daily Value
- Vitamin C: 2% of Daily Value
- Calcium: 4% of Daily Value
- Iron: 8% of Daily Value

Fish en Papillote

Yield: 4 servings **Prep Time:** 20 minutes **Cook Time:** 20 minutes

Ingredients
- 4 white fish fillets (such as cod, halibut, or tilapia, about 6 ounces each)
- 2 tablespoons olive oil
- 1 lemon, thinly sliced
- 1 small zucchini, julienned
- 1 small carrot, julienned
- 1 red bell pepper, thinly sliced
- 1 cup cherry tomatoes, halved
- 4 cloves garlic, minced
- 1/4 cup fresh parsley, chopped
- 1/4 cup fresh basil, chopped
- Salt and pepper to taste
- Parchment paper

Directions
1. Preheat the Oven: Preheat your oven to 400°F (200°C).
2. Prepare the Parchment Paper: Cut 4 large pieces of parchment paper, each about 15x20 inches.
3. Assemble the Packets: Place one fish fillet in the center of each piece of parchment paper. Drizzle each fillet with olive oil and season with salt and pepper.
   Arrange the lemon slices, julienned zucchini, julienned carrot, sliced red bell pepper, and cherry tomatoes evenly over and around each fillet.
   Sprinkle minced garlic, chopped fresh parsley, and chopped fresh basil over the top.
4. Seal the Packets: Fold the parchment paper over the fish and vegetables, then fold and crimp the edges to seal each packet tightly, creating a pouch to hold in the steam.
5. Bake: Place the sealed packets on a baking sheet and bake in the preheated oven for 18-20 minutes, or until the fish is cooked through and flakes easily with a fork.
6. Serve: Carefully open the packets, allowing the steam to escape. Transfer the fish and vegetables to plates and serve immediately.

Nutritional Information (per serving)
- Calories: 250
- Protein: 25g
- Carbohydrates: 10g
- Dietary Fiber: 3g
- Sugars: 5g
- Fat: 12g
- Saturated Fat: 2g
- Sodium: 150mg
- Potassium: 800mg
- Vitamin A: 40% of Daily Value
- Vitamin C: 70% of Daily Value
- Calcium: 6% of Daily Value
- Iron: 8% of Daily Value

Spicy Tuna Poke Bowl

Yield: 4 servings **Prep Time:** 20 minutes
Cook Time: 20 minutes (for rice)

Ingredients
For the Poke Bowl
- 1 pound sushi-grade tuna, diced
- 2 cups cooked brown rice or quinoa
- 1 avocado, diced
- 1 cucumber, diced
- 1 cup edamame, shelled
- 1/2 cup shredded carrots
- 2 green onions, chopped
- 1 tablespoon sesame seeds (optional, for garnish)
- 1 sheet nori (seaweed), cut into thin strips (optional, for garnish)

For the Spicy Sauce
- 1/4 cup mayonnaise (or vegan mayonnaise)
- 1 tablespoon sriracha sauce (adjust to taste)
- 1 teaspoon soy sauce or tamari (gluten-free if needed)
- 1 teaspoon sesame oil
- 1 teaspoon rice vinegar

For the Marinade
- 2 tablespoons soy sauce or tamari
- 1 tablespoon sesame oil
- 1 tablespoon rice vinegar
- 1 tablespoon fresh lemon juice
- 1 teaspoon honey or maple syrup
- 1 teaspoon grated fresh ginger
- 1 clove garlic, minced

Directions
1. Prepare the Spicy Sauce: In a small bowl, whisk together the mayonnaise, sriracha sauce, soy sauce or tamari, sesame oil, and rice vinegar. Adjust the sriracha to taste for desired spiciness. Set aside.
2. Marinate the Tuna: In a medium bowl, combine the soy sauce or tamari, sesame oil, rice vinegar, fresh lemon juice, honey or maple syrup, grated fresh ginger, and minced garlic. Add the diced tuna and toss to coat evenly. Marinate in the refrigerator for at least 10 minutes.
3. Prepare the Vegetables: While the tuna is marinating, prepare the vegetables by dicing the avocado and cucumber, and shelling the edamame if needed.
4. Assemble the Poke Bowls: Divide the cooked brown rice or quinoa among four bowls. Top each bowl with marinated tuna, diced avocado, diced cucumber, edamame, shredded carrots, and chopped green onions.
5. Drizzle with Spicy Sauce: Drizzle the spicy sauce over the poke bowls. Garnish with sesame seeds and nori strips if desired.
6. Serve: Serve immediately and enjoy.

Nutritional Information (per serving)
- Calories: 450
- Protein: 30g
- Carbohydrates: 40g
- Dietary Fiber: 8g
- Sugars: 5g
- Fat: 20g
- Saturated Fat: 3g
- Sodium: 800mg
- Potassium: 900mg
- Vitamin A: 60% of Daily Value
- Vitamin C: 25% of Daily Value
- Calcium: 10% of Daily Value
- Iron: 20% of Daily Value

Ginger Soy Steamed Fish

Yield: 4 servings **Prep Time:** 10 minutes
Cook Time: 15 minutes

Ingredients

- 4 white fish fillets (such as cod, halibut, or tilapia, about 6 ounces each)
- 3 tablespoons low-sodium soy sauce or tamari (gluten-free if needed)
- 2 tablespoons fresh lemon juice
- 1 tablespoon sesame oil
- 2 tablespoons fresh ginger, julienned
- 3 cloves garlic, minced
- 4 green onions, cut into 2-inch pieces
- 1 small red chili, thinly sliced (optional, for heat)
- Fresh cilantro, chopped (optional, for garnish)
- Lemon wedges (optional, for serving)

Directions

1. Prepare the Steaming Liquid: In a small bowl, whisk together the soy sauce or tamari, fresh lemon juice, and sesame oil. Set aside.
2. Prepare the Fish: Pat the fish fillets dry with paper towels and season lightly with salt.
3. Assemble the Steaming Dish: Place the fish fillets in a heatproof dish that fits inside your steamer. Scatter the julienned ginger, minced garlic, green onions, and sliced red chili (if using) over the fish fillets.
4. Add the Steaming Liquid: Pour the prepared steaming liquid over the fish and aromatics.
5. Steam the Fish: Fill a large pot or wok with about 2 inches of water and bring to a boil. Place the dish with the fish into the steamer basket and cover. Steam the fish for about 10-12 minutes, or until the fish is opaque and flakes easily with a fork.
6. Garnish and Serve: Carefully remove the dish from the steamer. Garnish with chopped fresh cilantro if desired. Serve with lemon wedges on the side.

Nutritional Information (per serving)

- Calories: 200
- Protein: 30g
- Carbohydrates: 3g
- Dietary Fiber: 1g
- Sugars: 0g
- Fat: 8g
- Saturated Fat: 1g
- Sodium: 600mg
- Potassium: 700mg
- Vitamin A: 4% of Daily Value
- Vitamin C: 10% of Daily Value
- Calcium: 4% of Daily Value
- Iron: 6% of Daily Value

Lemon Basil Shrimp Pasta

Yield: 4 servings **Prep Time:** 15 minutes
Cook Time: 20 minutes

Ingredients

- 8 ounces gluten-free pasta (such as brown rice or quinoa pasta)
- 1 pound large shrimp, peeled and deveined
- 2 tablespoons olive oil
- 3 cloves garlic, minced
- 1/4 teaspoon red pepper flakes (optional)
- Zest and juice of 1 large lemon
- 1/4 cup fresh basil leaves, chopped
- 1/4 cup fresh parsley, chopped
- Salt and pepper to taste
- 1/4 cup grated Parmesan cheese (optional, for serving)

Directions

1. Cook the Pasta: Bring a large pot of salted water to a boil. Add the gluten-free pasta and cook according to the package instructions until al dente. Drain and set aside.
2. Sauté the Shrimp: In a large skillet, heat the olive oil over medium-high heat. Add the shrimp and cook for about 2-3 minutes on each side, or until the shrimp are pink and opaque. Remove the shrimp from the skillet and set aside.
3. Cook the Aromatics: In the same skillet, add the minced garlic and red pepper flakes (if using). Sauté for about 1 minute until fragrant.
4. Add Lemon and Herbs: Stir in the lemon zest, lemon juice, chopped basil, and chopped parsley. Cook for another 1-2 minutes until heated through.
5. Combine Pasta and Shrimp: Add the cooked pasta and sautéed shrimp to the skillet. Toss everything together until well combined. Season with salt and pepper to taste.
6. Serve: Divide the pasta among four plates. Top with grated Parmesan cheese if desired. Serve warm.

Nutritional Information (per serving)

- Calories: 350
- Protein: 25g
- Carbohydrates: 40g
- Dietary Fiber: 5g
- Sugars: 2g
- Fat: 10g
- Saturated Fat: 1.5g
- Sodium: 600mg
- Potassium: 400mg
- Vitamin A: 15% of Daily Value
- Vitamin C: 25% of Daily Value
- Calcium: 10% of Daily Value
- Iron: 20% of Daily Value

Citrus Herb Grilled Swordfish

Yield: 4 servings **Prep Time:** 15 minutes (plus 30 minutes marinating time) **Cook Time:** 10 minutes

Ingredients
- 4 swordfish steaks (about 6 ounces each)
- 1/4 cup olive oil
- 2 tablespoons fresh lemon juice
- 2 tablespoons fresh orange juice
- 1 tablespoon fresh lime juice
- 2 cloves garlic, minced
- 1 tablespoon fresh thyme, chopped
- 1 tablespoon fresh rosemary, chopped
- 1 tablespoon fresh parsley, chopped
- 1 teaspoon lemon zest
- 1 teaspoon orange zest
- Salt and pepper to taste
- Lemon wedges (optional, for serving)
- Fresh herbs (optional, for garnish)

Directions
1. Prepare the Marinade: In a small bowl, whisk together the olive oil, fresh lemon juice, fresh orange juice, fresh lime juice, minced garlic, chopped thyme, chopped rosemary, chopped parsley, lemon zest, and orange zest. Season with salt and pepper to taste.
2. Marinate the Swordfish: Place the swordfish steaks in a shallow dish or resealable plastic bag. Pour the marinade over the steaks, ensuring they are well coated. Marinate in the refrigerator for at least 30 minutes, or up to 2 hours.
3. Preheat the Grill: Preheat your grill to medium-high heat. Lightly oil the grill grates to prevent sticking.
4. Grill the Swordfish: Remove the swordfish steaks from the marinade and shake off any excess. Place the steaks on the preheated grill. Grill for about 4-5 minutes per side, or until the fish is cooked through and has nice grill marks.
5. Serve: Remove the swordfish from the grill and let rest for a few minutes. Serve with lemon wedges and garnish with fresh herbs if desired. Serve warm.

Nutritional Information (per serving)
- Calories: 350
- Protein: 35g
- Carbohydrates: 3g
- Dietary Fiber: 1g
- Sugars: 1g
- Fat: 20g
- Saturated Fat: 3g
- Sodium: 150mg
- Potassium: 800mg
- Vitamin A: 6% of Daily Value
- Vitamin C: 25% of Daily Value
- Calcium: 4% of Daily Value
- Iron: 10% of Daily Value

Smoked Salmon and Avocado Toast

Yield: 4 servings **Prep Time:** 10 minutes **Cook Time:** None

Ingredients
- 4 slices whole grain bread, toasted
- 2 ripe avocados, mashed
- 8 ounces smoked salmon
- 1 tablespoon fresh lemon juice
- 1/4 teaspoon salt
- 1/4 teaspoon black pepper
- 1/4 teaspoon red pepper flakes (optional)
- 1/4 cup red onion, thinly sliced
- 2 tablespoons capers, drained
- Fresh dill, chopped (optional, for garnish)
- Lemon wedges (optional, for serving)

Directions
1. Prepare the Avocado: In a small bowl, combine the mashed avocados, fresh lemon juice, salt, black pepper, and red pepper flakes (if using). Mix well.
2. Toast the Bread: Toast the whole grain bread slices to your desired level of crispiness.
3. Assemble the Toast: Spread an even layer of the mashed avocado mixture onto each slice of toasted bread.
4. Add the Smoked Salmon: Top each slice with smoked salmon.
5. Garnish: Add thinly sliced red onion, capers, and fresh dill (if using) on top of the smoked salmon.
6. Serve: Serve immediately with lemon wedges on the side.

Nutritional Information (per serving)
- Calories: 300
- Protein: 15g
- Carbohydrates: 25g
- Dietary Fiber: 8g
- Sugars: 3g
- Fat: 18g
- Saturated Fat: 3g
- Sodium: 600mg
- Potassium: 600mg
- Vitamin A: 8% of Daily Value
- Vitamin C: 20% of Daily Value
- Calcium: 6% of Daily Value
- Iron: 10% of Daily Value

Poultry & Meat

Lean protein options that reduce inflammation

Lemon Herb Chicken

Yield: 4 servings **Prep Time:** 15 minutes (plus 30 minutes marinating time) **Cook Time:** 25 minutes

Ingredients
- 4 boneless, skinless chicken breasts
- 1/4 cup olive oil
- 1/4 cup fresh lemon juice
- 2 tablespoons fresh lemon zest
- 3 cloves garlic, minced
- 2 tablespoons fresh rosemary, chopped
- 2 tablespoons fresh thyme, chopped
- 1 tablespoon fresh parsley, chopped
- Salt and pepper to taste
- Lemon wedges (optional, for serving)
- Fresh herbs (optional, for garnish)

Directions
1. Prepare the Marinade: In a small bowl, whisk together the olive oil, fresh lemon juice, lemon zest, minced garlic, chopped rosemary, chopped thyme, chopped parsley, salt, and pepper.
2. Marinate the Chicken: Place the chicken breasts in a shallow dish or resealable plastic bag. Pour the marinade over the chicken, ensuring each breast is well coated. Marinate in the refrigerator for at least 30 minutes, or up to 2 hours.
3. Preheat the Oven: Preheat your oven to 400°F (200°C). Lightly grease a baking dish with olive oil.
4. Bake the Chicken: Remove the chicken from the marinade and place it in the prepared baking dish. Discard the remaining marinade. Bake in the preheated oven for 20-25 minutes, or until the chicken is cooked through and reaches an internal temperature of 165°F (74°C).
5. Serve: Remove from the oven and let rest for a few minutes. Serve with lemon wedges and garnish with fresh herbs if desired. Serve warm.

Nutritional Information (per serving)
- Calories: 300
- Protein: 28g
- Carbohydrates: 3g
- Dietary Fiber: 1g
- Sugars: 0g
- Fat: 18g
- Saturated Fat: 3g
- Sodium: 150mg
- Potassium: 600mg
- Vitamin A: 4% of Daily Value
- Vitamin C: 30% of Daily Value
- Calcium: 2% of Daily Value
- Iron: 6% of Daily Value

Turmeric Chicken Thighs

Yield: 4 servings **Prep Time:** 15 minutes (plus 30 minutes marinating time) **Cook Time:** 35 minutes

Ingredients
- 8 bone-in, skin-on chicken thighs
- 3 tablespoons olive oil
- 2 tablespoons ground turmeric
- 1 tablespoon fresh ginger, grated
- 3 cloves garlic, minced
- 1 teaspoon ground cumin
- 1 teaspoon ground coriander
- 1 teaspoon paprika
- 1 teaspoon salt
- 1/2 teaspoon black pepper
- 2 tablespoons fresh lemon juice
- Fresh cilantro, chopped (optional, for garnish)

Directions
1. Prepare the Marinade: In a large bowl, combine the olive oil, ground turmeric, grated ginger, minced garlic, ground cumin, ground coriander, paprika, salt, black pepper, and fresh lemon juice. Mix well to form a paste.
2. Marinate the Chicken: Add the chicken thighs to the bowl and rub the marinade all over the chicken, ensuring it is well coated. Cover and refrigerate for at least 30 minutes, or up to 2 hours.
3. Preheat the Oven: Preheat your oven to 400°F (200°C). Line a baking sheet with parchment paper or lightly grease it with olive oil.
4. Roast the Chicken: Arrange the marinated chicken thighs on the prepared baking sheet, skin side up. Roast in the preheated oven for 35-40 minutes, or until the chicken is cooked through and the skin is crispy and golden brown.
5. Serve: Remove the chicken from the oven and let rest for a few minutes. Garnish with chopped fresh cilantro if desired. Serve warm.

Nutritional Information (per serving)
- Calories: 400
- Protein: 30g
- Carbohydrates: 3g
- Dietary Fiber: 1g
- Sugars: 0g
- Fat: 28g
- Saturated Fat: 6g
- Sodium: 600mg
- Potassium: 400mg
- Vitamin A: 6% of Daily Value
- Vitamin C: 15% of Daily Value
- Calcium: 4% of Daily Value
- Iron: 15% of Daily Value

Balsamic Glazed Turkey Meatballs

Yield: 4 servings (makes about 20 meatballs) **Prep Time:** 20 minutes **Cook Time:** 25 minutes

Ingredients
For the Meatballs
- 1 pound ground turkey
- 1/2 cup almond flour
- 1/4 cup onion, finely chopped
- 2 cloves garlic, minced
- 1 large egg, beaten
- 2 tablespoons fresh parsley, chopped
- 1 teaspoon dried oregano
- 1 teaspoon dried basil
- 1/2 teaspoon salt
- 1/2 teaspoon black pepper

For the Balsamic Glaze
- 1/2 cup balsamic vinegar
- 2 tablespoons honey or maple syrup
- 1 teaspoon Dijon mustard
- 1 clove garlic, minced

Directions
1. Preheat the Oven: Preheat your oven to 400°F (200°C). Line a baking sheet with parchment paper or lightly grease it with olive oil.
2. Prepare the Meatballs: In a large bowl, combine the ground turkey, almond flour, finely chopped onion, minced garlic, beaten egg, chopped fresh parsley, dried oregano, dried basil, salt, and black pepper. Mix until well combined.
3. Form the Meatballs: Using your hands or a small ice cream scoop, form the mixture into approximately 20 meatballs and place them on the prepared baking sheet.
4. Bake the Meatballs: Bake in the preheated oven for 20-25 minutes, or until the meatballs are cooked through and golden brown.
5. Prepare the Balsamic Glaze: While the meatballs are baking, prepare the glaze. In a small saucepan, combine the balsamic vinegar, honey or maple syrup, Dijon mustard, and minced garlic. Bring to a simmer over medium heat and cook for about 5-7 minutes, or until the glaze has thickened slightly.
6. Glaze the Meatballs: Remove the meatballs from the oven and transfer them to a large bowl. Pour the balsamic glaze over the meatballs and toss gently to coat.
7. Serve: Serve the glazed meatballs warm. Garnish with additional fresh parsley if desired.

Nutritional Information (per serving)
- Calories: 320
- Protein: 25g
- Carbohydrates: 15g
- Dietary Fiber: 2g
- Sugars: 10g
- Fat: 18g
- Saturated Fat: 4g
- Sodium: 450mg
- Potassium: 600mg
- Vitamin A: 6% of Daily Value
- Vitamin C: 8% of Daily Value
- Calcium: 6% of Daily Value
- Iron: 10% of Daily Value

Garlic Rosemary Lamb Chops

Yield: 4 servings **Prep Time:** 15 minutes (plus 1 hour marinating time) **Cook Time:** 15 minutes

Ingredients
- 8 lamb chops (about 1-inch thick)
- 1/4 cup olive oil
- 4 cloves garlic, minced
- 2 tablespoons fresh rosemary, chopped
- 1 tablespoon fresh thyme, chopped
- 1 tablespoon fresh lemon juice
- Salt and pepper to taste

Directions
1. Prepare the Marinade: In a small bowl, whisk together the olive oil, minced garlic, chopped rosemary, chopped thyme, fresh lemon juice, salt, and pepper.
2. Marinate the Lamb Chops: Place the lamb chops in a shallow dish or resealable plastic bag. Pour the marinade over the lamb chops, ensuring they are well coated. Marinate in the refrigerator for at least 1 hour, or up to 4 hours for more flavor.
3. Preheat the Grill: Preheat your grill to medium-high heat. Lightly oil the grill grates to prevent sticking.
4. Grill the Lamb Chops: Remove the lamb chops from the marinade and shake off any excess. Place the lamb chops on the preheated grill and cook for about 4-5 minutes per side for medium-rare, or until the desired level of doneness is reached.
5. Serve: Remove the lamb chops from the grill and let rest for a few minutes before serving. Serve warm.

Nutritional Information (per serving)
- Calories: 350
- Protein: 30g
- Carbohydrates: 2g
- Dietary Fiber: 0g
- Sugars: 0g
- Fat: 25g
- Saturated Fat: 9g
- Sodium: 150mg
- Potassium: 450mg
- Vitamin A: 2% of Daily Value
- Vitamin C: 6% of Daily Value
- Calcium: 4% of Daily Value
- Iron: 15% of Daily Value

Herb Crusted Pork Tenderloin

Yield: 4 servings **Prep Time:** 15 minutes **Cook Time:** 30 minutes

Ingredients
- 1 1/2 pounds pork tenderloin
- 2 tablespoons olive oil
- 3 cloves garlic, minced
- 1 tablespoon fresh rosemary, chopped
- 1 tablespoon fresh thyme, chopped
- 1 tablespoon fresh parsley, chopped
- 1 teaspoon Dijon mustard
- 1 teaspoon salt
- 1/2 teaspoon black pepper
- Lemon wedges (optional, for serving)

Directions
1. Preheat the Oven: Preheat your oven to 400°F (200°C). Line a baking sheet with parchment paper or lightly grease it with olive oil.
2. Prepare the Herb Mixture: In a small bowl, combine the minced garlic, chopped rosemary, chopped thyme, chopped parsley, Dijon mustard, salt, and black pepper. Mix well to form a paste.
3. Prepare the Pork Tenderloin: Pat the pork tenderloin dry with paper towels. Rub the herb mixture all over the pork tenderloin, coating it evenly.
4. Sear the Pork: In a large skillet, heat the olive oil over medium-high heat. Add the pork tenderloin and sear on all sides until golden brown, about 2-3 minutes per side.
5. Roast the Pork: Transfer the seared pork tenderloin to the prepared baking sheet. Roast in the preheated oven for 20-25 minutes, or until the pork reaches an internal temperature of 145°F (63°C).
6. Rest and Serve: Remove the pork from the oven and let it rest for 5-10 minutes before slicing. Serve with lemon wedges if desired. Serve warm.

Nutritional Information (per serving)
- Calories: 250
- Protein: 30g
- Carbohydrates: 2g
- Dietary Fiber: 0g
- Sugars: 0g
- Fat: 13g
- Saturated Fat: 3g
- Sodium: 600mg
- Potassium: 550mg
- Vitamin A: 2% of Daily Value
- Vitamin C: 10% of Daily Value
- Calcium: 2% of Daily Value
- Iron: 10% of Daily Value

Ginger Lime Chicken Skewers

Yield: 4 servings **Prep Time:** 15 minutes (plus 1 hour marinating time) **Cook Time:** 15 minutes

Ingredients

- 1 1/2 pounds boneless, skinless chicken breasts, cut into 1-inch cubes
- 1/4 cup olive oil
- 2 tablespoons fresh lime juice
- 1 tablespoon lime zest
- 2 tablespoons fresh ginger, grated
- 3 cloves garlic, minced
- 2 tablespoons honey or maple syrup
- 2 tablespoons soy sauce or tamari (gluten-free if needed)
- 1 teaspoon ground cumin
- 1/4 teaspoon red pepper flakes (optional)
- Salt and pepper to taste
- Fresh cilantro, chopped (optional, for garnish)
- Lime wedges (optional, for serving)
- Skewers (if using wooden skewers, soak them in water for 30 minutes before use)

Directions

1. Prepare the Marinade: In a large bowl, whisk together the olive oil, fresh lime juice, lime zest, grated ginger, minced garlic, honey or maple syrup, soy sauce or tamari, ground cumin, red pepper flakes (if using), salt, and pepper.
2. Marinate the Chicken: Add the cubed chicken to the bowl and toss to coat well. Cover and refrigerate for at least 1 hour, or up to 4 hours for more flavor.
3. Preheat the Grill: Preheat your grill to medium-high heat. Lightly oil the grill grates to prevent sticking.
4. Prepare the Skewers: Thread the marinated chicken cubes onto the skewers, leaving a little space between each piece for even cooking.
5. Grill the Skewers: Place the chicken skewers on the preheated grill. Cook for about 5-7 minutes per side, or until the chicken is cooked through and has nice grill marks.
6. Serve: Remove the chicken skewers from the grill and let rest for a few minutes. Garnish with chopped fresh cilantro and serve with lime wedges if desired. Serve warm.

Nutritional Information (per serving)

- Calories: 300
- Protein: 28g
- Carbohydrates: 8g
- Dietary Fiber: 1g
- Sugars: 5g
- Fat: 18g
- Saturated Fat: 3g
- Sodium: 500mg
- Potassium: 450mg
- Vitamin A: 2% of Daily Value
- Vitamin C: 10% of Daily Value
- Calcium: 2% of Daily Value
- Iron: 6% of Daily Value

Cilantro Lime Turkey Burgers

Yield: 4 servings **Prep Time:** 15 minutes
Cook Time: 15 minutes

Ingredients
- 1 pound ground turkey
- 1/4 cup fresh cilantro, chopped
- 2 cloves garlic, minced
- 1 tablespoon fresh lime juice
- 1 teaspoon lime zest
- 1 teaspoon ground cumin
- 1/2 teaspoon paprika
- 1/2 teaspoon salt
- 1/4 teaspoon black pepper
- 1 tablespoon olive oil
- 8 large lettuce leaves (for wraps)
- Toppings: avocado slices, red onion, tomato slices, and any other preferred toppings

Directions
1. Prepare the Turkey Mixture: In a large bowl, combine the ground turkey, chopped fresh cilantro, minced garlic, fresh lime juice, lime zest, ground cumin, paprika, salt, and black pepper. Mix until all ingredients are well incorporated.
2. Form the Patties: Divide the turkey mixture into 4 equal portions and shape each portion into a patty.
3. Heat the Skillet: In a large skillet, heat the olive oil over medium-high heat.
4. Cook the Patties: Add the turkey patties to the skillet and cook for about 5-7 minutes on each side, or until the patties are cooked through and reach an internal temperature of 165°F (74°C).
5. Prepare the Lettuce Wraps: While the patties are cooking, prepare the lettuce leaves by washing and patting them dry.
6. Assemble the Burgers: Place each cooked turkey patty on a large lettuce leaf. Top with avocado slices, red onion, tomato slices, and any other preferred toppings. Fold the lettuce leaf around the burger to create a wrap.
7. Serve: Serve the cilantro lime turkey burgers warm.

Nutritional Information (per serving)
- Calories: 250
- Protein: 25g
- Carbohydrates: 4g
- Dietary Fiber: 2g
- Sugars: 1g
- Fat: 15g
- Saturated Fat: 3g
- Sodium: 500mg
- Potassium: 400mg
- Vitamin A: 8% of Daily Value
- Vitamin C: 15% of Daily Value
- Calcium: 2% of Daily Value
- Iron: 8% of Daily Value

Pesto Stuffed Chicken Breast

Yield: 4 servings **Prep Time:** 20 minutes
Cook Time: 25 minutes

Ingredients
For the Pesto
- 1 cup fresh basil leaves
- 1/4 cup pine nuts or walnuts
- 2 cloves garlic
- 1/4 cup grated Parmesan cheese (optional, for non-dairy-free)
- 1/4 cup extra virgin olive oil
- Salt and pepper to taste

For the Chicken
- 4 boneless, skinless chicken breasts
- 1 tablespoon olive oil
- Salt and pepper to taste
- Fresh basil leaves (optional, for garnish)
- Lemon wedges (optional, for serving)

Directions
1. Preheat the Oven: Preheat your oven to 375°F (190°C). Lightly grease a baking dish with olive oil.
2. Prepare the Pesto: In a food processor, combine the basil leaves, pine nuts or walnuts, garlic, and Parmesan cheese (if using). Pulse until finely chopped. With the processor running, gradually add the olive oil until the mixture is smooth and creamy. Season with salt and pepper to taste.
3. Prepare the Chicken Breasts: Using a sharp knife, carefully cut a pocket into each chicken breast by slicing horizontally, being careful not to cut all the way through.
4. Stuff the Chicken Breasts: Spoon a generous amount of pesto into each pocket, spreading it evenly. Secure the opening with toothpicks if needed.
5. Season the Chicken: Place the stuffed chicken breasts in the prepared baking dish. Drizzle with olive oil and season with salt and pepper.
6. Bake: Bake in the preheated oven for 25-30 minutes, or until the chicken is cooked through and reaches an internal temperature of 165°F (74°C).
7. Serve: Remove from the oven and let rest for a few minutes. Garnish with fresh basil leaves and serve with lemon wedges if desired. Serve warm.

Nutritional Information (per serving)
- Calories: 350
- Protein: 30g
- Carbohydrates: 2g
- Dietary Fiber: 1g
- Sugars: 0g
- Fat: 24g
- Saturated Fat: 4g
- Sodium: 250mg
- Potassium: 500mg
- Vitamin A: 15% of Daily Value
- Vitamin C: 10% of Daily Value
- Calcium: 6% of Daily Value
- Iron: 10% of Daily Value

Rosemary Lemon Roast Turkey Breast

Yield: 4 servings **Prep Time:** 15 minutes (plus 1 hour marinating time) **Cook Time:** 1 hour 30 minutes

Ingredients
- 1 turkey breast (about 3-4 pounds), bone-in and skin-on
- 1/4 cup olive oil
- 1/4 cup fresh lemon juice
- 2 tablespoons lemon zest
- 4 cloves garlic, minced
- 2 tablespoons fresh rosemary, chopped
- 1 tablespoon fresh thyme, chopped
- 1 teaspoon salt
- 1/2 teaspoon black pepper
- Lemon wedges (optional, for serving)
- Fresh rosemary sprigs (optional, for garnish)

Directions
1. Prepare the Marinade: In a small bowl, whisk together the olive oil, fresh lemon juice, lemon zest, minced garlic, chopped rosemary, chopped thyme, salt, and black pepper.
2. Marinate the Turkey Breast: Place the turkey breast in a large resealable plastic bag or a shallow dish. Pour the marinade over the turkey, making sure it is well coated. Seal the bag or cover the dish and marinate in the refrigerator for at least 1 hour, or up to overnight for more flavor.
3. Preheat the Oven: Preheat your oven to 350°F (175°C). Place a roasting rack in a roasting pan.
4. Roast the Turkey Breast: Remove the turkey breast from the marinade and place it on the roasting rack. Discard the remaining marinade. Roast in the preheated oven for about 1 hour and 30 minutes, or until the turkey reaches an internal temperature of 165°F (74°C) and the skin is golden brown and crispy. Baste the turkey occasionally with its juices during cooking.
5. Rest and Serve: Remove the turkey from the oven and let it rest for 15 minutes before carving. Garnish with lemon wedges and fresh rosemary sprigs if desired. Serve warm.

Nutritional Information (per serving)
- Calories: 350
- Protein: 50g
- Carbohydrates: 2g
- Dietary Fiber: 1g
- Sugars: 0g
- Fat: 15g
- Saturated Fat: 3g
- Sodium: 400mg
- Potassium: 500mg
- Vitamin A: 2% of Daily Value
- Vitamin C: 10% of Daily Value
- Calcium: 4% of Daily Value
- Iron: 10% of Daily Value

Spiced Moroccan Lamb Stew

Yield: 6 servings **Prep Time:** 20 minutes
Cook Time: 2 hours

Ingredients
- 2 pounds lamb shoulder, cut into 1-inch cubes
- 2 tablespoons olive oil
- 1 large onion, chopped
- 3 cloves garlic, minced
- 2 tablespoons fresh ginger, grated
- 2 teaspoons ground cumin
- 2 teaspoons ground coriander
- 1 teaspoon ground cinnamon
- 1 teaspoon ground turmeric
- 1/2 teaspoon ground paprika
- 1/2 teaspoon ground cayenne pepper (optional)
- 1 teaspoon salt
- 1/2 teaspoon black pepper
- 2 cups beef or lamb broth (low sodium)
- 1 (14.5-ounce) can diced tomatoes
- 1 (14-ounce) can chickpeas, drained and rinsed
- 2 large sweet potatoes, peeled and cut into 1-inch cubes
- 1/2 cup dried apricots, chopped
- 1/4 cup fresh cilantro, chopped (for garnish)
- 1/4 cup fresh parsley, chopped (for garnish)
- Cooked quinoa or couscous, for serving (optional)

Directions
1. Heat the Olive Oil: In a large Dutch oven or heavy-bottomed pot, heat the olive oil over medium-high heat.
2. Brown the Lamb: Add the lamb cubes to the pot and brown on all sides, about 5-7 minutes. Remove the lamb from the pot and set aside.
3. Sauté the Onions and Spices: In the same pot, add the chopped onion and sauté for about 5 minutes until softened. Add the minced garlic and grated ginger, and sauté for another 1-2 minutes until fragrant. Add the ground cumin, ground coriander, ground cinnamon, ground turmeric, ground paprika, ground cayenne pepper (if using), salt, and black pepper. Stir to combine and cook for 1 minute.
4. Deglaze and Combine: Add the broth and diced tomatoes, stirring to deglaze the pot. Return the browned lamb to the pot, and add the chickpeas, sweet potatoes, and chopped dried apricots. Stir to combine.
5. Simmer: Bring the stew to a boil, then reduce the heat to low. Cover and simmer for about 1 1/2 to 2 hours, or until the lamb and sweet potatoes are tender.
6. Serve: Remove from heat and stir in the chopped cilantro and parsley. Serve the stew warm, over cooked quinoa or couscous if desired.

Nutritional Information (per serving)
- Calories: 450
- Protein: 30g
- Carbohydrates: 35g
- Dietary Fiber: 8g
- Sugars: 10g
- Fat: 20g
- Saturated Fat: 6g
- Sodium: 600mg
- Potassium: 1000mg
- Vitamin A: 200% of Daily Value
- Vitamin C: 25% of Daily Value
- Calcium: 10% of Daily Value
- Iron: 25% of Daily Value

Chicken and Vegetable Stir-Fry

Yield: 4 servings **Prep Time:** 15 minutes
Cook Time: 15 minutes

Ingredients

- 1 1/2 pounds boneless, skinless chicken breasts, cut into thin strips
- 2 tablespoons olive oil, divided
- 1 red bell pepper, thinly sliced
- 1 yellow bell pepper, thinly sliced
- 1 small broccoli head, cut into florets
- 1 large carrot, julienned
- 1 cup snap peas
- 3 cloves garlic, minced
- 1 tablespoon fresh ginger, grated
- 1/4 cup low-sodium soy sauce or tamari (gluten-free if needed)
- 2 tablespoons rice vinegar
- 1 tablespoon honey or maple syrup
- 1 tablespoon cornstarch mixed with 2 tablespoons water (optional, for thickening)
- 2 green onions, chopped
- 1 tablespoon sesame seeds (optional, for garnish)
- Cooked brown rice or quinoa, for serving (optional)

Directions

1. Prepare the Sauce: In a small bowl, whisk together the soy sauce or tamari, rice vinegar, and honey or maple syrup. Set aside.
2. Cook the Chicken: In a large skillet or wok, heat 1 tablespoon of olive oil over medium-high heat. Add the chicken strips and cook for about 5-7 minutes, or until the chicken is cooked through and lightly browned. Remove the chicken from the skillet and set aside.
3. Stir-Fry the Vegetables: In the same skillet, add the remaining 1 tablespoon of olive oil. Add the minced garlic and grated ginger, and sauté for about 1 minute until fragrant. Add the red bell pepper, yellow bell pepper, broccoli florets, julienned carrot, and snap peas. Stir-fry for about 5 minutes, or until the vegetables are tender-crisp.
4. Combine and Cook: Return the cooked chicken to the skillet. Pour the prepared sauce over the chicken and vegetables, stirring to combine. If you prefer a thicker sauce, add the cornstarch mixture and cook for another 1-2 minutes until the sauce has thickened.
5. Serve: Remove from heat and stir in the chopped green onions. Garnish with sesame seeds if desired. Serve the stir-fry warm over cooked brown rice or quinoa if desired.

Nutritional Information (per serving)

- Calories: 350
- Protein: 30g
- Carbohydrates: 20g
- Dietary Fiber: 5g
- Sugars: 8g
- Fat: 15g
- Saturated Fat: 2.5g
- Sodium: 700mg
- Potassium: 800mg
- Vitamin A: 100% of Daily Value
- Vitamin C: 150% of Daily Value
- Calcium: 6% of Daily Value
- Iron: 10% of Daily Value

Lemon Dill Turkey Cutlets

Yield: 4 servings **Prep Time:** 10 minutes
Cook Time: 15 minutes

Ingredients
- 1 1/2 pounds turkey cutlets
- 2 tablespoons olive oil
- 2 cloves garlic, minced
- Zest and juice of 1 large lemon
- 2 tablespoons fresh dill, chopped
- 1/2 cup low-sodium chicken broth
- Salt and pepper to taste
- Lemon wedges (optional, for serving)
- Fresh dill sprigs (optional, for garnish)

Directions
1. Season the Turkey Cutlets: Pat the turkey cutlets dry with paper towels. Season both sides with salt and pepper.
2. Heat the Olive Oil: In a large skillet, heat the olive oil over medium-high heat.
3. Cook the Turkey Cutlets: Add the turkey cutlets to the skillet and cook for about 3-4 minutes on each side, or until they are golden brown and cooked through. Remove the turkey cutlets from the skillet and set aside.
4. Sauté the Garlic: In the same skillet, add the minced garlic and sauté for about 1 minute until fragrant.
5. Add Lemon and Dill: Add the lemon zest, lemon juice, and fresh dill to the skillet. Stir to combine.
6. Deglaze with Broth: Pour in the chicken broth, stirring to deglaze the skillet. Bring the mixture to a simmer.
7. Combine and Heat Through: Return the turkey cutlets to the skillet and spoon the lemon dill sauce over the top. Cook for another 2-3 minutes until everything is heated through and well coated.
8. Serve: Remove from heat and transfer the turkey cutlets to a serving platter. Garnish with lemon wedges and fresh dill sprigs if desired. Serve warm.

Nutritional Information (per serving)
- Calories: 250
- Protein: 30g
- Carbohydrates: 2g
- Dietary Fiber: 1g
- Sugars: 0g
- Fat: 12g
- Saturated Fat: 2g
- Sodium: 300mg
- Potassium: 600mg
- Vitamin A: 2% of Daily Value
- Vitamin C: 20% of Daily Value
- Calcium: 2% of Daily Value
- Iron: 6% of Daily Value

Apple Cider Vinegar Chicken

Yield: 4 servings **Prep Time:** 15 minutes (plus 1 hour marinating time) **Cook Time:** 35 minutes

Ingredients
- 8 bone-in, skin-on chicken thighs
- 1/2 cup apple cider vinegar
- 1/4 cup olive oil
- 4 cloves garlic, minced
- 1 tablespoon fresh rosemary, chopped
- 1 tablespoon fresh thyme, chopped
- 1 tablespoon fresh parsley, chopped
- 1 tablespoon honey or maple syrup
- 1 teaspoon salt
- 1/2 teaspoon black pepper
- Lemon wedges (optional, for serving)
- Fresh herbs (optional, for garnish)

Directions
1. Prepare the Marinade: In a large bowl, whisk together the apple cider vinegar, olive oil, minced garlic, chopped rosemary, chopped thyme, chopped parsley, honey or maple syrup, salt, and black pepper.
2. Marinate the Chicken: Place the chicken thighs in a resealable plastic bag or a shallow dish. Pour the marinade over the chicken, ensuring each thigh is well coated. Seal the bag or cover the dish and refrigerate for at least 1 hour, or up to 4 hours for more flavor.
3. Preheat the Oven: Preheat your oven to 400°F (200°C). Line a baking sheet with parchment paper or lightly grease it with olive oil.
4. Bake the Chicken: Remove the chicken from the marinade and place it on the prepared baking sheet, skin side up. Discard the remaining marinade. Bake in the preheated oven for 35-40 minutes, or until the chicken is cooked through and the skin is crispy and golden brown.
5. Serve: Remove the chicken from the oven and let it rest for a few minutes. Serve with lemon wedges and garnish with fresh herbs if desired. Serve warm.

Nutritional Information (per serving)
- Calories: 350
- Protein: 30g
- Carbohydrates: 4g
- Dietary Fiber: 0g
- Sugars: 2g
- Fat: 22g
- Saturated Fat: 5g
- Sodium: 600mg
- Potassium: 400mg
- Vitamin A: 4% of Daily Value
- Vitamin C: 8% of Daily Value
- Calcium: 4% of Daily Value
- Iron: 10% of Daily Value

Lemon Garlic Shrimp and Chicken

Yield: 4 servings **Prep Time:** 15 minutes
Cook Time: 20 minutes

Ingredients

- 1 pound boneless, skinless chicken breasts, cut into bite-sized pieces
- 1 pound large shrimp, peeled and deveined
- 3 tablespoons olive oil, divided
- 4 cloves garlic, minced
- Zest and juice of 2 lemons
- 1 teaspoon dried oregano
- 1/2 teaspoon salt
- 1/2 teaspoon black pepper
- 1/4 teaspoon red pepper flakes (optional)
- 1/4 cup fresh parsley, chopped
- Lemon wedges (optional, for serving)

Directions

1. Prepare the Chicken and Shrimp: Pat the chicken and shrimp dry with paper towels. Season both with salt and pepper.
2. Cook the Chicken: In a large skillet, heat 2 tablespoons of olive oil over medium-high heat. Add the chicken pieces and cook for about 5-7 minutes, or until the chicken is cooked through and browned. Remove the chicken from the skillet and set aside.
3. Cook the Shrimp: In the same skillet, add the remaining 1 tablespoon of olive oil. Add the shrimp and cook for about 2-3 minutes on each side, or until the shrimp are pink and opaque. Remove the shrimp from the skillet and set aside.
4. Sauté the Garlic: In the same skillet, add the minced garlic and sauté for about 1 minute until fragrant.
5. Combine and Add Lemon: Return the chicken and shrimp to the skillet. Add the lemon zest, lemon juice, dried oregano, and red pepper flakes (if using). Stir well to combine and cook for another 2-3 minutes until everything is heated through.
6. Garnish and Serve: Remove from heat and stir in the chopped fresh parsley. Serve the lemon garlic shrimp and chicken with lemon wedges if desired.

Nutritional Information (per serving)

- Calories: 350
- Protein: 40g
- Carbohydrates: 3g
- Dietary Fiber: 1g
- Sugars: 0g
- Fat: 18g
- Saturated Fat: 3g
- Sodium: 600mg
- Potassium: 650mg
- Vitamin A: 8% of Daily Value
- Vitamin C: 40% of Daily Value
- Calcium: 15% of Daily Value
- Iron: 20% of Daily Value

Spicy Thai Basil Chicken

Yield: 4 servings **Prep Time:** 15 minutes
Cook Time: 15 minutes

Ingredients

- 1 1/2 pounds boneless, skinless chicken thighs, cut into bite-sized pieces
- 3 tablespoons olive oil or coconut oil, divided
- 4 cloves garlic, minced
- 2-3 Thai chilies, sliced (adjust to taste)
- 1 red bell pepper, thinly sliced
- 1 cup green beans, trimmed and cut into 2-inch pieces
- 1/4 cup low-sodium soy sauce or tamari (gluten-free if needed)
- 1 tablespoon fish sauce
- 1 tablespoon honey or maple syrup
- 1 tablespoon fresh lime juice
- 1 cup fresh Thai basil leaves
- Cooked brown rice or quinoa, for serving (optional)

Directions

1. Prepare the Sauce: In a small bowl, whisk together the soy sauce or tamari, fish sauce, honey or maple syrup, and fresh lime juice. Set aside.
2. Cook the Chicken: In a large skillet or wok, heat 2 tablespoons of oil over medium-high heat. Add the chicken pieces and cook for about 5-7 minutes, or until the chicken is cooked through and lightly browned. Remove the chicken from the skillet and set aside.
3. Sauté the Aromatics: In the same skillet, add the remaining 1 tablespoon of oil. Add the minced garlic and sliced Thai chilies, and sauté for about 1 minute until fragrant.
4. Add the Vegetables: Add the sliced red bell pepper and green beans to the skillet. Stir-fry for about 3-4 minutes, or until the vegetables are tender-crisp.
5. Combine and Add Sauce: Return the cooked chicken to the skillet. Pour the prepared sauce over the chicken and vegetables, stirring well to combine. Cook for another 2-3 minutes until everything is heated through.
6. Add Thai Basil: Remove from heat and stir in the fresh Thai basil leaves until wilted.
7. Serve: Serve the spicy Thai basil chicken warm over cooked brown rice or quinoa if desired.

Nutritional Information (per serving)

- Calories: 350
- Protein: 30g
- Carbohydrates: 12g
- Dietary Fiber: 3g
- Sugars: 5g
- Fat: 20g
- Saturated Fat: 5g
- Sodium: 800mg
- Potassium: 600mg
- Vitamin A: 30% of Daily Value
- Vitamin C: 60% of Daily Value
- Calcium: 6% of Daily Value
- Iron: 15% of Daily Value

Rosemary Garlic Roast Pork Loin

Yield: 4 servings **Prep Time:** 15 minutes **Cook Time:** 1 hour 15 minutes

Ingredients
- 1 1/2 pounds pork loin
- 3 tablespoons olive oil
- 4 cloves garlic, minced
- 2 tablespoons fresh rosemary, chopped
- 1 tablespoon fresh thyme, chopped
- 1 teaspoon salt
- 1/2 teaspoon black pepper
- 1/2 teaspoon paprika
- Lemon wedges (optional, for serving)
- Fresh herbs (optional, for garnish)

Directions
1. Preheat the Oven: Preheat your oven to 375°F (190°C). Line a roasting pan with parchment paper or lightly grease it with olive oil.
2. Prepare the Herb Mixture: In a small bowl, combine the minced garlic, chopped rosemary, chopped thyme, salt, black pepper, and paprika. Add 2 tablespoons of olive oil and mix well to form a paste.
3. Season the Pork Loin: Pat the pork loin dry with paper towels. Rub the herb mixture all over the pork loin, coating it evenly.
4. Roast the Pork Loin: Place the pork loin in the prepared roasting pan. Drizzle the remaining 1 tablespoon of olive oil over the top. Roast in the preheated oven for about 1 hour and 15 minutes, or until the pork reaches an internal temperature of 145°F (63°C).
5. Rest and Serve: Remove the pork loin from the oven and let it rest for 10 minutes before slicing. Serve with lemon wedges and garnish with fresh herbs if desired. Serve warm.

Nutritional Information (per serving)
- Calories: 300
- Protein: 30g
- Carbohydrates: 1g
- Dietary Fiber: 0g
- Sugars: 0g
- Fat: 20g
- Saturated Fat: 5g
- Sodium: 600mg
- Potassium: 500mg
- Vitamin A: 2% of Daily Value
- Vitamin C: 4% of Daily Value
- Calcium: 2% of Daily Value
- Iron: 8% of Daily Value

Mustard Herb Grilled Chicken

Yield: 4 servings **Prep Time:** 15 minutes (plus 1 hour marinating time) **Cook Time:** 15 minutes

Ingredients
- 4 boneless, skinless chicken breasts
- 1/4 cup Dijon mustard
- 2 tablespoons whole grain mustard
- 1/4 cup olive oil
- 2 tablespoons fresh lemon juice
- 2 cloves garlic, minced
- 1 tablespoon fresh rosemary, chopped
- 1 tablespoon fresh thyme, chopped
- 1 tablespoon fresh parsley, chopped
- 1/2 teaspoon salt
- 1/2 teaspoon black pepper

Directions
1. Prepare the Marinade: In a small bowl, whisk together the Dijon mustard, whole grain mustard, olive oil, fresh lemon juice, minced garlic, chopped rosemary, chopped thyme, chopped parsley, salt, and black pepper.
2. Marinate the Chicken: Place the chicken breasts in a resealable plastic bag or a shallow dish. Pour the marinade over the chicken, ensuring each breast is well coated. Seal the bag or cover the dish and refrigerate for at least 1 hour, or up to 4 hours for more flavor.
3. Preheat the Grill: Preheat your grill to medium-high heat. Lightly oil the grill grates to prevent sticking.
4. Grill the Chicken: Remove the chicken from the marinade and discard any remaining marinade. Place the chicken breasts on the preheated grill and cook for about 6-7 minutes per side, or until the chicken is cooked through and reaches an internal temperature of 165°F (74°C).
5. Serve: Remove the chicken from the grill and let rest for a few minutes before serving. Serve warm.

Nutritional Information (per serving)
- Calories: 280
- Protein: 30g
- Carbohydrates: 3g
- Dietary Fiber: 1g
- Sugars: 1g
- Fat: 15g
- Saturated Fat: 2.5g
- Sodium: 500mg
- Potassium: 600mg
- Vitamin A: 4% of Daily Value
- Vitamin C: 15% of Daily Value
- Calcium: 2% of Daily Value
- Iron: 6% of Daily Value

Coconut Curry Chicken

Yield: 4 servings **Prep Time:** 15 minutes
Cook Time: 25 minutes

Ingredients

- 1 1/2 pounds boneless, skinless chicken breasts or thighs, cut into bite-sized pieces
- 2 tablespoons coconut oil or olive oil
- 1 large onion, chopped
- 3 cloves garlic, minced
- 1 tablespoon fresh ginger, grated
- 2 tablespoons red curry paste
- 1 (14-ounce) can full-fat coconut milk
- 1 cup chicken broth (low sodium)
- 1 red bell pepper, thinly sliced
- 1 yellow bell pepper, thinly sliced
- 1 zucchini, sliced
- 1 cup cherry tomatoes, halved
- 2 tablespoons fish sauce (optional)
- 1 tablespoon lime juice
- 1/4 cup fresh cilantro, chopped (for garnish)
- Cooked brown rice or quinoa, for serving (optional)

Directions

1. Heat the Oil: In a large skillet or wok, heat the coconut oil over medium-high heat.
2. Cook the Chicken: Add the chicken pieces to the skillet and cook for about 5-7 minutes, or until the chicken is browned and cooked through. Remove the chicken from the skillet and set aside.
3. Sauté the Aromatics: In the same skillet, add the chopped onion, minced garlic, and grated ginger. Sauté for about 3-4 minutes until the onion is translucent and fragrant.
4. Add the Curry Paste: Stir in the red curry paste and cook for another 1-2 minutes until well combined.
5. Simmer the Sauce: Pour in the coconut milk and chicken broth, stirring to combine. Bring the mixture to a simmer.
6. Add the Vegetables: Add the sliced red bell pepper, yellow bell pepper, zucchini, and cherry tomatoes to the skillet. Simmer for about 5-7 minutes until the vegetables are tender.
7. Combine and Finish: Return the cooked chicken to the skillet. Stir in the fish sauce (if using) and lime juice. Simmer for another 2-3 minutes until everything is heated through.
8. Serve: Remove from heat and garnish with chopped fresh cilantro. Serve the coconut curry chicken warm over cooked brown rice or quinoa if desired.

Nutritional Information (per serving)

- Calories: 400
- Protein: 30g
- Carbohydrates: 12g
- Dietary Fiber: 3g
- Sugars: 5g
- Fat: 28g
- Saturated Fat: 20g
- Sodium: 700mg
- Potassium: 700mg
- Vitamin A: 50% of Daily Value
- Vitamin C: 100% of Daily Value
- Calcium: 4% of Daily Value
- Iron: 15% of Daily Value

Ginger Soy Chicken Thighs

Yield: 4 servings **Prep Time:** 15 minutes (plus 1 hour marinating time) **Cook Time:** 35 minutes

Ingredients

- 8 bone-in, skin-on chicken thighs
- 1/4 cup low-sodium soy sauce or tamari (gluten-free if needed)
- 1/4 cup honey or maple syrup
- 2 tablespoons fresh ginger, grated
- 4 cloves garlic, minced
- 2 tablespoons rice vinegar
- 1 tablespoon sesame oil
- 1 tablespoon olive oil
- 1 teaspoon ground black pepper
- 1/4 teaspoon red pepper flakes (optional)
- Green onions, chopped (for garnish)
- Sesame seeds (optional, for garnish)

Directions

1. Prepare the Marinade: In a large bowl, whisk together the soy sauce or tamari, honey or maple syrup, grated ginger, minced garlic, rice vinegar, sesame oil, olive oil, ground black pepper, and red pepper flakes (if using).
2. Marinate the Chicken: Place the chicken thighs in a resealable plastic bag or a shallow dish. Pour the marinade over the chicken, ensuring each thigh is well coated. Seal the bag or cover the dish and refrigerate for at least 1 hour, or up to 4 hours for more flavor.
3. Preheat the Oven: Preheat your oven to 375°F (190°C). Line a baking sheet with parchment paper or lightly grease it with olive oil.
4. Bake the Chicken: Remove the chicken from the marinade and place it on the prepared baking sheet, skin side up. Discard the remaining marinade. Bake in the preheated oven for 35-40 minutes, or until the chicken is cooked through and the skin is crispy and golden brown.
5. Serve: Remove the chicken from the oven and let it rest for a few minutes. Garnish with chopped green onions and sesame seeds if desired. Serve warm.

Nutritional Information (per serving)

- Calories: 350
- Protein: 25g
- Carbohydrates: 12g
- Dietary Fiber: 0g
- Sugars: 8g
- Fat: 22g
- Saturated Fat: 5g
- Sodium: 600mg
- Potassium: 400mg
- Vitamin A: 2% of Daily Value
- Vitamin C: 4% of Daily Value
- Calcium: 4% of Daily Value
- Iron: 10% of Daily Value

Balsamic Glazed Pork Chops

Yield: 4 servings **Prep Time:** 15 minutes
Cook Time: 30 minutes

Ingredients
For the Pork Chops
- 4 boneless pork chops (about 1 inch thick)
- 2 tablespoons olive oil
- Salt and pepper to taste

For the Balsamic Glaze
- 1/2 cup balsamic vinegar
- 2 tablespoons honey or maple syrup
- 1 teaspoon Dijon mustard
- 2 cloves garlic, minced

For the Roasted Vegetables
- 2 cups broccoli florets
- 2 cups baby carrots
- 1 red bell pepper, chopped
- 1 tablespoon olive oil
- Salt and pepper to taste

Directions:
1. Preheat the Oven: Preheat your oven to 400°F (200°C). Line a baking sheet with parchment paper or lightly grease it with olive oil.
2. Prepare the Vegetables: In a large bowl, combine the broccoli florets, baby carrots, and chopped red bell pepper. Drizzle with olive oil and season with salt and pepper. Toss to coat evenly. Spread the vegetables in a single layer on the prepared baking sheet. Roast in the preheated oven for 20-25 minutes, or until the vegetables are tender and slightly caramelized.
3. Prepare the Balsamic Glaze: While the vegetables are roasting, prepare the balsamic glaze. In a small saucepan, combine the balsamic vinegar, honey or maple syrup, Dijon mustard, and minced garlic. Bring to a simmer over medium heat and cook for about 5-7 minutes, or until the glaze has thickened slightly. Remove from heat and set aside.
4. Cook the Pork Chops: In a large skillet, heat the olive oil over medium-high heat. Season the pork chops with salt and pepper on both sides. Add the pork chops to the skillet and cook for about 4-5 minutes on each side, or until they are golden brown and cooked through.
5. Glaze the Pork Chops: Reduce the heat to low and pour the balsamic glaze over the pork chops in the skillet. Turn the pork chops to coat them evenly with the glaze. Cook for another 1-2 minutes until the glaze is heated through and the pork chops are well coated.
6. Serve: Remove the pork chops from the skillet and let them rest for a few minutes. Serve the balsamic glazed pork chops warm, alongside the roasted vegetables.

Nutritional Information (per serving)
- Calories: 400
- Protein: 30g
- Carbohydrates: 20g
- Dietary Fiber: 4g
- Sugars: 12g
- Fat: 20g
- Saturated Fat: 4g
- Sodium: 450mg
- Potassium: 800mg
- Vitamin A: 200% of Daily Value
- Vitamin C: 150% of Daily Value
- Calcium: 8% of Daily Value
- Iron: 10% of Daily Value

Mediterranean Chicken

Yield: 4 servings **Prep Time:** 15 minutes
Cook Time: 30 minutes

Ingredients

- 4 boneless, skinless chicken breasts
- 2 tablespoons olive oil
- 1 pint cherry tomatoes, halved
- 1/2 cup Kalamata olives, pitted and halved
- 1/4 cup red onion, thinly sliced
- 3 cloves garlic, minced
- 1 tablespoon fresh oregano, chopped
- 1 tablespoon fresh basil, chopped
- 1 teaspoon fresh thyme, chopped
- 1/4 cup crumbled feta cheese (optional)
- Salt and pepper to taste
- Lemon wedges (optional, for serving)

Directions

1. Preheat the Oven: Preheat your oven to 375°F (190°C). Lightly grease a baking dish with olive oil.
2. Prepare the Chicken: Pat the chicken breasts dry with paper towels. Season both sides with salt and pepper.
3. Assemble the Dish: Place the chicken breasts in the prepared baking dish. Arrange the halved cherry tomatoes, Kalamata olives, and sliced red onion around the chicken. Sprinkle the minced garlic, chopped oregano, chopped basil, and chopped thyme over the chicken and vegetables. Drizzle with olive oil.
4. Bake the Chicken: Bake in the preheated oven for 25-30 minutes, or until the chicken is cooked through and reaches an internal temperature of 165°F (74°C). If using, sprinkle the crumbled feta cheese over the chicken during the last 5 minutes of baking.
5. Serve: Remove the chicken from the oven and let it rest for a few minutes. Serve with lemon wedges and garnish with additional fresh herbs if desired. Serve warm.

Nutritional Information (per serving)

- Calories: 320
- Protein: 30g
- Carbohydrates: 8g
- Dietary Fiber: 2g
- Sugars: 4g
- Fat: 18g
- Saturated Fat: 3g
- Sodium: 500mg
- Potassium: 700mg
- Vitamin A: 15% of Daily Value
- Vitamin C: 40% of Daily Value
- Calcium: 10% of Daily Value
- Iron: 8% of Daily Value

Paprika Lime Chicken

Yield: 4 servings **Prep Time:** 15 minutes (plus 30 minutes marinating time) **Cook Time:** 15 minutes

Ingredients

- 4 boneless, skinless chicken breasts
- 2 tablespoons olive oil
- 2 tablespoons lime juice
- 1 tablespoon lime zest
- 2 teaspoons paprika
- 1 teaspoon ground cumin
- 1 teaspoon garlic powder
- 1/2 teaspoon onion powder
- 1/2 teaspoon salt
- 1/2 teaspoon black pepper
- Fresh cilantro, chopped (optional, for garnish)
- Lime wedges (optional, for serving)

Directions

1. Prepare the Marinade: In a small bowl, whisk together the olive oil, lime juice, lime zest, paprika, ground cumin, garlic powder, onion powder, salt, and black pepper.
2. Marinate the Chicken: Place the chicken breasts in a resealable plastic bag or a shallow dish. Pour the marinade over the chicken, ensuring each breast is well coated. Seal the bag or cover the dish and refrigerate for at least 30 minutes, or up to 4 hours for more flavor.
3. Preheat the Grill: Preheat your grill to medium-high heat. Lightly oil the grill grates to prevent sticking.
4. Grill the Chicken: Remove the chicken from the marinade and discard any remaining marinade. Place the chicken breasts on the preheated grill and cook for about 6-7 minutes per side, or until the chicken is cooked through and reaches an internal temperature of 165°F (74°C).
5. Serve: Remove the chicken from the grill and let it rest for a few minutes. Garnish with chopped fresh cilantro and serve with lime wedges if desired. Serve warm.

Nutritional Information (per serving)

- Calories: 280
- Protein: 30g
- Carbohydrates: 2g
- Dietary Fiber: 1g
- Sugars: 0g
- Fat: 15g
- Saturated Fat: 2.5g
- Sodium: 500mg
- Potassium: 600mg
- Vitamin A: 15% of Daily Value
- Vitamin C: 15% of Daily Value
- Calcium: 2% of Daily Value
- Iron: 6% of Daily Value

Spicy Moroccan Chicken

Yield: 4 servings **Prep Time:** 15 minutes (plus 1 hour marinating time) **Cook Time:** 15 minutes

Ingredients
- 4 boneless, skinless chicken breasts
- 3 tablespoons olive oil
- 2 tablespoons fresh lemon juice
- 1 tablespoon lemon zest
- 3 cloves garlic, minced
- 1 tablespoon ground cumin
- 1 tablespoon ground coriander
- 1 teaspoon ground cinnamon
- 1 teaspoon ground turmeric
- 1 teaspoon paprika
- 1/2 teaspoon ground ginger
- 1/4 teaspoon cayenne pepper (adjust to taste)
- 1 teaspoon salt
- 1/2 teaspoon black pepper
- Fresh cilantro, chopped (optional, for garnish)
- Lemon wedges (optional, for serving)

Directions
1. Prepare the Marinade: In a large bowl, whisk together the olive oil, fresh lemon juice, lemon zest, minced garlic, ground cumin, ground coriander, ground cinnamon, ground turmeric, paprika, ground ginger, cayenne pepper, salt, and black pepper.
2. Marinate the Chicken: Place the chicken breasts in a resealable plastic bag or a shallow dish. Pour the marinade over the chicken, ensuring each breast is well coated. Seal the bag or cover the dish and refrigerate for at least 1 hour, or up to 4 hours for more flavor.
3. Preheat the Grill: Preheat your grill to medium-high heat. Lightly oil the grill grates to prevent sticking.
4. Grill the Chicken: Remove the chicken from the marinade and discard any remaining marinade. Place the chicken breasts on the preheated grill and cook for about 6-7 minutes per side, or until the chicken is cooked through and reaches an internal temperature of 165°F (74°C).
5. Serve: Remove the chicken from the grill and let it rest for a few minutes. Garnish with chopped fresh cilantro and serve with lemon wedges if desired. Serve warm.

Nutritional Information (per serving)
- Calories: 290
- Protein: 30g
- Carbohydrates: 2g
- Dietary Fiber: 1g
- Sugars: 0g
- Fat: 16g
- Saturated Fat: 2.5g
- Sodium: 550mg
- Potassium: 600mg
- Vitamin A: 15% of Daily Value
- Vitamin C: 20% of Daily Value
- Calcium: 2% of Daily Value
- Iron: 8% of Daily Value

Herb Marinated Lamb Kebabs

Yield: 4 servings **Prep Time:** 20 minutes (plus 1 hour marinating time) **Cook Time:** 15 minutes

Ingredients
- 1 1/2 pounds lamb shoulder, cut into 1-inch cubes
- 1/4 cup olive oil
- 3 tablespoons fresh lemon juice
- 2 tablespoons fresh rosemary, chopped
- 2 tablespoons fresh thyme, chopped
- 2 tablespoons fresh mint, chopped
- 4 cloves garlic, minced
- 1 teaspoon ground cumin
- 1 teaspoon ground coriander
- 1 teaspoon salt
- 1/2 teaspoon black pepper
- Wooden or metal skewers (if using wooden skewers, soak them in water for 30 minutes before use)

Directions
1. Prepare the Marinade: In a large bowl, whisk together the olive oil, fresh lemon juice, chopped rosemary, chopped thyme, chopped mint, minced garlic, ground cumin, ground coriander, salt, and black pepper.
2. Marinate the Lamb: Add the lamb cubes to the bowl and toss to coat well. Cover and refrigerate for at least 1 hour, or up to 4 hours for more flavor.
3. Preheat the Grill: Preheat your grill to medium-high heat. Lightly oil the grill grates to prevent sticking.
4. Prepare the Kebabs: Thread the marinated lamb cubes onto the skewers, leaving a little space between each piece for even cooking.
5. Grill the Kebabs: Place the lamb kebabs on the preheated grill and cook for about 10-15 minutes, turning occasionally, until the lamb is cooked to your desired level of doneness.
6. Serve: Remove the lamb kebabs from the grill and let them rest for a few minutes. Serve warm with your favorite sides.

Nutritional Information (per serving)
- Calories: 350
- Protein: 28g
- Carbohydrates: 2g
- Dietary Fiber: 0g
- Sugars: 0g
- Fat: 25g
- Saturated Fat: 8g
- Sodium: 600mg
- Potassium: 500mg
- Vitamin A: 4% of Daily Value
- Vitamin C: 10% of Daily Value
- Calcium: 4% of Daily Value
- Iron: 20% of Daily Value

Lemon Thyme Turkey Meatballs

Yield: 4 servings (makes about 20 meatballs) **Prep Time:** 20 minutes **Cook Time:** 25 minutes

Ingredients
- 1 pound ground turkey
- 1/2 cup almond flour
- 1/4 cup onion, finely chopped
- 2 cloves garlic, minced
- 1 large egg, beaten
- 1 tablespoon fresh thyme, chopped
- 1 tablespoon fresh lemon zest
- 1 tablespoon fresh parsley, chopped
- 1 tablespoon fresh lemon juice
- 1 teaspoon salt
- 1/2 teaspoon black pepper
- Olive oil spray or 1 tablespoon olive oil (for greasing)

Directions
1. Preheat the Oven: Preheat your oven to 400°F (200°C). Line a baking sheet with parchment paper or lightly grease it with olive oil.
2. Prepare the Meatball Mixture: In a large bowl, combine the ground turkey, almond flour, finely chopped onion, minced garlic, beaten egg, chopped fresh thyme, lemon zest, chopped parsley, lemon juice, salt, and black pepper. Mix until well combined.
3. Form the Meatballs: Using your hands or a small ice cream scoop, form the mixture into approximately 20 meatballs and place them on the prepared baking sheet.
4. Bake the Meatballs: Bake in the preheated oven for 20-25 minutes, or until the meatballs are cooked through and golden brown.
5. Serve: Remove the meatballs from the oven and let them rest for a few minutes. Serve warm, garnished with additional fresh herbs if desired.

Nutritional Information (per serving)
- Calories: 250
- Protein: 25g
- Carbohydrates: 6g
- Dietary Fiber: 2g
- Sugars: 1g
- Fat: 14g
- Saturated Fat: 3g
- Sodium: 600mg
- Potassium: 500mg
- Vitamin A: 4% of Daily Value
- Vitamin C: 10% of Daily Value
- Calcium: 6% of Daily Value
- Iron: 10% of Daily Value

Pomegranate Glazed Chicken

Yield: 4 servings **Prep Time:** 15 minutes
Cook Time: 30 minutes

Ingredients

- 4 boneless, skinless chicken breasts
- 1 cup pomegranate juice
- 1/4 cup balsamic vinegar
- 2 tablespoons honey or maple syrup
- 2 cloves garlic, minced
- 1 tablespoon fresh rosemary, chopped
- 1 tablespoon olive oil
- Salt and pepper to taste
- Pomegranate seeds (optional, for garnish)
- Fresh parsley or mint (optional, for garnish)

Directions

1. Preheat the Oven: Preheat your oven to 375°F (190°C). Lightly grease a baking dish with olive oil.
2. Prepare the Pomegranate Glaze: In a small saucepan, combine the pomegranate juice, balsamic vinegar, honey or maple syrup, minced garlic, and chopped rosemary. Bring to a simmer over medium heat and cook for about 10 minutes, or until the sauce has reduced and thickened slightly. Remove from heat and set aside.
3. Season the Chicken: Pat the chicken breasts dry with paper towels. Season both sides with salt and pepper.
4. Sear the Chicken: In a large skillet, heat the olive oil over medium-high heat. Add the chicken breasts and sear for about 2-3 minutes on each side, or until golden brown.
5. Glaze and Bake the Chicken: Transfer the seared chicken breasts to the prepared baking dish. Brush the pomegranate glaze generously over the chicken. Bake in the preheated oven for 20-25 minutes, or until the chicken is cooked through and reaches an internal temperature of 165°F (74°C).
6. Serve: Remove the chicken from the oven and let it rest for a few minutes. Garnish with pomegranate seeds and fresh parsley or mint if desired. Serve warm.

Nutritional Information (per serving)

- Calories: 320
- Protein: 30g
- Carbohydrates: 18g
- Dietary Fiber: 1g
- Sugars: 16g
- Fat: 12g
- Saturated Fat: 2.5g
- Sodium: 350mg
- Potassium: 600mg
- Vitamin A: 4% of Daily Value
- Vitamin C: 8% of Daily Value
- Calcium: 4% of Daily Value
- Iron: 8% of Daily Value

Sage and Apple Pork Chops

Yield: 4 servings **Prep Time:** 15 minutes
Cook Time: 25 minutes

Ingredients

- 4 boneless pork chops (about 1-inch thick)
- 2 tablespoons olive oil
- 1 large apple, cored and thinly sliced
- 1 small onion, thinly sliced
- 3 cloves garlic, minced
- 1 tablespoon fresh sage, chopped
- 1/2 cup low-sodium chicken broth
- 1/4 cup apple cider vinegar
- 1 tablespoon honey or maple syrup
- Salt and pepper to taste
- Fresh sage leaves (optional, for garnish)

Directions

1. Season the Pork Chops: Pat the pork chops dry with paper towels. Season both sides with salt and pepper.
2. Sear the Pork Chops: In a large skillet, heat the olive oil over medium-high heat. Add the pork chops and sear for about 3-4 minutes on each side, or until golden brown. Remove the pork chops from the skillet and set aside.
3. Sauté the Aromatics and Apples: In the same skillet, add the sliced apple and onion. Sauté for about 5 minutes, or until the onion is softened and the apple slices are slightly caramelized. Add the minced garlic and chopped sage, and sauté for another 1-2 minutes until fragrant.
4. Deglaze and Simmer: Pour in the chicken broth, apple cider vinegar, and honey or maple syrup. Stir to combine, scraping up any browned bits from the bottom of the skillet. Bring the mixture to a simmer.
5. Cook the Pork Chops: Return the seared pork chops to the skillet, nestling them into the apple and onion mixture. Reduce the heat to medium-low, cover, and simmer for about 10-12 minutes, or until the pork chops are cooked through and reach an internal temperature of 145°F (63°C).
6. Serve: Remove the pork chops from the skillet and let them rest for a few minutes. Serve warm, garnished with fresh sage leaves if desired.

Nutritional Information (per serving)

- Calories: 350
- Protein: 30g
- Carbohydrates: 15g
- Dietary Fiber: 2g
- Sugars: 10g
- Fat: 20g
- Saturated Fat: 5g
- Sodium: 500mg
- Potassium: 600mg
- Vitamin A: 2% of Daily Value
- Vitamin C: 8% of Daily Value
- Calcium: 4% of Daily Value
- Iron: 8% of Daily Value

Ginger Turmeric Chicken Soup

Yield: 6 servings **Prep Time:** 15 minutes
Cook Time: 45 minutes

Ingredients

- 1 1/2 pounds boneless, skinless chicken thighs or breasts
- 2 tablespoons olive oil
- 1 large onion, chopped
- 3 cloves garlic, minced
- 2 tablespoons fresh ginger, grated
- 1 tablespoon ground turmeric
- 4 cups low-sodium chicken broth
- 2 cups water
- 2 large carrots, sliced
- 2 celery stalks, sliced
- 1 large zucchini, diced
- 1 cup spinach or kale, chopped
- 1/2 cup fresh parsley, chopped
- Juice of 1 lemon
- Salt and pepper to taste

Directions

1. Prepare the Chicken: Cut the chicken into bite-sized pieces. Season with salt and pepper.
2. Sauté the Aromatics: In a large pot, heat the olive oil over medium heat. Add the chopped onion and sauté for about 5 minutes, or until softened. Add the minced garlic, grated ginger, and ground turmeric. Sauté for another 1-2 minutes until fragrant.
3. Cook the Chicken: Add the chicken pieces to the pot and cook for about 5-7 minutes, or until the chicken is browned on all sides.
4. Add the Broth and Vegetables: Pour in the chicken broth and water. Add the sliced carrots, celery, and zucchini. Bring the soup to a boil, then reduce the heat and let it simmer for about 25-30 minutes, or until the vegetables are tender and the chicken is cooked through.
5. Add the Greens and Herbs: Stir in the chopped spinach or kale and fresh parsley. Let the soup simmer for another 5 minutes until the greens are wilted.
6. Finish with Lemon Juice: Stir in the lemon juice and season with additional salt and pepper to taste.
7. Serve: Ladle the soup into bowls and serve warm.

Nutritional Information (per serving)

- Calories: 250
- Protein: 25g
- Carbohydrates: 10g
- Dietary Fiber: 3g
- Sugars: 4g
- Fat: 12g
- Saturated Fat: 2g
- Sodium: 500mg
- Potassium: 800mg
- Vitamin A: 110% of Daily Value
- Vitamin C: 35% of Daily Value
- Calcium: 6% of Daily Value
- Iron: 10% of Daily Value

Garlic Herb Roasted Chicken

Yield: 4-6 servings **Prep Time:** 15 minutes
Cook Time: 1 hour 30 minutes

Ingredients
- 1 whole chicken (about 4-5 pounds)
- 4 tablespoons olive oil
- 6 cloves garlic, minced
- 2 tablespoons fresh rosemary, chopped
- 2 tablespoons fresh thyme, chopped
- 2 tablespoons fresh parsley, chopped
- 1 tablespoon fresh lemon zest
- 1 tablespoon fresh lemon juice
- 1 teaspoon salt
- 1/2 teaspoon black pepper
- 1 lemon, quartered
- 1 onion, quartered
- Fresh herbs (optional, for garnish)

Directions
1. Preheat the Oven: Preheat your oven to 375°F (190°C). Place a rack in a roasting pan.
2. Prepare the Garlic Herb Mixture: In a small bowl, combine the olive oil, minced garlic, chopped rosemary, chopped thyme, chopped parsley, lemon zest, lemon juice, salt, and black pepper. Mix well to form a paste.
3. Season the Chicken: Pat the chicken dry with paper towels. Rub the garlic herb mixture all over the chicken, making sure to coat the outside and inside of the cavity. Stuff the cavity with the quartered lemon and onion.
4. Roast the Chicken: Place the chicken on the rack in the roasting pan, breast side up. Roast in the preheated oven for about 1 hour and 30 minutes, or until the chicken is golden brown and the internal temperature reaches 165°F (74°C) in the thickest part of the thigh.
5. Rest the Chicken: Remove the chicken from the oven and let it rest for 10-15 minutes before carving.
6. Serve: Carve the chicken and serve warm, garnished with fresh herbs if desired.

Nutritional Information (per serving)
- Calories: 400
- Protein: 35g
- Carbohydrates: 2g
- Dietary Fiber: 1g
- Sugars: 0g
- Fat: 26g
- Saturated Fat: 6g
- Sodium: 600mg
- Potassium: 450mg
- Vitamin A: 4% of Daily Value
- Vitamin C: 15% of Daily Value
- Calcium: 4% of Daily Value
- Iron: 10% of Daily Value

Cilantro Lime Chicken Tacos

Yield: 4 servings **Prep Time:** 20 minutes (plus 30 minutes marinating time) **Cook Time:** 15 minutes

Ingredients
- 1 1/2 pounds boneless, skinless chicken breasts, cut into bite-sized pieces
- 2 tablespoons olive oil
- 1/4 cup fresh lime juice
- 1 tablespoon lime zest
- 3 cloves garlic, minced
- 1/4 cup fresh cilantro, chopped
- 1 teaspoon ground cumin
- 1/2 teaspoon ground paprika
- 1/2 teaspoon salt
- 1/2 teaspoon black pepper
- 8 large lettuce leaves (for wraps)
- Toppings: avocado slices, diced tomatoes, red onion, and extra chopped cilantro

Directions
1. Prepare the Marinade: In a large bowl, whisk together the olive oil, fresh lime juice, lime zest, minced garlic, chopped cilantro, ground cumin, ground paprika, salt, and black pepper.
2. Marinate the Chicken: Add the chicken pieces to the bowl and toss to coat well. Cover and refrigerate for at least 30 minutes, or up to 2 hours for more flavor.
3. Cook the Chicken: In a large skillet, heat a little olive oil over medium-high heat. Add the marinated chicken pieces and cook for about 10-12 minutes, or until the chicken is cooked through and golden brown.
4. Prepare the Lettuce Wraps: While the chicken is cooking, prepare the lettuce leaves by washing and patting them dry.
5. Assemble the Tacos: Place a portion of the cooked chicken in each lettuce leaf. Top with avocado slices, diced tomatoes, red onion, and extra chopped cilantro.
6. Serve: Serve the cilantro lime chicken tacos warm.

Nutritional Information (per serving)
- Calories: 300
- Protein: 30g
- Carbohydrates: 8g
- Dietary Fiber: 4g
- Sugars: 2g
- Fat: 18g
- Saturated Fat: 3g
- Sodium: 600mg
- Potassium: 700mg
- Vitamin A: 15% of Daily Value
- Vitamin C: 35% of Daily Value
- Calcium: 4% of Daily Value
- Iron: 10% of Daily Value

Snacks & Sweets

Healthy and satisfying snack ideas and desserts

Coconut Macaroons

Yield: 20 macaroons **Prep Time:** 15 minutes
Cook Time: 20 minutes

Ingredients
- 3 cups unsweetened shredded coconut
- 1/2 cup almond flour
- 1/2 cup maple syrup
- 1/4 cup coconut oil, melted
- 1 teaspoon vanilla extract
- 1/4 teaspoon sea salt

Directions
1. Preheat the Oven: Preheat your oven to 325°F (160°C). Line a baking sheet with parchment paper.
2. Mix the Ingredients: In a large bowl, combine the shredded coconut, almond flour, maple syrup, melted coconut oil, vanilla extract, and sea salt. Mix until well combined.
3. Form the Macaroons: Using a small cookie scoop or your hands, form the mixture into small balls (about 1 inch in diameter) and place them on the prepared baking sheet. Flatten each ball slightly to form a round shape.
4. Bake: Bake in the preheated oven for 18-20 minutes, or until the edges are golden brown.
5. Cool: Remove from the oven and let the macaroons cool on the baking sheet for a few minutes before transferring them to a wire rack to cool completely.
6. Serve: Enjoy the macaroons once they are completely cooled. Store any leftovers in an airtight container at room temperature for up to 1 week.

Nutritional Information (per macaroon)
- Calories: 100
- Protein: 1g
- Carbohydrates: 9g
- Dietary Fiber: 2g
- Sugars: 7g
- Fat: 7g
- Saturated Fat: 5g
- Sodium: 25mg
- Potassium: 60mg
- Vitamin A: 0% of Daily Value
- Vitamin C: 0% of Daily Value
- Calcium: 1% of Daily Value
- Iron: 2% of Daily Value

Baked Apple Chips

Yield: 4 servings **Prep Time:** 10 minutes
Cook Time: 2 hours

Ingredients
- 4 large apples (any variety)
- 1 teaspoon ground cinnamon

Directions
1. Preheat the Oven: Preheat your oven to 225°F (110°C). Line two baking sheets with parchment paper.
2. Slice the Apples: Using a mandoline slicer or a sharp knife, thinly slice the apples crosswise into 1/8-inch thick rounds. Remove any seeds.
3. Arrange on Baking Sheets: Lay the apple slices in a single layer on the prepared baking sheets, ensuring they do not overlap.
4. Sprinkle with Cinnamon: Lightly sprinkle the ground cinnamon over the apple slices.
5. Bake: Bake in the preheated oven for about 1.5 to 2 hours, or until the apple slices are dry and crisp. Flip the apple slices halfway through the baking time to ensure even crispness.
6. Cool: Remove the apple chips from the oven and let them cool completely on the baking sheets. They will continue to crisp up as they cool.
7. Serve: Enjoy the apple chips once they are completely cooled. Store any leftovers in an airtight container at room temperature for up to 1 week.

Nutritional Information (per serving)
- Calories: 95
- Protein: 0g
- Carbohydrates: 25g
- Dietary Fiber: 4g
- Sugars: 19g
- Fat: 0g
- Saturated Fat: 0g
- Sodium: 0mg
- Potassium: 195mg
- Vitamin A: 2% of Daily Value
- Vitamin C: 8% of Daily Value
- Calcium: 1% of Daily Value
- Iron: 1% of Daily Value

Avocado Chocolate Mousse

Yield: 4 servings **Prep Time:** 10 minutes **Cook Time:** 0 minutes

Ingredients
- 2 ripe avocados, peeled and pitted
- 1/4 cup unsweetened cocoa powder
- 1/4 cup honey or maple syrup
- 1/4 cup almond milk (or any dairy-free milk)
- 1 teaspoon vanilla extract
- Pinch of sea salt
- Fresh berries or mint leaves (optional, for garnish)

Directions
1. Blend Ingredients: In a blender or food processor, combine the ripe avocados, cocoa powder, honey or maple syrup, almond milk, vanilla extract, and sea salt. Blend until smooth and creamy.
2. Adjust Consistency: If the mousse is too thick, add a little more almond milk, one tablespoon at a time, until the desired consistency is reached.
3. Chill: Spoon the mousse into individual serving bowls. Cover and refrigerate for at least 30 minutes to allow the flavors to meld and the mousse to firm up slightly.
4. Serve: Serve chilled, topped with fresh berries or mint leaves if desired.

Nutritional Information (per serving)
- Calories: 180
- Protein: 2g
- Carbohydrates: 25g
- Dietary Fiber: 7g
- Sugars: 15g
- Fat: 10g
- Saturated Fat: 2g
- Sodium: 45mg
- Potassium: 550mg
- Vitamin A: 2% of Daily Value
- Vitamin C: 15% of Daily Value
- Calcium: 4% of Daily Value
- Iron: 10% of Daily Value

Golden Milk Popsicles

Yield: 6 popsicles **Prep Time:** 10 minutes **Cook Time:** 0 minutes (plus freezing time)

Ingredients
- 2 cups unsweetened almond milk
- 1 teaspoon ground turmeric
- 1 teaspoon ground ginger
- 1/2 teaspoon ground cinnamon
- 2 tablespoons honey or maple syrup
- 1 teaspoon vanilla extract
- Pinch of black pepper (to enhance turmeric absorption)

Directions
1. Blend Ingredients: In a blender, combine the almond milk, ground turmeric, ground ginger, ground cinnamon, honey or maple syrup, vanilla extract, and a pinch of black pepper. Blend until well combined.
2. Pour into Molds: Pour the mixture into popsicle molds, filling each mold almost to the top.
3. Insert Sticks and Freeze: Insert popsicle sticks into the molds. Freeze for at least 4 hours, or until completely frozen.
4. Serve: To remove the popsicles from the molds, run warm water over the outside of the molds for a few seconds. Gently pull on the sticks to release the popsicles.

Nutritional Information (per popsicle)
- Calories: 50
- Protein: 1g
- Carbohydrates: 10g
- Dietary Fiber: 1g
- Sugars: 8g
- Fat: 1.5g
- Saturated Fat: 0g
- Sodium: 50mg
- Potassium: 100mg
- Vitamin A: 2% of Daily Value
- Vitamin C: 0% of Daily Value
- Calcium: 10% of Daily Value
- Iron: 2% of Daily Value

Spiced Almonds

Yield: 4 servings **Prep Time:** 5 minutes
Cook Time: 15 minutes

Ingredients
- 2 cups raw almonds
- 1 tablespoon olive oil
- 1 teaspoon ground turmeric
- 1 teaspoon ground cumin
- 1/2 teaspoon ground paprika
- 1/2 teaspoon ground cinnamon
- 1/4 teaspoon cayenne pepper (optional, for extra heat)
- 1/2 teaspoon sea salt
- 1/4 teaspoon black pepper

Directions
1. Preheat the Oven: Preheat your oven to 350°F (175°C). Line a baking sheet with parchment paper.
2. Prepare the Almonds: In a large bowl, combine the raw almonds and olive oil. Toss to coat the almonds evenly.
3. Add the Spices: In a small bowl, mix together the ground turmeric, ground cumin, ground paprika, ground cinnamon, cayenne pepper (if using), sea salt, and black pepper. Sprinkle the spice mixture over the almonds and toss until the almonds are evenly coated.
4. Bake: Spread the spiced almonds in a single layer on the prepared baking sheet. Bake in the preheated oven for 15-20 minutes, stirring halfway through, until the almonds are golden and fragrant.
5. Cool: Remove the baking sheet from the oven and let the almonds cool completely. They will become crispier as they cool.
6. Serve: Enjoy the spiced almonds as a healthy snack. Store any leftovers in an airtight container at room temperature for up to 1 week.

Nutritional Information (per serving)
- Calories: 200
- Protein: 7g
- Carbohydrates: 7g
- Dietary Fiber: 4g
- Sugars: 1g
- Fat: 18g
- Saturated Fat: 1.5g
- Sodium: 150mg
- Potassium: 250mg
- Vitamin A: 2% of Daily Value
- Vitamin C: 0% of Daily Value
- Calcium: 8% of Daily Value
- Iron: 6% of Daily Value

Turmeric Ginger Energy Balls

Yield: 20 energy balls **Prep Time:** 15 minutes
Cook Time: 0 minutes

Ingredients
- 1 cup Medjool dates, pitted
- 1 cup almonds or cashews
- 1/4 cup shredded coconut
- 1 tablespoon chia seeds
- 1 tablespoon ground flaxseed
- 1 tablespoon coconut oil
- 1 teaspoon ground turmeric
- 1 teaspoon ground ginger
- 1 teaspoon cinnamon
- 1 teaspoon vanilla extract
- 1/4 teaspoon sea salt

Directions
1. Prepare the Dates: If the dates are dry, soak them in warm water for about 10 minutes to soften. Drain well.
2. Process the Nuts: In a food processor, pulse the almonds or cashews until they are finely chopped.
3. Add Remaining Ingredients: Add the dates, shredded coconut, chia seeds, ground flaxseed, coconut oil, ground turmeric, ground ginger, cinnamon, vanilla extract, and sea salt to the food processor.
4. Blend: Process the mixture until it is well combined and starts to come together in a sticky dough. If the mixture is too dry, add a small amount of water (a teaspoon at a time) until the desired consistency is reached.
5. Form the Balls: Using your hands, roll the mixture into small balls, about 1 inch in diameter.
6. Chill: Place the energy balls on a baking sheet lined with parchment paper and refrigerate for at least 30 minutes to firm up.
7. Serve: Enjoy the energy balls as a healthy snack. Store any leftovers in an airtight container in the refrigerator for up to 1 week.

Nutritional Information (per energy ball)
- Calories: 80
- Protein: 2g
- Carbohydrates: 10g
- Dietary Fiber: 2g
- Sugars: 6g
- Fat: 4g
- Saturated Fat: 1g
- Sodium: 30mg
- Potassium: 100mg
- Vitamin A: 0% of Daily Value
- Vitamin C: 0% of Daily Value
- Calcium: 2% of Daily Value
- Iron: 4% of Daily Value

Pumpkin Seed Brittle

Yield: 12 servings **Prep Time:** 10 minutes
Cook Time: 20 minutes

Ingredients
- 1 cup raw pumpkin seeds (pepitas)
- 1/2 cup honey or maple syrup
- 1/4 cup coconut sugar
- 1 tablespoon coconut oil
- 1/2 teaspoon vanilla extract
- 1/4 teaspoon ground cinnamon
- 1/4 teaspoon sea salt
- 1/4 teaspoon baking soda

Directions
1. Prepare a Baking Sheet: Line a baking sheet with parchment paper or a silicone baking mat. Set aside.
2. Toast the Pumpkin Seeds: In a dry skillet over medium heat, toast the pumpkin seeds for about 3-5 minutes, stirring frequently, until they are golden brown and fragrant. Be careful not to burn them. Remove from heat and set aside.
3. Heat the Honey and Sugar: In a medium saucepan, combine the honey (or maple syrup), coconut sugar, and coconut oil. Cook over medium heat, stirring constantly until the mixture comes to a boil. Once it starts boiling, stop stirring and let it boil for 2-3 minutes until it reaches a deep amber color.
4. Add the Spices and Baking Soda: Remove the saucepan from heat and immediately stir in the vanilla extract, ground cinnamon, sea salt, and baking soda. The mixture will bubble up.
5. Combine with Pumpkin Seeds: Quickly stir in the toasted pumpkin seeds until they are fully coated with the caramel mixture.
6. Spread the Mixture: Pour the mixture onto the prepared baking sheet and spread it out evenly with a spatula.
7. Cool: Let the brittle cool completely at room temperature, about 30 minutes.
8. Break into Pieces: Once the brittle is fully cooled and hardened, break it into pieces.
9. Serve: Enjoy the pumpkin seed brittle as a healthy snack. Store any leftovers in an airtight container at room temperature for up to 1 week.

Nutritional Information (per serving)
- Calories: 120
- Protein: 2g
- Carbohydrates: 17g
- Dietary Fiber: 1g
- Sugars: 14g
- Fat: 6g
- Saturated Fat: 2g
- Sodium: 50mg
- Potassium: 90mg
- Vitamin A: 0% of Daily Value
- Vitamin C: 0% of Daily Value
- Calcium: 2% of Daily Value
- Iron: 4% of Daily Value

Chia Seed Pudding

Yield: 4 servings **Prep Time:** 10 minutes
Cook Time: 0 minutes (plus 4 hours chilling time)

Ingredients
- 1/2 cup chia seeds
- 2 cups unsweetened almond milk
- 1 teaspoon vanilla extract
- 2 tablespoons honey or maple syrup
- 1 cup fresh berries (strawberries, blueberries, raspberries, or a mix)
- Fresh mint leaves (optional, for garnish)

Directions
1. Prepare the Pudding Base: In a medium bowl, whisk together the chia seeds, almond milk, vanilla extract, and honey or maple syrup until well combined.
2. Chill: Cover the bowl and refrigerate for at least 4 hours, or overnight, until the mixture thickens to a pudding-like consistency. Stir occasionally to prevent clumping.
3. Serve: Divide the chia seed pudding into 4 serving bowls. Top with fresh berries and garnish with mint leaves if desired. Drizzle with additional honey or maple syrup if desired.

Nutritional Information (per serving)
- Calories: 180
- Protein: 4g
- Carbohydrates: 22g
- Dietary Fiber: 10g
- Sugars: 10g
- Fat: 8g
- Saturated Fat: 0.5g
- Sodium: 80mg
- Potassium: 220mg
- Vitamin A: 2% of Daily Value
- Vitamin C: 25% of Daily Value
- Calcium: 20% of Daily Value
- Iron: 10% of Daily Value

Cucumber Hummus Bites

Yield: 4 servings (approximately 16 bites)
Prep Time: 15 minutes **Cook Time:** 0 minutes

Ingredients
- 1 large cucumber
- 1 cup homemade hummus (recipe below)
- 1/2 teaspoon paprika
- Fresh parsley, chopped (optional, for garnish)

Homemade Hummus
- 1 can (15 ounces) chickpeas, drained and rinsed
- 1/4 cup tahini
- 2 tablespoons olive oil
- 2 tablespoons fresh lemon juice
- 2 cloves garlic, minced
- 1/2 teaspoon ground cumin
- 1/2 teaspoon salt
- 2-3 tablespoons water (as needed for consistency)

Directions
To Make the Hummus
1. Blend Ingredients: In a food processor, combine the chickpeas, tahini, olive oil, lemon juice, minced garlic, ground cumin, and salt. Blend until smooth.
2. Adjust Consistency: Add water, one tablespoon at a time, until the hummus reaches your desired consistency.
3. Taste and Adjust: Taste the hummus and adjust the seasoning if needed. Set aside.

To Assemble the Cucumber Hummus Bites
1. Prepare the Cucumber: Wash the cucumber thoroughly. Slice it into rounds about 1/4-inch thick.
2. Top with Hummus: Spread about a teaspoon of hummus on top of each cucumber slice.
3. Garnish: Sprinkle a pinch of paprika on top of the hummus for color and flavor. Garnish with chopped fresh parsley if desired.
4. Serve: Arrange the cucumber hummus bites on a serving platter and serve immediately.

Nutritional Information (per serving)
- Calories: 150
- Protein: 5g
- Carbohydrates: 12g
- Dietary Fiber: 4g
- Sugars: 2g
- Fat: 10g
- Saturated Fat: 1.5g
- Sodium: 300mg
- Potassium: 250mg
- Vitamin A: 6% of Daily Value
- Vitamin C: 10% of Daily Value
- Calcium: 4% of Daily Value
- Iron: 8% of Daily Value

Berry Yogurt Parfait

Yield: 4 servings **Prep Time:** 10 minutes
Cook Time: 0 minutes

Ingredients
- 2 cups dairy-free yogurt (such as almond, coconut, or cashew yogurt)
- 2 cups mixed berries (strawberries, blueberries, raspberries, blackberries)
- 1 cup granola (gluten-free if needed)
- 2 tablespoons honey or maple syrup (optional, for added sweetness)
- Fresh mint leaves (optional, for garnish)

Directions
1. Prepare the Ingredients: Wash and dry the berries. If using larger berries like strawberries, slice them into smaller pieces.
2. Layer the Parfait: In 4 serving glasses or bowls, layer the ingredients as follows: Start with a spoonful of yogurt at the bottom.
Add a layer of mixed berries.
Add a layer of granola.
Repeat the layers until the glasses are filled, finishing with a layer of yogurt on top.
3. Drizzle with Honey or Maple Syrup: If desired, drizzle a little honey or maple syrup on top of each parfait for added sweetness.
4. Garnish: Garnish with fresh mint leaves if desired.
5. Serve: Serve immediately and enjoy!

Nutritional Information (per serving)
- Calories: 200
- Protein: 5g
- Carbohydrates: 30g
- Dietary Fiber: 5g
- Sugars: 15g
- Fat: 8g
- Saturated Fat: 1.5g
- Sodium: 50mg
- Potassium: 250mg
- Vitamin A: 2% of Daily Value
- Vitamin C: 35% of Daily Value
- Calcium: 15% of Daily Value
- Iron: 8% of Daily Value

Dark Chocolate Bark

Yield: 16 servings **Prep Time:** 10 minutes
Cook Time: 5 minutes (plus cooling time)

Ingredients

- 8 ounces dark chocolate (70% cocoa or higher), chopped
- 1/4 cup almonds, chopped
- 1/4 cup walnuts, chopped
- 1/4 cup dried cranberries
- 1/4 cup dried apricots, chopped
- 1 tablespoon chia seeds
- 1 tablespoon shredded coconut (unsweetened)
- Pinch of sea salt

Directions

1. Melt the Chocolate: In a double boiler or a heatproof bowl set over a pot of simmering water, melt the chopped dark chocolate, stirring occasionally until smooth. Alternatively, you can melt the chocolate in the microwave in 30-second intervals, stirring between each interval until fully melted.
2. Prepare the Baking Sheet: Line a baking sheet with parchment paper.
3. Spread the Chocolate: Pour the melted chocolate onto the prepared baking sheet and spread it into an even layer, about 1/4-inch thick.
4. Add the Toppings: Sprinkle the chopped almonds, walnuts, dried cranberries, dried apricots, chia seeds, shredded coconut, and a pinch of sea salt evenly over the melted chocolate.
5. Set the Bark: Place the baking sheet in the refrigerator for about 30 minutes, or until the chocolate is fully set and hardened.
6. Break into Pieces: Once the chocolate is set, remove it from the refrigerator and break it into pieces.
7. Serve: Enjoy the dark chocolate bark as a healthy snack. Store any leftovers in an airtight container in the refrigerator for up to 1 week.

Nutritional Information (per serving)

- Calories: 120
- Protein: 2g
- Carbohydrates: 12g
- Dietary Fiber: 3g
- Sugars: 7g
- Fat: 8g
- Saturated Fat: 3g
- Sodium: 20mg
- Potassium: 150mg
- Vitamin A: 0% of Daily Value
- Vitamin C: 0% of Daily Value
- Calcium: 2% of Daily Value
- Iron: 10% of Daily Value

Turmeric Roasted Chickpeas

Yield: 4 servings **Prep Time:** 10 minutes
Cook Time: 40 minutes

Ingredients

- 1 can (15 ounces) chickpeas, drained and rinsed
- 2 tablespoons olive oil
- 1 teaspoon ground turmeric
- 1/2 teaspoon ground cumin
- 1/2 teaspoon paprika
- 1/4 teaspoon cayenne pepper (optional, for extra heat)
- 1/2 teaspoon garlic powder
- 1/2 teaspoon sea salt
- 1/4 teaspoon black pepper

Directions

1. Preheat the Oven: Preheat your oven to 400°F (200°C). Line a baking sheet with parchment paper.
2. Prepare the Chickpeas: Pat the chickpeas dry with paper towels. Removing as much moisture as possible will help them get crispy in the oven.
3. Season the Chickpeas: In a large bowl, toss the chickpeas with olive oil, ground turmeric, ground cumin, paprika, cayenne pepper (if using), garlic powder, sea salt, and black pepper until evenly coated.
4. Spread on Baking Sheet: Spread the seasoned chickpeas in a single layer on the prepared baking sheet.
5. Roast: Roast in the preheated oven for 35-40 minutes, stirring halfway through, until the chickpeas are golden brown and crispy.
6. Cool and Serve: Remove from the oven and let the chickpeas cool completely on the baking sheet. They will continue to crisp up as they cool.
7. Serve: Enjoy the turmeric roasted chickpeas as a healthy snack. Store any leftovers in an airtight container at room temperature for up to 1 week.

Nutritional Information (per serving)

- Calories: 140
- Protein: 5g
- Carbohydrates: 17g
- Dietary Fiber: 5g
- Sugars: 1g
- Fat: 6g
- Saturated Fat: 1g
- Sodium: 300mg
- Potassium: 230mg
- Vitamin A: 4% of Daily Value
- Vitamin C: 2% of Daily Value
- Calcium: 4% of Daily Value
- Iron: 10% of Daily Value

Banana Oat Cookies

Yield: 12 cookies **Prep Time:** 10 minutes
Cook Time: 15 minutes

Ingredients
- 2 ripe bananas, mashed
- 1 1/2 cups rolled oats (gluten-free if needed)
- 1/4 cup almond butter or peanut butter
- 1/4 cup honey or maple syrup
- 1 teaspoon vanilla extract
- 1 teaspoon ground cinnamon
- 1/2 teaspoon baking powder
- 1/4 teaspoon sea salt
- 1/4 cup dark chocolate chips or raisins (optional)
- 1/4 cup chopped nuts (optional)

Directions
1. Preheat the Oven: Preheat your oven to 350°F (175°C). Line a baking sheet with parchment paper.
2. Mash the Bananas: In a large bowl, mash the ripe bananas until smooth.
3. Combine Ingredients: Add the rolled oats, almond butter, honey or maple syrup, vanilla extract, ground cinnamon, baking powder, and sea salt to the mashed bananas. Mix until well combined.
4. Add Mix-ins: Fold in the dark chocolate chips or raisins and chopped nuts, if using.
5. Form the Cookies: Scoop out tablespoon-sized portions of the dough and place them onto the prepared baking sheet. Flatten each scoop slightly with the back of a spoon to form cookie shapes.
6. Bake: Bake in the preheated oven for 12-15 minutes, or until the cookies are golden brown and set.
7. Cool: Remove the baking sheet from the oven and let the cookies cool on the sheet for a few minutes before transferring them to a wire rack to cool completely.
8. Serve: Enjoy the cookies once they are completely cooled. Store any leftovers in an airtight container at room temperature for up to 3 days.

Nutritional Information (per cookie)
- Calories: 90
- Protein: 2g
- Carbohydrates: 15g
- Dietary Fiber: 2g
- Sugars: 6g
- Fat: 3.5g
- Saturated Fat: 0.5g
- Sodium: 60mg
- Potassium: 115mg
- Vitamin A: 0% of Daily Value
- Vitamin C: 2% of Daily Value
- Calcium: 2% of Daily Value
- Iron: 4% of Daily Value

Almond Butter Stuffed Dates

Yield: 12 stuffed dates **Prep Time:** 10 minutes
Cook Time: 0 minutes

Ingredients
- 12 Medjool dates
- 1/2 cup almond butter
- 1/4 teaspoon sea salt
- Optional toppings: shredded coconut, chopped nuts, dark chocolate drizzle

Directions
1. Prepare the Dates: Carefully slice each Medjool date lengthwise, creating a small opening. Remove the pits and discard them.
2. Stuff the Dates: Using a small spoon or a piping bag, fill each date with about a teaspoon of almond butter.
3. Sprinkle with Sea Salt: Lightly sprinkle a pinch of sea salt over the stuffed dates.
4. Optional Toppings: If desired, top the stuffed dates with shredded coconut, chopped nuts, or a drizzle of melted dark chocolate for added flavor and texture.
5. Serve: Arrange the stuffed dates on a serving platter and enjoy immediately. Store any leftovers in an airtight container in the refrigerator for up to 1 week.

Nutritional Information (per stuffed date)
- Calories: 110
- Protein: 2g
- Carbohydrates: 18g
- Dietary Fiber: 3g
- Sugars: 16g
- Fat: 4g
- Saturated Fat: 0.5g
- Sodium: 40mg
- Potassium: 200mg
- Vitamin A: 0% of Daily Value
- Vitamin C: 0% of Daily Value
- Calcium: 2% of Daily Value
- Iron: 2% of Daily Value

Matcha Green Tea Energy Bars

Yield: 12 bars **Prep Time:** 15 minutes
Cook Time: 0 minutes (plus chilling time)

Ingredients
- 1 cup almonds
- 1 cup cashews
- 1/2 cup pumpkin seeds
- 1/4 cup chia seeds
- 1/4 cup flaxseeds
- 1/4 cup shredded coconut (unsweetened)
- 1/4 cup honey or maple syrup
- 1/4 cup almond butter or peanut butter
- 2 tablespoons coconut oil, melted
- 1 tablespoon matcha green tea powder
- 1 teaspoon vanilla extract
- Pinch of sea salt

Directions
1. Prepare the Pan: Line an 8x8 inch baking pan with parchment paper, leaving some overhang on the sides for easy removal.
2. Process the Nuts and Seeds: In a food processor, pulse the almonds, cashews, pumpkin seeds, chia seeds, flaxseeds, and shredded coconut until they are finely chopped but still have some texture.
3. Combine Wet Ingredients: In a large bowl, mix together the honey or maple syrup, almond butter, melted coconut oil, matcha green tea powder, vanilla extract, and a pinch of sea salt until well combined.
4. Mix Everything Together: Add the chopped nuts and seeds to the bowl with the wet ingredients. Stir until everything is well combined and the mixture is sticky.
5. Press into Pan: Transfer the mixture to the prepared baking pan. Use a spatula or your hands to press it down firmly and evenly.
6. Chill: Place the pan in the refrigerator for at least 1 hour, or until the mixture is firm and set.
7. Cut into Bars: Once the mixture is set, use the parchment paper overhang to lift it out of the pan. Place on a cutting board and cut into 12 bars.
8. Serve: Enjoy the energy bars immediately, or store them in an airtight container in the refrigerator for up to 1 week.

Nutritional Information (per bar)
- Calories: 200
- Protein: 6g
- Carbohydrates: 12g
- Dietary Fiber: 4g
- Sugars: 7g
- Fat: 15g
- Saturated Fat: 4g
- Sodium: 30mg
- Potassium: 200mg
- Vitamin A: 0% of Daily Value
- Vitamin C: 0% of Daily Value
- Calcium: 6% of Daily Value
- Iron: 8% of Daily Value

Pineapple Coconut Smoothie

Yield: 2 servings **Prep Time:** 5 minutes
Cook Time: 0 minutes

Ingredients
- 2 cups fresh or frozen pineapple chunks
- 1 cup unsweetened coconut milk
- 1/2 cup coconut water
- 1 tablespoon fresh ginger, grated
- 1 tablespoon honey or maple syrup (optional, for added sweetness)
- Ice cubes (optional, for a thicker smoothie)
- Fresh mint leaves (optional, for garnish)

Directions
1. Blend Ingredients: In a blender, combine the pineapple chunks, coconut milk, coconut water, grated ginger, and honey or maple syrup (if using). Add ice cubes if a thicker consistency is desired.
2. Blend Until Smooth: Blend on high speed until the mixture is smooth and creamy.
3. Serve: Pour the smoothie into two glasses. Garnish with fresh mint leaves if desired.
4. Enjoy: Serve immediately and enjoy!

Nutritional Information (per serving)
- Calories: 140
- Protein: 1g
- Carbohydrates: 30g
- Dietary Fiber: 3g
- Sugars: 25g
- Fat: 5g
- Saturated Fat: 4g
- Sodium: 20mg
- Potassium: 230mg
- Vitamin A: 2% of Daily Value
- Vitamin C: 90% of Daily Value
- Calcium: 4% of Daily Value
- Iron: 6% of Daily Value

Cashew Coconut Bites

Yield: 20 bites **Prep Time:** 15 minutes
Cook Time: 0 minutes

Ingredients
- 1 cup raw cashews
- 1 cup Medjool dates, pitted
- 1/2 cup shredded coconut (unsweetened)
- 1 tablespoon coconut oil
- 1 teaspoon vanilla extract
- 1/2 teaspoon ground cinnamon
- Pinch of sea salt

Directions
1. Prepare the Ingredients: If the dates are dry, soak them in warm water for about 10 minutes to soften. Drain well.
2. Process the Cashews: In a food processor, pulse the cashews until they are finely chopped.
3. Add Remaining Ingredients: Add the dates, shredded coconut, coconut oil, vanilla extract, ground cinnamon, and sea salt to the food processor. Process until the mixture is well combined and starts to stick together.
4. Form the Bites: Using your hands, roll the mixture into small bite-sized balls, about 1 inch in diameter.
5. Chill: Place the bites on a baking sheet lined with parchment paper and refrigerate for at least 30 minutes to firm up.
6. Serve: Enjoy the cashew coconut bites as a healthy snack. Store any leftovers in an airtight container in the refrigerator for up to 1 week.

Nutritional Information (per bite)
- Calories: 90
- Protein: 1.5g
- Carbohydrates: 10g
- Dietary Fiber: 2g
- Sugars: 6g
- Fat: 5g
- Saturated Fat: 2.5g
- Sodium: 20mg
- Potassium: 110mg
- Vitamin A: 0% of Daily Value
- Vitamin C: 0% of Daily Value
- Calcium: 1% of Daily Value
- Iron: 3% of Daily Value

Sweet Potato Chips

Yield: 4 servings **Prep Time:** 10 minutes
Cook Time: 25 minutes

Ingredients
- 2 large sweet potatoes, thinly sliced
- 2 tablespoons olive oil or coconut oil
- 1/2 teaspoon sea salt
- 1/2 teaspoon ground paprika (optional)
- 1/2 teaspoon garlic powder (optional)
- Fresh rosemary or thyme (optional, for garnish)

Directions
1. Preheat the Oven: Preheat your oven to 400°F (200°C). Line two baking sheets with parchment paper.
2. Prepare the Sweet Potatoes: Wash and peel the sweet potatoes. Using a mandoline slicer or a sharp knife, thinly slice the sweet potatoes into rounds about 1/8-inch thick.
3. Season the Slices: In a large bowl, toss the sweet potato slices with olive oil or coconut oil until they are evenly coated. Sprinkle with sea salt, ground paprika, and garlic powder, and toss again to coat evenly.
4. Arrange on Baking Sheets: Arrange the sweet potato slices in a single layer on the prepared baking sheets, ensuring they do not overlap.
5. Bake: Bake in the preheated oven for 20-25 minutes, or until the chips are crispy and golden brown. Flip the chips halfway through the baking time to ensure even crisping.
6. Cool: Remove the baking sheets from the oven and let the chips cool for a few minutes. They will continue to crisp up as they cool.
7. Serve: Transfer the sweet potato chips to a serving bowl and garnish with fresh rosemary or thyme if desired. Serve immediately.

Nutritional Information (per serving)
- Calories: 150
- Protein: 2g
- Carbohydrates: 25g
- Dietary Fiber: 4g
- Sugars: 5g
- Fat: 6g
- Saturated Fat: 1g
- Sodium: 300mg
- Potassium: 400mg
- Vitamin A: 350% of Daily Value
- Vitamin C: 4% of Daily Value
- Calcium: 4% of Daily Value
- Iron: 4% of Daily Value

Mango Chia Popsicles

Yield: 6 popsicles **Prep Time:** 10 minutes
Cook Time: 0 minutes (plus freezing time)

Ingredients
- 2 ripe mangoes, peeled and pitted
- 1 cup unsweetened coconut milk or almond milk
- 2 tablespoons chia seeds
- 1 tablespoon honey or maple syrup (optional, for added sweetness)
- 1 teaspoon fresh lime juice

Directions
1. Prepare the Mango Puree: In a blender, combine the mangoes, coconut milk or almond milk, honey or maple syrup (if using), and lime juice. Blend until smooth.
2. Add Chia Seeds: Stir in the chia seeds until evenly distributed.
3. Fill the Molds: Pour the mixture into popsicle molds, filling each mold almost to the top.
4. Insert Sticks and Freeze: Insert popsicle sticks into the molds. Freeze for at least 4 hours, or until completely frozen.
5. Serve: To remove the popsicles from the molds, run warm water over the outside of the molds for a few seconds. Gently pull on the sticks to release the popsicles.

Nutritional Information (per popsicle)
- Calories: 70
- Protein: 1g
- Carbohydrates: 12g
- Dietary Fiber: 3g
- Sugars: 8g
- Fat: 2.5g
- Saturated Fat: 2g
- Sodium: 10mg
- Potassium: 180mg
- Vitamin A: 25% of Daily Value
- Vitamin C: 45% of Daily Value
- Calcium: 2% of Daily Value
- Iron: 2% of Daily Value

Carrot Cake Bites

Yield: 20 bites **Prep Time:** 15 minutes
Cook Time: 0 minutes

Ingredients
- 1 cup shredded carrots
- 1 cup Medjool dates, pitted
- 1 cup raw walnuts or pecans
- 1/2 cup unsweetened shredded coconut
- 1/4 cup almond flour
- 1 tablespoon coconut oil, melted
- 1 teaspoon ground cinnamon
- 1/2 teaspoon ground ginger
- 1/4 teaspoon ground nutmeg
- 1/4 teaspoon sea salt
- 1 teaspoon vanilla extract
- 1/4 cup raisins (optional)

Directions
1. Prepare the Dates: If the dates are dry, soak them in warm water for about 10 minutes to soften. Drain well.
2. Process the Nuts: In a food processor, pulse the walnuts or pecans until they are finely chopped.
3. Add Remaining Ingredients: Add the shredded carrots, dates, shredded coconut, almond flour, melted coconut oil, ground cinnamon, ground ginger, ground nutmeg, sea salt, vanilla extract, and raisins (if using) to the food processor. Process until the mixture is well combined and starts to stick together.
4. Form the Bites: Using your hands, roll the mixture into small bite-sized balls, about 1 inch in diameter.
5. Chill: Place the bites on a baking sheet lined with parchment paper and refrigerate for at least 30 minutes to firm up.
6. Serve: Enjoy the carrot cake bites as a healthy snack. Store any leftovers in an airtight container in the refrigerator for up to 1 week.

Nutritional Information (per bite)
- Calories: 90
- Protein: 1.5g
- Carbohydrates: 11g
- Dietary Fiber: 2g
- Sugars: 7g
- Fat: 5g
- Saturated Fat: 1.5g
- Sodium: 30mg
- Potassium: 150mg
- Vitamin A: 25% of Daily Value
- Vitamin C: 1% of Daily Value
- Calcium: 2% of Daily Value
- Iron: 2% of Daily Value

Zucchini Chips

Yield: 4 servings **Prep Time:** 10 minutes
Cook Time: 2 hours

Ingredients
- 2 large zucchinis
- 2 tablespoons olive oil
- 1/2 teaspoon sea salt
- 1/2 teaspoon garlic powder (optional)
- 1/2 teaspoon paprika (optional)

Directions
1. Preheat the Oven: Preheat your oven to 225°F (110°C). Line two baking sheets with parchment paper.
2. Prepare the Zucchini: Wash and dry the zucchinis. Using a mandoline slicer or a sharp knife, thinly slice the zucchinis into rounds about 1/8-inch thick.
3. Season the Slices: In a large bowl, toss the zucchini slices with olive oil until they are evenly coated. Sprinkle with sea salt, garlic powder, and paprika, and toss again to coat evenly.
4. Arrange on Baking Sheets: Arrange the zucchini slices in a single layer on the prepared baking sheets, ensuring they do not overlap.
5. Bake: Bake in the preheated oven for about 2 hours, or until the zucchini slices are dry and crispy. Flip the slices halfway through the baking time to ensure even crisping.
6. Cool: Remove the baking sheets from the oven and let the zucchini chips cool completely. They will continue to crisp up as they cool.
7. Serve: Transfer the zucchini chips to a serving bowl and enjoy immediately. Store any leftovers in an airtight container at room temperature for up to 1 week.

Nutritional Information (per serving)
- Calories: 70
- Protein: 1g
- Carbohydrates: 6g
- Dietary Fiber: 2g
- Sugars: 3g
- Fat: 5g
- Saturated Fat: 1g
- Sodium: 300mg
- Potassium: 250mg
- Vitamin A: 4% of Daily Value
- Vitamin C: 20% of Daily Value
- Calcium: 2% of Daily Value
- Iron: 2% of Daily Value

Pomegranate Yogurt Bark

Yield: 12 servings **Prep Time:** 10 minutes
Cook Time: 0 minutes (plus freezing time)

Ingredients
- 2 cups dairy-free yogurt (such as almond, coconut, or cashew yogurt)
- 1/2 cup pomegranate seeds
- 1/4 cup chopped nuts (such as almonds, walnuts, or pistachios)
- 2 tablespoons honey or maple syrup (optional, for added sweetness)
- 1 teaspoon vanilla extract

Directions
1. Prepare the Baking Sheet: Line a baking sheet with parchment paper.
2. Mix the Yogurt: In a bowl, mix the dairy-free yogurt with honey or maple syrup (if using) and vanilla extract until well combined.
3. Spread the Yogurt: Pour the yogurt mixture onto the prepared baking sheet and spread it out evenly to about 1/4-inch thickness.
4. Add the Toppings: Sprinkle the pomegranate seeds and chopped nuts evenly over the yogurt.
5. Freeze: Place the baking sheet in the freezer for at least 2 hours, or until the yogurt is completely frozen.
6. Break into Pieces: Once the yogurt bark is frozen, remove it from the freezer and break it into pieces.
7. Serve: Enjoy immediately or store the yogurt bark in an airtight container in the freezer for up to 1 month.

Nutritional Information (per serving)
- Calories: 60
- Protein: 2g
- Carbohydrates: 7g
- Dietary Fiber: 1g
- Sugars: 4g
- Fat: 3g
- Saturated Fat: 1g
- Sodium: 20mg
- Potassium: 100mg
- Vitamin A: 0% of Daily Value
- Vitamin C: 4% of Daily Value
- Calcium: 6% of Daily Value
- Iron: 2% of Daily Value

Spicy Pumpkin Seeds

Yield: 4 servings **Prep Time:** 10 minutes
Cook Time: 25 minutes

Ingredients
- 1 cup raw pumpkin seeds (pepitas)
- 1 tablespoon olive oil
- 1 teaspoon chili powder
- 1/2 teaspoon smoked paprika
- 1/2 teaspoon ground cumin
- 1/2 teaspoon garlic powder
- 1/4 teaspoon cayenne pepper (optional, for extra heat)
- 1/2 teaspoon sea salt
- 1/4 teaspoon black pepper

Directions
1. Preheat the Oven: Preheat your oven to 300°F (150°C). Line a baking sheet with parchment paper.
2. Prepare the Pumpkin Seeds: In a medium bowl, combine the pumpkin seeds and olive oil. Toss to coat the seeds evenly.
3. Add the Spices: Add the chili powder, smoked paprika, ground cumin, garlic powder, cayenne pepper (if using), sea salt, and black pepper to the bowl. Toss again to evenly coat the pumpkin seeds with the spice mixture.
4. Spread on Baking Sheet: Spread the seasoned pumpkin seeds in a single layer on the prepared baking sheet.
5. Bake: Bake in the preheated oven for 20-25 minutes, stirring halfway through, until the pumpkin seeds are golden brown and crispy.
6. Cool: Remove from the oven and let the pumpkin seeds cool completely on the baking sheet. They will continue to crisp up as they cool.
7. Serve: Enjoy the spicy pumpkin seeds as a healthy snack. Store any leftovers in an airtight container at room temperature for up to 1 week.

Nutritional Information (per serving)
- Calories: 150
- Protein: 6g
- Carbohydrates: 5g
- Dietary Fiber: 2g
- Sugars: 0g
- Fat: 13g
- Saturated Fat: 2g
- Sodium: 300mg
- Potassium: 150mg
- Vitamin A: 6% of Daily Value
- Vitamin C: 0% of Daily Value
- Calcium: 2% of Daily Value
- Iron: 15% of Daily Value

Frozen Grapes

Yield: 4 servings **Prep Time:** 5 minutes
Cook Time: 0 minutes (plus freezing time)

Ingredients
- 2 cups seedless grapes (red or green)

Directions
1. Prepare the Grapes: Wash the grapes thoroughly under cold water and remove them from the stems. Pat them dry with a paper towel.
2. Freeze the Grapes: Spread the grapes in a single layer on a baking sheet lined with parchment paper. Place the baking sheet in the freezer and freeze the grapes for at least 2 hours, or until completely frozen.
3. Store the Grapes: Once the grapes are frozen, transfer them to a resealable plastic bag or airtight container. Keep them in the freezer until ready to serve.
4. Serve: Enjoy the frozen grapes straight from the freezer as a sweet and refreshing snack.

Nutritional Information (per serving)
- Calories: 60
- Protein: 0.5g
- Carbohydrates: 16g
- Dietary Fiber: 1g
- Sugars: 15g
- Fat: 0g
- Saturated Fat: 0g
- Sodium: 2mg
- Potassium: 150mg
- Vitamin A: 2% of Daily Value
- Vitamin C: 10% of Daily Value
- Calcium: 1% of Daily Value
- Iron: 1% of Daily Value

Apple Cinnamon Overnight Oats

Yield: 2 servings **Prep Time:** 10 minutes
Cook Time: 0 minutes (plus overnight soaking time)

Ingredients
- 1 cup rolled oats (gluten-free if needed)
- 1 cup unsweetened almond milk
- 1 apple, grated or finely chopped
- 1 tablespoon chia seeds
- 1 tablespoon maple syrup or honey
- 1 teaspoon ground cinnamon
- 1/2 teaspoon vanilla extract
- 1/4 teaspoon ground nutmeg (optional)
- 2 tablespoons chopped nuts (such as walnuts or almonds, for topping)
- Fresh apple slices (for topping, optional)

Directions
1. Prepare the Mixture: In a medium bowl, combine the rolled oats, almond milk, grated or chopped apple, chia seeds, maple syrup or honey, ground cinnamon, vanilla extract, and ground nutmeg (if using). Stir well to combine.
2. Divide into Jars: Divide the mixture evenly between two mason jars or airtight containers.
3. Soak Overnight: Cover the jars or containers with lids and place them in the refrigerator to soak overnight, or for at least 4 hours.
4. Serve: In the morning, give the oats a good stir. Top with chopped nuts and fresh apple slices if desired. Enjoy cold or heat up in the microwave for a warm breakfast.

Nutritional Information (per serving)
- Calories: 250
- Protein: 6g
- Carbohydrates: 45g
- Dietary Fiber: 8g
- Sugars: 15g
- Fat: 7g
- Saturated Fat: 0.5g
- Sodium: 70mg
- Potassium: 300mg
- Vitamin A: 2% of Daily Value
- Vitamin C: 8% of Daily Value
- Calcium: 20% of Daily Value
- Iron: 10% of Daily Value

Cacao Nib Trail Mix

Yield: 4 servings **Prep Time:** 5 minutes
Cook Time: 0 minutes

Ingredients
- 1/2 cup raw almonds
- 1/2 cup raw walnuts
- 1/4 cup raw pumpkin seeds
- 1/4 cup raw sunflower seeds
- 1/4 cup unsweetened dried cranberries
- 1/4 cup cacao nibs
- 1/4 cup unsweetened shredded coconut
- 1/4 cup dark chocolate chips (optional)

Directions
1. Mix Ingredients: In a large bowl, combine the raw almonds, raw walnuts, raw pumpkin seeds, raw sunflower seeds, unsweetened dried cranberries, cacao nibs, unsweetened shredded coconut, and dark chocolate chips (if using).
2. Combine Well: Stir the mixture until all ingredients are evenly distributed.
3. Store and Serve: Transfer the trail mix to an airtight container. Store at room temperature for up to 2 weeks. Enjoy as a healthy snack.

Nutritional Information (per serving)
- Calories: 230
- Protein: 6g
- Carbohydrates: 14g
- Dietary Fiber: 5g
- Sugars: 6g
- Fat: 18g
- Saturated Fat: 4g
- Sodium: 5mg
- Potassium: 250mg
- Vitamin A: 0% of Daily Value
- Vitamin C: 2% of Daily Value
- Calcium: 6% of Daily Value
- Iron: 10% of Daily Value

Baked Plantain Chips

Yield: 4 servings **Prep Time:** 10 minutes
Cook Time: 20 minutes

Ingredients
- 2 green plantains
- 2 tablespoons olive oil or coconut oil, melted
- 1/2 teaspoon sea salt
- 1/2 teaspoon ground paprika (optional)
- 1/4 teaspoon garlic powder (optional)

Directions
1. Preheat the Oven: Preheat your oven to 375°F (190°C). Line a baking sheet with parchment paper.
2. Prepare the Plantains: Peel the plantains and slice them thinly into rounds, about 1/8-inch thick. You can use a mandoline slicer for even slices.
3. Season the Slices: In a large bowl, toss the plantain slices with the olive oil or melted coconut oil, sea salt, ground paprika, and garlic powder until evenly coated.
4. Arrange on Baking Sheet: Spread the plantain slices in a single layer on the prepared baking sheet, ensuring they do not overlap.
5. Bake: Bake in the preheated oven for about 15-20 minutes, flipping the slices halfway through, until the plantains are golden brown and crispy.
6. Cool: Remove from the oven and let the plantain chips cool completely on the baking sheet. They will continue to crisp up as they cool.
7. Serve: Enjoy the plantain chips immediately, or store them in an airtight container at room temperature for up to 1 week.

Nutritional Information (per serving)
- Calories: 150
- Protein: 1g
- Carbohydrates: 22g
- Dietary Fiber: 2g
- Sugars: 0g
- Fat: 7g
- Saturated Fat: 2g
- Sodium: 150mg
- Potassium: 350mg
- Vitamin A: 20% of Daily Value
- Vitamin C: 20% of Daily Value
- Calcium: 0% of Daily Value
- Iron: 2% of Daily Value

Lemon Coconut Energy Balls

Yield: 20 energy balls **Prep Time:** 15 minutes
Cook Time: 0 minutes

Ingredients
- 1 cup Medjool dates, pitted
- 1 cup raw cashews or almonds
- 1/2 cup shredded coconut (unsweetened)
- 1 tablespoon coconut oil
- Zest of 1 large lemon
- Juice of 1/2 large lemon
- 1 teaspoon vanilla extract
- Pinch of sea salt

Directions
1. Prepare the Dates: If the dates are dry, soak them in warm water for about 10 minutes to soften. Drain well.
2. Process the Nuts: In a food processor, pulse the cashews or almonds until they are finely chopped.
3. Add Remaining Ingredients: Add the dates, shredded coconut, coconut oil, lemon zest, lemon juice, vanilla extract, and sea salt to the food processor. Process until the mixture is well combined and starts to stick together.
4. Form the Balls: Using your hands, roll the mixture into small bite-sized balls, about 1 inch in diameter.
5. Chill: Place the energy balls on a baking sheet lined with parchment paper and refrigerate for at least 30 minutes to firm up.
6. Serve: Enjoy the lemon coconut energy balls as a healthy snack. Store any leftovers in an airtight container in the refrigerator for up to 1 week.

Nutritional Information (per energy ball)
- Calories: 90
- Protein: 1.5g
- Carbohydrates: 12g
- Dietary Fiber: 2g
- Sugars: 8g
- Fat: 4.5g
- Saturated Fat: 2.5g
- Sodium: 10mg
- Potassium: 120mg
- Vitamin A: 0% of Daily Value
- Vitamin C: 2% of Daily Value
- Calcium: 1% of Daily Value
- Iron: 2% of Daily Value

Berry Smoothie Bowl

Yield: 2 servings **Prep Time:** 10 minutes
Cook Time: 0 minutes

Ingredients
For the Smoothie
- 1 cup frozen mixed berries (strawberries, blueberries, raspberries, blackberries)
- 1 banana, sliced
- 1/2 cup unsweetened almond milk or coconut milk
- 1/2 cup dairy-free yogurt (such as almond or coconut yogurt)
- 1 tablespoon chia seeds
- 1 tablespoon honey or maple syrup (optional)

For the Toppings
- 1/2 cup fresh berries (strawberries, blueberries, raspberries, blackberries)
- 2 tablespoons chopped nuts (such as almonds, walnuts, or pecans)
- 1 tablespoon pumpkin seeds
- 1 tablespoon shredded coconut (unsweetened)
- 1 tablespoon cacao nibs (optional)

Directions
1. Blend the Smoothie: In a blender, combine the frozen mixed berries, banana, almond milk or coconut milk, dairy-free yogurt, chia seeds, and honey or maple syrup (if using). Blend until smooth and creamy. If the mixture is too thick, add a little more almond milk to reach the desired consistency.
2. Pour into Bowls: Pour the smoothie mixture into two bowls.
3. Add Toppings: Top each smoothie bowl with fresh berries, chopped nuts, pumpkin seeds, shredded coconut, and cacao nibs (if using).
4. Serve: Enjoy immediately with a spoon.

Nutritional Information (per serving)
- Calories: 250
- Protein: 6g
- Carbohydrates: 38g
- Dietary Fiber: 8g
- Sugars: 22g
- Fat: 10g
- Saturated Fat: 3g
- Sodium: 60mg
- Potassium: 450mg
- Vitamin A: 2% of Daily Value
- Vitamin C: 60% of Daily Value
- Calcium: 15% of Daily Value
- Iron: 10% of Daily Value

Cinnamon Spiced Pears

Yield: 4 servings **Prep Time:** 10 minutes
Cook Time: 25 minutes

Ingredients
- 4 ripe pears
- 2 tablespoons coconut oil or butter, melted
- 2 tablespoons honey or maple syrup
- 1 teaspoon ground cinnamon
- 1/4 teaspoon ground nutmeg (optional)
- 1/4 teaspoon ground ginger (optional)
- 1/4 teaspoon sea salt
- Fresh lemon juice (optional, to prevent browning)

Directions
1. Preheat the Oven: Preheat your oven to 375°F (190°C). Line a baking sheet with parchment paper.
2. Prepare the Pears: Wash and core the pears. Slice them into 1/4-inch thick slices. If desired, sprinkle the slices with a little fresh lemon juice to prevent browning.
3. Mix the Topping: In a small bowl, mix the melted coconut oil or butter, honey or maple syrup, ground cinnamon, ground nutmeg, ground ginger, and sea salt.
4. Coat the Pears: Place the pear slices in a large bowl. Pour the spiced mixture over the pears and toss gently to coat evenly.
5. Arrange on Baking Sheet: Arrange the pear slices in a single layer on the prepared baking sheet.
6. Bake: Bake in the preheated oven for 20-25 minutes, or until the pears are tender and slightly caramelized. Flip the slices halfway through the baking time to ensure even baking.
7. Serve: Remove from the oven and let the pears cool for a few minutes before serving. Enjoy warm or at room temperature.

Nutritional Information (per serving)
- Calories: 140
- Protein: 1g
- Carbohydrates: 29g
- Dietary Fiber: 5g
- Sugars: 20g
- Fat: 4g
- Saturated Fat: 3g
- Sodium: 70mg
- Potassium: 210mg
- Vitamin A: 2% of Daily Value
- Vitamin C: 10% of Daily Value
- Calcium: 2% of Daily Value
- Iron: 2% of Daily Value

Exercises to Reduce Inflammation

Physical activity plays a crucial role in managing inflammation. Regular exercise can significantly reduce the levels of inflammatory markers in the body. This doesn't mean you need to become a marathon runner or a gym fanatic. Even moderate, consistent exercise can make a big difference in how you feel and how your body handles inflammation.

One of the primary benefits of exercise is its ability to help regulate your immune system. When you exercise, your body produces anti-inflammatory substances that help counteract the inflammation process. Regular physical activity also helps reduce fat tissue, which is known to release pro-inflammatory substances. Additionally, exercise enhances circulation, helping to clear out cellular debris and reduce the inflammatory response.

Exercise also offers numerous other benefits that indirectly contribute to reduced inflammation. It helps improve cardiovascular health, supports healthy blood sugar levels, and boosts mental well-being, all of which can have a positive impact on inflammation. Plus, regular movement helps maintain a healthy weight, which is crucial since excess body fat can be a significant source of inflammation.

The key to reaping these benefits is consistency. Aim to incorporate physical activity into your daily routine, making it a regular part of your lifestyle. It doesn't have to be intense or time-consuming; even small amounts of movement throughout the day can add up to substantial benefits.

Types of Exercises to Include

When it comes to reducing inflammation, a variety of exercises can be beneficial. You don't need to stick to one type of activity; mixing things up can keep your routine interesting and work different parts of your body.

Aerobic exercises, like walking, cycling, and swimming, are great for overall cardiovascular health. They get your heart rate up, improve circulation, and help manage weight. Aim for at least 30 minutes of moderate aerobic activity most days of the week.

Strength training is also important. Building muscle helps boost your metabolism and reduce body fat. Activities like lifting weights, using resistance bands, or doing body-weight exercises such as squats and push-ups can be highly effective. Try to include strength training exercises at least two days a week.

Flexibility and balance exercises, such as yoga and Pilates, are excellent for reducing muscle tension and improving overall body function. These exercises help enhance flexibility, balance, and core strength, which can reduce the risk of injuries and improve posture. Incorporate these activities a few times a week to complement your aerobic and strength training routines.

Low-impact activities, like tai chi and gentle stretching, can be particularly beneficial for those dealing with chronic inflammation or joint pain. These exercises are gentle on the body but still help improve mobility and reduce stress.

Sample Exercise Routines

Creating a routine that incorporates various types of exercise can help keep you motivated and ensure you're getting a well-rounded workout. Here are some easy-to-follow exercise plans to help you get started:

Morning Routine: Start Your Day Right

- 5-minute warm-up: Light stretching or a brisk walk around your house.
- 10-minute aerobic activity: Try a short walk, a few minutes on a stationary bike, or a quick swim if you have access to a pool.
- 5-minute strength training: Do a set of body-weight exercises like squats, lunges, or push-ups.

Midday Movement: Break Up Your Day

- 10-minute walk: After lunch, take a quick walk around your neighborhood or office.
- 5-minute stretching: Focus on stretching major muscle groups to relieve any tension that's built up.

Evening Routine: Wind Down

- 10-minute yoga session: Follow a gentle yoga routine to help relax and stretch your muscles.
- 5-minute balance exercises: Practice standing on one leg, or try tai chi movements to improve your balance and core strength.

Weekend Routine: Longer Sessions

- 30-minute hike or bike ride: Take advantage of your free time to enjoy a longer aerobic activity.
- 20-minute strength training: Use this time for a more extended strength training session, incorporating various exercises for different muscle groups.
- 10-minute flexibility session: End your workout with yoga or stretching to enhance flexibility and prevent muscle soreness.

Remember, the best exercise routine is one that you enjoy and can stick with consistently. Listen to your body and adjust the intensity and duration of your workouts as needed. If you're new to exercise or have any health concerns, it's always a good idea to consult with a healthcare provider before starting a new fitness program.

Incorporating regular physical activity into your routine can have a profound impact on reducing inflammation and improving your overall health. Start small, stay consistent, and enjoy the benefits that come with a more active lifestyle.

Conclusion

Recap and Encouragement

As you reach the end of this book, take a moment to reflect on the transformative journey you've embarked on. From the early days of understanding inflammation and its profound impact on your health to exploring a wide variety of anti-inflammatory foods and integrating them into your diet, you've made significant strides toward a healthier, more vibrant life.

Throughout these pages, we've delved into the science behind inflammation, demystifying how certain foods and lifestyle choices can either fuel the fire of inflammation or help extinguish it. You now know that an anti-inflammatory diet isn't just a temporary fix or a fad—it's a sustainable way of living that supports your body's natural healing processes.

You've equipped yourself with an arsenal of delicious and nutritious recipes, from hearty breakfasts that kickstart your day to satisfying lunches and dinners that keep you fueled and nourished. These recipes aren't just meals; they're tools for your wellness, carefully crafted to help you reduce inflammation, boost your immune system, and maintain a healthy weight.

In addition to dietary changes, we've emphasized the importance of regular physical activity. Exercise isn't just about losing weight or building muscle; it's a powerful anti-inflammatory tool that enhances circulation, reduces fat tissue, and helps regulate your immune system. By incorporating a mix of aerobic exercises, strength training, and flexibility routines, you're setting yourself up for a balanced and healthy life.

The 4-weeks meal plan provided a structured yet flexible approach to help you implement these changes. It was designed to ease you into this new lifestyle, offering a roadmap to follow while you get accustomed to new habits. Each day was carefully planned to ensure you're getting a variety of nutrients from different foods, keeping your meals interesting and your motivation high.

But beyond the recipes and the meal plans, this journey has also been about mindset. Changing your diet and lifestyle isn't always easy. It requires commitment, patience, and sometimes a bit of creativity. But by now, you should feel empowered. You've seen that making these changes is possible and that the benefits are worth the effort. Improved energy levels, reduced pain, better digestion, and a lower risk of chronic diseases are just a few of the rewards awaiting you.

Remember, this is just the beginning. Maintaining your new lifestyle requires ongoing commitment. Keep experimenting with new recipes, stay active, and continue educating yourself about anti-inflammatory living. The more you immerse yourself in this lifestyle, the more natural it will become. Surround yourself with supportive friends and family, and don't hesitate to seek out new resources and communities that share your goals.

As you continue your journey, you'll find that there are many resources available to help you stay on track and deepen your understanding of anti-inflammatory living. Consider exploring additional books and articles on the subject.

Online communities can also be a valuable source of support and information. Platforms host groups dedicated to anti-inflammatory diets where you can share your experiences, seek advice, and find motivation from others who are on the same path. Engaging with these communities can provide you with ongoing encouragement and fresh ideas.

Summarize the Book

In this book, you have gained a comprehensive understanding of how to reduce inflammation through diet and lifestyle changes. We've covered the science of inflammation, provided a variety of delicious and nutritious recipes, highlighted the importance of regular physical activity, and offered a structured 4-weeks meal plan to guide you. These strategies, when implemented consistently, can significantly improve your overall health, reduce the risk of chronic diseases, and enhance your quality of life.

Now that you have the right knowledge, it's time to put it into practice. Start incorporating these changes into your daily routine and witness the transformation in your health and well-being. Remember, the journey to a healthier, inflammation-free life is a marathon, not a sprint. Take it one step at a time, celebrate your successes, and learn from any setbacks.

If you found this book helpful, please consider leaving a review on Amazon. Your feedback not only helps others discover the book but also supports the ongoing effort to share valuable health information with a wider audience.

Thank you for allowing this book to be a part of your journey toward better health. Embrace the changes, stay committed, and enjoy the vibrant, healthy life that comes with reducing inflammation. Here's to your health and happiness!

Appendices

Allergen-Aware Labels

Navigating food allergies and sensitivities can be tricky, but understanding allergen-aware labels can make it easier. These labels indicate whether a product contains common allergens or is free from them, helping you make safer and healthier choices.

Gluten-free labels mean the product doesn't contain wheat, barley, rye, or their hybrids, which is crucial for those with celiac disease or gluten sensitivity. **Dairy-free** labels indicate the absence of milk and milk-derived ingredients, important for those with lactose intolerance or milk allergies. **Nut-free** labels ensure the product is free of tree nuts and peanuts, vital for people with nut allergies. **Soy-free** labels signify that the product doesn't contain soy or soy-derived ingredients, beneficial for individuals with soy allergies. **Egg-free** labels mean the product doesn't include eggs or egg products, essential for those with egg allergies.

Reading labels carefully and understanding these designations can help you make informed choices, especially if you or your loved ones have food allergies or sensitivities.

Glossary

To help you better understand the concepts and terminology related to an anti-inflammatory diet, here are definitions of key terms used throughout this book.

Anti-inflammatory refers to foods or substances that help reduce inflammation in the body. **Chronic inflammation** is a prolonged inflammatory response that can lead to tissue damage and various health issues. **Omega-3 fatty acids** are essential fats found in fatty fish and some plant sources that have anti-inflammatory properties. **Antioxidants** are compounds found in foods that help fight oxidative stress and reduce inflammation. The **glycemic index** measures how quickly foods raise blood sugar levels, with low glycemic index foods being better for managing inflammation. **Phytochemicals** are naturally occurring compounds in plants that have health benefits, including anti-inflammatory effects. **Probiotics** are beneficial bacteria found in fermented foods that support gut health and can reduce inflammation.

Index

To make it easier for you to find recipes tailored to your specific dietary needs, here is an index of recipes sorted by special needs like dairy-free, gluten-free, vegetarian, vegan, and low-sugar options.

Dairy-Free Recipes include Overnight Oats with Blueberries and Chia Seeds, Quinoa Salad with Mixed Greens and Lemon-Tahini Dressing, and Grilled Chicken and Vegetable Stir-Fry.

Gluten-Free Recipes feature Spinach and Feta Omelette, Baked Salmon with Roasted Brussels Sprouts and Sweet Potatoes, and Turmeric and Coconut Chicken Curry.

Vegetarian Recipes offer Chia Pudding with Mango and Coconut Flakes, Zucchini Noodles with Pesto and Cherry Tomatoes, and Sweet Potato and Kale Hash.

Vegan Recipes include Green Smoothie with Spinach, Banana, and Flax Seeds, Black Bean and Sweet Potato Enchiladas, and Lentil Soup with Mixed Greens.

Low-Sugar Recipes highlight Greek Yogurt with Honey and Walnuts, Stuffed Bell Peppers with Ground Turkey and Brown Rice, and Shrimp Stir-Fry with Bell Peppers, Broccoli, and Brown Rice.

This index will help you quickly find recipes that suit your dietary preferences and needs, making meal planning and preparation easier and more enjoyable.

By understanding what to eat and what to avoid, navigating allergen-aware labels, and using the glossary and index, you can confidently continue your journey towards a healthier, inflammation-free lifestyle.

Thank you for joining me on this journey. Stay healthy and happy!

Printed in Dunstable, United Kingdom